Critical Perspectives on Human Security

This new book presents critical approaches towards Human Security, which has become one of the key areas for policy and academic debate within Security Studies and IR.

The Human Security paradigm has had considerable significance for academics, policy-makers and practitioners. Under the rubric of Human Security, security policy practices seem to have transformed their goals and approaches, re-prioritising economic and social welfare issues that were marginal to the state-based geopolitical rivalries of the Cold War era. Human Security has reflected and reinforced the reconceptualisation of international security, both broadening and deepening it, and, in so doing, it has helped extend and shape the space within which security concerns inform international policy practices. However, in its wider use, Human Security has become an amorphous and unclear political concept, seen by some as progressive and radical and by others as tainted by association with the imposition of neo-liberal practices and values on non-western spaces or as legitimising attacks on Iraq and Afghanistan.

This book is concerned with critical perspectives towards Human Security, highlighting some of the tensions which can emerge between critical perspectives which discursively radicalise Human Security within frameworks of emancipatory possibility and those which attempt to deconstruct Human Security within the framework of an externally imposed attempt to regulate and order the globe on behalf of hegemonic power. The chapters gathered in this edited collection represent a range of critical approaches which bring together alternative understandings of human security.

This book will be of great interest to students of human security studies and critical security studies, war and conflict studies and International Relations.

David Chandler is Professor of International Relations at the University of Westminster. He is author of several books and edits the *Journal of Statebuilding and Intervention*.

Nik Hynek is Research Fellow at the Institute of International Relations in Prague and Lecturer at Charles University and Metropolitan University. Previously, he conducted research at the Saltzman Institute of War and Peace Studies (SIWPS) at Columbia University and at the BIOS Institute of the LSE. He has widely published on international security and theories of IR.

PRIO New Security Studies
Series Editor: J. Peter Burgess
PRIO, Oslo

The aim of this book series is to gather state-of-the-art theoretical reflexion and empirical research into a core set of volumes that respond vigorously and dynamically to the new challenges to security scholarship.

The Geopolitics of American Insecurity
Terror, power and foreign policy
Edited by François Debrix and Mark J. Lacy

Security, Risk and the Biometric State
Governing borders and bodies
Benjamin Muller

Security and Global Governmentality
Globalization, governance and the state
Miguel de Larrinaga and Marc G. Doucet

Critical Perspectives on Human Security
Rethinking emancipation and power in international relations
Edited by David Chandler and Nik Hynek

Critical Perspectives on Human Security

Rethinking emancipation and power in international relations

Edited by David Chandler and Nik Hynek

LONDON AND NEW YORK

First published 2011
by Routledge
2 Park Square, Milton Park, Abingdon, Oxfordshire OX14 4RN

Simultaneously published in the USA and Canada
by Routledge
711 Third Avenue, New York, NY 10017

*Routledge is an imprint of the Taylor & Francis Group,
an informa business*

First issued in paperback 2011

© 2011 David Chandler and Nik Hynek

The right of the editors to be identified as the authors of the editorial material, and of the authors for their individual chapters, has been asserted in accordance with sections 77 and 78 of the Copyright, Designs and Patents Act 1988.

Typeset in Baskerville by Swales & Willis Ltd, Exeter, Devon

All rights reserved. No part of this book may be reprinted or reproduced or utilised in any form or by any electronic, mechanical, or other means, now known or hereafter invented, including photocopying and recording, or in any information storage or retrieval system, without permission in writing from the publishers.

British Library Cataloguing in Publication Data
A catalogue record for this book is available from the British Library

Library of Congress Cataloging-in-Publication Data
Critical perspectives on human security : rethinking emancipation and power in international relations / edited by David Chandler and Nik Hynek.
p. cm.
1. Security, International. 2. International relations. 3. Human security. 4. Human rights. I. Chandler, David, 1962– II. Hynek, Nik.
JZ5595.C76 2010
327.1—dc22
2010001794

ISBN13: 978-0-415-56734-3 (hbk)
ISBN13: 978-0-415-53251-8 (pbk)
ISBN13: 978-0-203-84758-9 (ebk)

Contents

List of contributors   vii

1 **Introduction: Emancipation and power in human security**   1
NIK HYNEK AND DAVID CHANDLER

PART I   11

2 **'We the peoples': Contending discourses of security in human rights theory and practice**   13
TIM DUNNE AND NICHOLAS J. WHEELER

3 **Development of the human security field: A critical examination**   28
DAVID BOSOLD

4 **Post-colonial hybridity and the return of human security**   43
OLIVER P. RICHMOND

5 **Securitizing 'bare life': Critical perspectives on human security discourse**   56
GIORGIO SHANI

6 **Human security, biopoverty and the possibility for emancipation**   69
DAVID ROBERTS

7 **Institutionalised and co-opted: Why human security has lost its way**   83
MANDY TURNER, NEIL COOPER AND MICHAEL PUGH

PART II 97

8 **The limits to emancipation in the human security framework** 99
TARA MCCORMACK

9 **Rethinking global discourses of security** 114
DAVID CHANDLER

10 **Human security and the securing of human life: Tracing global sovereign and biopolitical rule** 129
MARC G. DOUCET AND MIGUEL DE LARRINAGA

11 **Problematizing life under biopower: A Foucauldian versus an Agambenite critique of human security** 144
SUVI ALT

12 **Rethinking human security: History, economy, governmentality** 157
NIK HYNEK

13 **Human security: Sovereignty and disorder** 172
KYLE GRAYSON

14 **Inhuman security** 186
MARK NEOCLEOUS

Further reading 198
Index 202

Contributors

Suvi Alt is a Doctoral Candidate in International Relations at the University of Lapland, Finland.

David Bosold is the Head of International Forum on Strategic Thinking at the German Council on Foreign Relations, Germany.

David Chandler is Professor of International Relations at the University of Westminster, United Kingdom. He is author of several books and edits the *Journal of Statebuilding and Intervention*.

Neil Cooper is Reader at the Department of Peace Studies of the University of Bradford, United Kingdom.

Miguel de Larrinaga is Lecturer at the School of Political Studies of the University of Ottawa, Canada.

Marc G. Doucet is Associate Professor at the Political Science department of Saint Mary's University, Canada.

Tim Dunne is Professor of International Relations and Head of Humanities and Social Sciences at the University of Exeter, United Kingdom.

Kyle Grayson is Lecturer in International Politics at the School of Geography, Politics and Sociology of Newcastle University, United Kingdom.

Nik Hynek is Research Fellow at the IIR Prague, Lecturer at Charles University and Doctoral Candidate at the Department of Peace Studies of the University of Bradford. Previously, he conducted research at Columbia University and LSE.

Tara McCormack is Lecturer at the Department of Politics and International Relations of the University of Leicester, United Kingdom.

Mark Neocleous is Professor of the Critique of Political Economy and Head of the Department of Politics and History at Brunel University, United Kingdom.

Michael Pugh is Research Professor at the Department of Peace Studies of the University of Bradford, United Kingdom.

Oliver P. Richmond is Professor of Peace and Conflict Studies at the School of International Relations of the University of St Andrews, United Kingdom.

David Roberts is Senior Lecturer in International Politics at the University of Ulster, United Kingdom.

Giorgio Shani is Associate Professor of International Development and Peacebuilding at the Department of Politics and International Relations of the International Christian University, Japan.

Mandy Turner is Lecturer at the Department of Peace Studies of the University of Bradford, United Kingdom.

Nicholas J. Wheeler is the Director of the David Davies Memorial Institute of International Studies in the Department of International Politics at Aberystwyth University, United Kingdom.

1 Introduction
Emancipation and power in human security

Nik Hynek and David Chandler

Introduction

Human security appears to be one of the central categories through which the changing nature of security discourses and policy practices is understood and analysed. This book is concerned with critical perspectives towards human security, highlighting some of the tensions which can emerge between critical perspectives which discursively radicalise human security within frameworks of emancipatory possibility and those which attempt to deconstruct human security within the framework of an externally imposed attempt to regulate and order the globe on behalf of hegemonic power. The chapters gathered in this edited collection represent a range of critical approaches which bring together alternative understandings of human security.

The human security paradigm has had considerable significance for academics, policy-makers and practitioners, with practical as well as theoretical effects. Under the rubric of human security, both the understanding of security and its policy practice have become transformed in ways which have reconstituted and politicised the subject, re-prioritising issues that formerly had low status. Human security has reflected and reinforced the reconceptualisation of liberal security, both broadening and deepening it, and in so doing it has helped extend and shape the space within which critical studies of peace and security have developed. However, like 'sustainable development', human security has also become an amorphous and unclear political concept, at risk of becoming an 'empty signifier' tainted by associations ranging from the imposition of neo-liberal practices and values on non-western spaces to the legitimisation for attacks on Iraq and Afghanistan.

Human security has also been encumbered with a number of conceptual problems from its very early articulation; these problems are central to the discussion and debate generated by the critical approaches collected here. For example, there has been a surprising paucity of theoretically rich explorations of human security. This situation has largely been given by the fact that almost none of the existing 'theoretical' reflections on human security have been able to break free from policy-making discourses and the analytical categories which they have used. In other words, human security started as a policy-making project and academics have often tended to participate in the overall entrenchment of human security as a political project rather than in its intellectually autonomous, critical investigation. A further difficulty has been the commonly held belief that human security and national security are mutually exclusive paradigms and that they are in a competitive relationship. This binary logic, in which human security seems to be rooted, has presented a dichotomy between state-centred national security and people-centred human security while not acknowledging other types of tension and interconnection. Another problem is that, in spite of the declared universality of human security, its focus on the abstract individual with an assumption of unspecified contact with society – a position derived from western classical liberal assumptions, has inevitably led to its problematisation in relationship to the imperatives of expanded international intervention under the rubric of liberal peace, in which human security frameworks have played an ever more important role.

This leaves us with the question: 'Where do we go from here?' Can human security discourses provide an avenue for critical approaches to international relations or are critical approaches imbricated in the reproduction and extension of power as long as they do not break from the connection between 'security' and the needs of the 'human'. This edited volume provides a range of theoretically-informed critical exploration of the mechanisms, frameworks and possibilities that emerge when critical studies in human security are deployed. The collection establishes a robust theoretical linkage and practical investigation into the securitisation of human security and critically examines existing discourses and practices in the issue area. At the forefront of this task stands a critical examination of tensions between critical perspectives which discursively radicalise human security within frameworks of emancipatory possibility (largely surveyed and discussed in part 1 of the book) and those which attempt to deconstruct human security within the framework of its necessary reproduction of power relations (part 2 of the book).

Human security and the challenge to power

The first part of the book analyses how the emancipatory aims of human security have become linked to human rights and how human security itself has emerged from normative and emancipatory attempts to escape the logic of neo-liberal peacebuilding and prevailing modes upon which the current security/development nexus is founded. Importantly, apart from promises of the emancipatory human security discourse, its limits are exposed and examined in detail too.

An emancipatory approach to human security is said to encompass alternative notions of life (the individual, community, the biosphere and planetary environment) and alternative understandings of the political economy of human security. Additionally, a critically-oriented emancipatory approach to human security does not take liberalism as the only normative construct. It creates space for other agendas and non-western security approaches and allows for the historically and spatially contingent transformation of varied societies. Such an approach necessarily includes a reconfiguration of the global economic system that empowers communities to have more control over their resources. Also, it embraces critiques of economic forces (finance capitalism, corporate power). In particular, a key issue has been to identify the modes of negotiation (or lack of it) between external and internal interlocutors, and the impacts of global and dominant international norms on the 'recipient' populations. Answers to the question: 'whose peace?' are clearly related to asymmetries of power that help determine the normative project of liberal peacebuilding, the securitisation of welfare, and local responses that involve the incorporation of external values but also resistances.

Some contributors outline a radical emancipatory and empathetic version of human security which envisages genuine local empowerment based on the needs of everyday life. As a result, a new, unsecuritised paradigm is outlined. As far as its advantages, it demands to take local voices seriously, it rejects universalism in favour of heterodoxy, and it reconceptualises the abstract individual as a social being, thus limiting damage to planetary life. According to the proponents, such a perspective would lead to a two-fold paradigm shift: from the 'liddism' of liberal peace to critical political economies of human security; and from universalist panaceas (which result in dysfunctional hybrid forms of political economy) to engaging with heterogeneity. This approach essentially aims at the return of the political in the theoretical analysis of human security as well as to the practical policy lessons which can be drawn from it.

Other contributors stress the limits to the emancipatory possibilities of human security, highlighting that the liberal discourses within which human security is structured cannot be overcome through the extension of its securitising approach. These contributors argue that critical approaches to human security can only be emancipatory by challenging the assumptions at the heart of the human security discourse. It is suggested that the promise of emancipation by the intervention of external, western actors, on the basis of their ability to engage with the local and to challenge structured inequalities neglects the problems of autonomy and agency so central to emancipation. Even at its most radical then, the human security framework posits and reproduces the bifurcated liberal world view of liberator and liberated, emancipator and emancipated.

Human security and the reproduction of power

The commentators in the second part of the book seek to constitute a critical approach to human security which is not posited on the liberal assumptions of an external agency of emancipation, with many explicitly drawing upon the work of Michel Foucault to provide an alternative framework of analysis. This approach challenges the asserted critical counterposition of human security to neo-liberal orthodoxy and liberal peace. From a discussion of sovereign power and biopower through the analysis of economy of power in human security to its biologisation, dehumanisation and globalisation, the second part of the book examines claims that highlight the operation of regimes of liberal power within the area of human security.

Foucaultian approaches to human security intimately connect security discourses and practices to varied sociopolitical regimes of power while paying greater attention to the examination of wider, structural sociopolitical processes, and the forms of life itself. This type of exploration claims to incorporate the concerns about freedom, liberal values and liberal political economy encompassed by human security. Additionally, Foucaultian examinations of human security disavow the 'problem-solving' agendas that focus on the abstract individual and the neo-liberal imperatives of the 'liberal peace'. They also bring new analytical insights and disciplinary areas into the picture, particularly the life sciences and economy. Life sciences focus on physiological and biological processes and on the exercise and circulation of power that has as its aim the introduction of self-discipline ('soft regulation') rather than the economically-imposed external compulsion of the market.

What is more, Foucaultian analysis of human security connects to economic frameworks of rational choice analysis because this is how freedom is being understood and validated in both core western and developing countries. However, the examination of economy here is not primarily about the power of economic forces but rather the 'economy of power'. The economy of power can be expressed as different forms of governmentality (the techniques and technologies used by governments) organised in frameworks of welfare liberalism or neo-liberalism, for example. Here it is often highlighted that neo-liberal 'economies of power' utilise a more subtle technique of regulating society through governments 'decentralising' to facilitate the market choices of individuals and 'empowering' NGOs; here emancipation itself is problematised as merely reproducing power hierarchies through the mechanisms through which the emancipated individual becomes the focal point of new forms of regulation.

The structure of the book

In chapter 2, Tim Dunne and Nicholas Wheeler set up the section on critical emancipatory approaches to human security through arguing the importance of putting humans at the centre of security. This chapter develops a critical conception of security by showing the limits of traditional realist and pluralist discourses. It does this by exploring the deficiencies of realist and pluralist approaches when it comes to thinking about the promotion of human rights. Realism leads to moral indifference and a myopic approach to security and pluralism is complacent about how the rules and norms of international society exclude humanitarian concerns. The chapter argues for a critical approach to security that places human rights at the centre of theory and praxis, reflecting the fundamental indivisibility of security and human rights. The chapter concludes by reflecting on the implications for agency of this position.

Chapter 3 by David Bosold provides a critical policy analysis of the development of human security. This chapter questions the commonly held wisdom that the origin of the human security concept has been the United Nations Development Programme's human development report of 1994. It argues that the main reason for this myth-turned-reality has been a naïve focus on the semantic dimension, i.e. a focus on the term 'human security'. Put differently, the emergence of human security as a broader understanding of security has been studied more in terms of a rhetorical re-branding of security than as a shift in the general thinking of what constitutes security and the ultimate referent object. A closer re-reading of documents calling for new security paradigms in the framework of the United Nations reveals that a more inclusive form and multifaceted nature of security has actually been promoted since the late 1970s. It was, however, not before the end of the Cold War when these previously conceptualised forms of security were actually increasingly accepted and addressed in the framework of new security strategies and policies. A genealogy of human security also reveals an additional irony, namely that due to the lack of clear practices outlined in the UNDP report, the adoption of human security by countries such as Canada actually led to a silencing of a number of issues that were raised at the outset by the UNDP and eventually resulted in a national human security policy that has been more strongly rooted in old security practices than one would expect from a seemingly progressive security concept.

Oliver Richmond, in chapter 4, extends the analysis of emancipatory approaches to human security through a consideration of the limits of liberal peacebuilding. Agreeing with Bosold's analysis regarding the co-option of liberal peacebuilding, he suggests that an appeal to the emancipatory aspect of human security offers some hope for the concept's revitalisation in an international system (or western-oriented international community) that still remains concerned with helping or 'saving' others. However, significant obstacles remain if this emancipatory version of it is to be framed by the liberal peace, by liberal statebuilding, and by western interveners' capacities (or lack thereof), interests, norms, policies and theories. If this community is to determine and provide for its others in conflict settings, emancipatory human security should not operate as if its subjects are helpless and incapacitated would-be liberals, but instead should help determine an approach to security on post-liberal terms and which enables local autonomous agencies (self-government and self-determination) in negotiation with international norms. A post-colonial version of HS should emerge, in other words, capable of organising hybrid understandings of security in relation to the human subjects they produce rather than falling back on the often empty securitisation of western forms of liberalism and realism.

In chapter 5, Giorgio Shani follows Richmond's focus on a post-colonial approach to human security. He argues that at the heart of conventional discourses on human security is a concern with the individual and that the individual is viewed as 'unencumbered', abstracted from the social and cultural mores of his or her community, and invested with formal political equality. While the 'narrow approach' to human security seeks to 'protect' the individual from external threats to their 'physical security or safety', the 'broader approach' seeks both to protect 'the vital core of all human lives in ways that enhance human freedoms and human fulfilment' and 'to empower them to act on their own behalf'. However, the cultural context within which the individual realises his/her self-consciousness or is 'empowered' is either ignored or downplayed. The de-historicised and deracinated individual – it is argued – is consequently reduced to 'bare life'. He argues that human dignity remains, despite the homogenising impulses of neo-liberal globalisation, embedded in the 'thick' values of cultural and religious communities. A major source of human insecurity, it is claimed, comes from the failure of states, in the North as well as the

South, to recognise the increasing cultural diversity of their populations which has resulted from globalisation. This is illustrated by highlighting the difficulties faced by Sikhs in France in gaining recognition of their culturally distinct way of life from an assimilationist state committed to laïcité.

In chapter 6, David Roberts seeks to circumvent the limits of universal, community and individual-orientated imaginings of human security to articulate a policy by transposing Foucault's classification of state populations with shared contingencies and characteristics to pan-national sub-state human groups that face similar contingencies of biopoverty (the civil-institutional denial of physiological necessity), and which consequently share similar biopolitical needs. These human security groupings can then be prioritised around highest mortality rates. The chapter then proposes that such groups exhibiting similarly treatable physiological contingencies, understood in terms of lethal biopoverty, can be enhanced by mobilising indigenous capacity through World Bank credits aimed at local and regional private sector solutions activating community-orientated clean water and sanitation provision. World Bank cooperation is generated by western civil-society-inspired, state-led norms entrepreneurialism via the Bank's Board of Governors. This approach recognises the role of asymmetric power, but co-opts neo-liberal control technologies to bypass the theoretical impasses in human security while framing high-impact, high-yield policies and outcomes focused on millions of everyday lives.

In chapter 7, the concluding chapter of part 1, Mandy Turner, Neil Cooper and Michael Pugh argue that human security has become too co-opted by power to provide the basis for an emancipatory approach and that it has been rapidly mainstreamed by power largely because of its perceived radicalism. It allows bureaucrats working in government and international institutions to highlight and target some issues traditionally ignored in the state security discourse, while not challenging their positions or that of their governments/organisations, or straying into the dangerous waters of critiquing the global structures of economic and political power. Human security is a malleable concept, which is where its strength – and the source of its co-option – lies. The chapter explores this co-option and institutionalisation through an analysis of peacebuilding, arms control and economic development. The authors emphasise that human security has lost its way through an analysis which uncovers identical processes at work in the three different policy arenas and argue that, despite its original radical promise, the human security discourse has been applied in ways that has meant the prioritisation and politicisation of some issues, and the depoliticisation of, and relative silence about, others. Rather than being open to the charge that human security frameworks are too amorphous, in prioritising everything and thus nothing, they argue that the key to understanding human security's dominance is in considering what is prioritised and what is left out. Such a paradigm shift would need to operate at two levels: continuous and equitable engagement with diverse local, cultural and welfare dynamics on the one hand, and restructuring or disempowerment of the existing financial hegemony at a global level. This chapter therefore concludes by proposing the necessity of a new research agenda configured around the development of a 'life welfare' paradigm –

one that is value-based, that coexists with civil society and that de-securitises the human in human security.

In chapter 8, the opening chapter of part 2 on the dangers of linking security with protecting humanity at risk is by Tara McCormack. She begins by emphasising that the concept of human security has traditionally been understood to be a progressive step away from the narrow conceptions of military and territorial security that have dominated international relations. In this logic, the human security framework is argued to have the potential to empower and emancipate individuals through putting the individual at the centre of policy, analysis and debate, and addressing the real problems faced by individuals in their daily lives. McCormack, nevertheless, demonstrates in her chapter that the human security framework cannot live up to its promises to empower the citizens of poor and developing countries. In concrete terms, she argues that whilst the human security framework problematises the relationship between the state and its citizens, it puts in its place unaccountable relationships with other states or international agencies, effectively further disempowering citizens in weak or unstable states. Therefore, the human security framework serves to enforce international power inequalities and renders intervention by powerful states and international institutions less clear and accountable. Finally, McCormack generalises her arguments in maintaining that emancipatory approaches to security are deeply problematic with regard to agency.

Chapter 9, by David Chandler, argues that the history of the radical challenge of 'human security' is often written by its advocates – from its first usage, in the United Nations Development Programme's 1994 Human Development Report, until today – in terms, which pose the centrality of the struggle between realist, traditional, state-based, interest-based approaches and new, liberal, cosmopolitan, de-territorialised, values-based approaches, which focus on individual human needs. For some authors, this struggle is still at the heart of how they conceive of international relations and questions of security; and one which, after 9/11 and with the ongoing disaster of Iraq, is more important than ever. This struggle for the heart and soul of global policy-making is often posed, by its advocates, as one between two different 'paradigms', two entirely different outlooks on the world: one paradigm reproducing current power relations and inequalities and insecurities, the other paradigm challenging this view, recognising the interconnectedness, interdependence and mutual vulnerabilities of security threats and the need for collective, collaborative, human-centred responses. More recently, the frameworks of human security advocates have been challenged by radical critics, asserting that rather than universal claims of 'human security' empowering individuals, they, in fact, represent the expansion of new relations and technologies of governance, through which global regulatory norms operate on behalf of neo-liberal capitalism, framed through the 'biopolitical' imperative of securing populations rather than the security of states. The universal framing of human security therefore has been understood as constitutive of a new globalised international order, both by the radical advocates and radical critics of 'human security'. This chapter first highlights the success of constructivism in challenging traditional rationalist framings of security and then draws out how the move to idealist constructions has been reinforced through approaches which have sought to criticise human security on the basis of its universalising claims.

In chapter 10, Marc Doucet and Miguel de Larrinaga argue that, in shifting its referent from the state to the individual, the concept and discourse of human security has often been conceived by its advocates as opening the possibility of mobilising the high political capital of security on behalf of humanitarian goals. In this light, the concept was understood as a progressive move away from the traditional state-sponsored notion of security, which was often secured through the massive loss of human life, towards a more human-centred conception that would be deployed as a means of safeguarding life. In having the health and welfare of the individual as its target, human security also sought to qualify the relationship between state sovereignty and security in such a way as to make sovereignty conditional on the state's ability to first provide security for its population rather than for itself. Thus, the concept of human security was meant to qualify sovereignty, and by extension set the ground for the authorisation of international intervention in the name of preserving human life. This chapter deploys the work of Michel Foucault and Giorgio Agamben in order to explore how, contrary to its claims of a progressive move towards bringing security onto the grounds of humanitarian emancipatory concerns, the concept and discourse of human security are bound up with an assemblage of global sovereign and biopolitical rule which further extend forms of domination

Suvi Alt, in chapter 11, takes a slightly different tack to Doucet and de Larringa's deployment of Foucault and Agamben to critique human security as an instrument of the contemporary assemblage of biopower and sovereign power. While this chapter too recognises the intimate relationship between biopower and sovereign power, the aim here is to problematise this conflation of Foucault with Agamben, suggesting that Foucaultian and Agambenite perspectives offer in fact very different kinds of critiques of human security. Whereas Doucet and de Larrinaga's focus on human security as the 'responsibility to protect' leads them to emphasise the role of sovereign power, this chapter, in contrast, examines material that offers a broader conception of human security, hence allowing for a critique of human security that is more interested in the workings of biopower. A Foucaultian reading offers an account of the human in the human security discourse as the object of a power exercised through both technologies of the self and technologies of domination. An Agambenite reading, on the other hand, places the discussion on human security around the concept of 'bare life'; the politicised form of pure biological life. But Doucet and de Larrinaga's account leaves the implications of ascribing bare life to human security unexamined. This chapter will make explicit how Agamben's philosophical radicalism is in danger of turning into political passivism when applied as a political analytical tool. In contrast, a Foucaultian account, especially when drawing from his later works, leaves more room for the political agency of the subjects of human security. While the works of both Foucault and Agamben can be used in reading the discourse of human security as limiting the potentiality of being human, it is nevertheless necessary to recognise the very different implications for politics these readings entail.

In chapter 12, Nik Hynek investigates human security as an intellectual project having certain practical effects. It begins by arguing that the conventional understanding of human security (HS) as a policy-making pet project *par excellence* – including the associated, problem-solving academic derivatives – has considerably limited its possible heuristic potential and has steered analysts' attention away from deeper structural levels from which human security has emerged, grown and sedimented. The observation on which the chapter rests is that attention needs to be directed to deeper levels from which a certain version of human security emerged, to which it later retreated, and from which it, again, re-emerged in its most recent manifestation of an explicit and successfully sedimented doctrine. Hynek argues that human security needs to be analysed through an examination of individuals in their dual, hybrid quality of subjects of security and objects of security against the backdrop of liberal order. In order to do so, historical trajectories of economic and political liberalism and their links to political and security rationalities are central to the analysis. Hynek therefore discusses the relevant conceptualisation of civil society and the state in the work of Michel Foucault and follows this with a historical treatment of human security, highlighting how nineteenth century security discourses can be seen to have visible echoes in the post-Cold War world, which represents a powerful mixture of old elements and distinctively new characteristics.

In chapter 13, Kyle Grayson explores how the theory and practice of human security is linked to more general disciplinary and biopolitical relations of power. Taking human security's own narrative of origins as a starting point, this chapter asks – paraphrasing Foucault: does human security act in opposition to power mechanisms that had operated unimpeded prior to its political emergence, or is it a part of the same historico-political network as those things it denounces? He argues that the narrative of emergence, including its inclusions and exclusions, is shared by many in the field and shapes contemporary understandings of what is at stake in discussions of human security and the function or role of human security in contemporary global politics. From this analysis, two observations are made. First – and perhaps paradoxically – that human security is unable to escape from specific forms of the sovereign state as the referent objects of security policy. Second, human security cannot meaningfully express an understanding of individualised security that is not tied to the sovereign state through the concept of citizenship (i.e. citizenship is a precursor for security). Within the literature, this lingering presence of the state is not seen to be problematic; many have argued both within the academic and policy communities that human security and state security are complementary. In contrast, Grayson conducts a critical investigation of the type of state and human that ideally is supposed to be conceived and produced through the theory and practice of human security. He concludes by asking if human security has, in fact, shed the geopolitical baggage of state security's primary concern with containment of perceived disorder, suggesting that this framing sheds light on what exactly is being provided through the practices of human security provision.

In chapter 14, the concluding chapter of this collection, Mark Neocleous challenges the assumption that security should be a key concept in a politics of emancipation, an assumption that runs through much of the debate about 'human security'. He does this by offering a reading of security's fascist moment, by interpreting the Third Reich as a security project par excellence. This fascist moment reveals that far from emancipation, security more easily lends itself to a politics of dehumanisation, in which humans are objects to be slaughtered rather than subjects to be emancipated. The outcome of this is the argument that we should abandon the logic of security altogether rather than attempt to 'humanise' it.

Part I

2 'We the peoples'

Contending discourses of security in human rights theory and practice

Tim Dunne and Nicholas J. Wheeler[1]

'Security is the first word which occurs to me if I look back on my youth – security not only in family relations, but in a sense scarcely imaginable since 1914.' This autobiographical reflection, by one of the greatest thinkers in the history of academic International Relations, is revealing for the way in which E. H. Carr attached significance to security in a very personal sense as well as the more traditional notion of security 'out there' in world politics. It also concentrates the reader's mind on the fact that there has been so much *insecurity* produced in the intervening years. And contrary to the hopes of the earliest professors of International Relations, the discipline has for the most part been muted in its response to the culture of violence that conditions the lives of the majority of the earth's inhabitants. The fact that the study of International Relations all too often sided with the status quo was one of the reasons why Carr abandoned the discipline in preference for the study of the Soviet Union which at least, in his view, promised a new and more equal society.

It is regrettable that Carr did not see the emergence of a 'critical' approach to International Relations that first began to stir around the time of his death in 1982.[2] Critical theory makes the familiar seem strange, asks how our ideas about common sense are constructed, and recognizes an imperative to change the world. In place of the traditional ontology of soldiers and diplomats, one view of critical theory 'places the victims at the centre of its enquiries' (Wyn Jones 1995). As this special issue demonstrates, when applied to security, critical theory provides a radically different theoretical account of the meaning and production of security. A key claim of critical security theorists is that the rules, norms and institutions of the society of states are a permissive cause of political violence because they provide a protected space in which individuals can be subjected to inhuman treatment with virtual impunity.

The crucial contribution of critical conceptions of security is to shift the referent object from the state to individuals who constitute humanity as a whole. Rather than taking for granted the traditional assumption that the state has a monopoly over our loyalty and identity, critical security perspectives extend our moral horizons beyond national-based conceptions of citizenship. This shift in ontology from an exclusivist 'us and them' identity relationship to an internationalist or cosmopolitan 'we the peoples' is embodied in the Preamble to the United Nations Charter and has subsequently been echoed by various voices in global civil society. 'We the peoples' not only represented a significant advance in the normative vocabulary of international relations; it also permeated the framing of the human rights regime that developed after 1945.[3] In the various documents which constitute the regime, an explicit link is made between human rights and security. This is clear from Article 3 of the 1948 Universal Declaration of Human Rights (UDHR) that proclaims 'the right to life, liberty and security of person' to all human beings.

The creation of law-making international institutions committed to the protection of human rights was predicated upon the assumption that sovereign states would stand guard over the security of their citizens and promote human rights internationally. The experience of the post-1945 world has shown this to be naive at best, morally complacent at worst. Realist thinking on security has proved to be more resilient than defenders of human rights had hoped. After 11 September 2001, and crucially the American response in the form of the 'war on terror', realism seems once again to be in the ascendancy. The ensuing cycle of terror attacks and attacks on terror prompted the usually optimistic liberal writer, Michael Ignatieff, to ask if the human rights era had come to an end (Ignatieff 2002). We argue that such a judgement is premature: even states engaged in the war against global terrorism recognize that human rights remain an important objective.[4] Rather than seeing one discourse triumph over another, a more sophisticated account of security after 9/11 would show how national security and humanitarianism uneasily coexist in practice, and that critical theory offers a possibility of overcoming such a tension.

This article begins by showing how the sovereign prerogatives of the society of states have frustrated the promise of solidarity implicit in 'we the peoples'. Having used critical theory to expose such flaws in traditional conceptions of security, the second half of the article will reflect on the immanent possibilities for constituting a new discourse of human security. We argue that the project of unifying human rights and security requires a multidimensional approach to agency. It is not a matter of humanity versus statism, as Richard Falk once put it, but instead requires an alliance of states and transnational civil society cooperating to achieve security for common humanity.

Discourses of security

In this section we examine the two dominant discourses of security and the practices they have legitimated. By discourse, we mean an authoritative narrative mobilized by political elites to justify a particular set of prescriptions for action (or inaction) (Crawford and Lipschutz 1997: 167).

Realism and the discourse of national security

All forms of critical theory purport to 'think against' the prevailing current. Critical security studies is no exception. What it wants to resist, transcend and defeat are theories of security which take for granted *who* is to be secured (the state), *how* security is to be achieved (by defending core 'national' values, forcibly if necessary) and from *whom* security is needed (the enemy). This understanding of security was neatly encapsulated by Walter Lippmann writing in 1943: 'A nation is secure to the extent to which it is not in danger of having to sacrifice core values, if it wishes to avoid war, and is able, if challenged, to maintain them in a victory in such a war' (Lippmann 1943, quoted in Ayoob 1997).

There is no better example of traditional thinking than the discourse of 'national security' which framed US thinking on defence and foreign policy during the Cold War. Promoting national security implied a desire to prevail over enemies who threatened the values of the 'nation'. Security, in this sense, was the protective shield of American society. The values of that society were thought to be self-evident, and were subject to minimal reflection by realist theorists. It was assumed by the realist strategists, that the Cold War was a permanent condition of international relations, one in which self-help and power politics were the only games in town. All means were acceptable to attain national security, including strategies of nuclear war-fighting which were justified on the highly dubious grounds that the Soviet Union was developing the capabilities to fight and win a nuclear war. The logic of this was that western deterrence required fashioning a theory and strategy of nuclear victory for the US and its allies.

Realists got it wrong. The Cold War was not a permanent condition. Nor was it a structural necessity; rather, it was a confrontation that they had played a significant part in creating and reproducing. But the discourse of 'national security' has not died despite the revisioning of East–West relations: the *who* of security has remained stable. The state is still the condition for the survival of 'national' core values. The *how* has become the subject of some debate, however. Not, of course, the assumption that the US needs a strong defence, and has to be prepared to use force. But there has been a debate among realists as to whether the proliferation of weapons of mass destruction strengthens or undermines national security. On the side of the former, there is the 'more is better' brigade which believes that the benefits of nuclear deterrence should be extended to stabilize relations between enemy states. In the opposite camp stand realists in the Pentagon who worry about the spread of weapons of mass destruction (WMD) – and their means of ballistic missile delivery – to 'rogue' states like Iraq, Iran and North Korea.

After 9/11 this threat assessment is reinforced by the very real concern that such weapons could find their way – either through deliberate intention or inadvertence – into the hands of terrorist groups like al-Qaeda. For realists like US Secretary of Defense Donald Rumsfeld, the only means of addressing the threat posed by rogue states and terrorist groups armed with WMDs is to ensure that such capabilities are never developed in the first place. This is the logic that drives the current US strategy of preventive war – first set out by President George W. Bush in his West Point speech of June 2002, and subsequently elaborated in the National Security Strategy of September 2002.[5] By naming the threat posed by states like Iraq, Iran and North Korea as an 'axis of evil', the Bush Administration has sought to legitimate the spending of billions of dollars on developing a defence posture that is capable of supporting the President's declared goal of regime change in these states. This demonstrates how the Cold War discourse of national security is being reinvented as a struggle between an America that represents a force for good in the world and the evil enemy represented by global terrorism and its state sponsors.

Where do human rights fit into this realist picture of security? Realist proponents of national security do not deny the existence of human rights norms such as those embodied in the Universal Declaration of Human Rights. But crucially, realism argues that they are norms which are not binding on states when they collide with other interests (such as trade or national security). Hans J. Morgenthau, the godfather of realism, argued that:

> the principle of the defense of human rights cannot be consistently applied in foreign policy because it can and must come in conflict with other interests that may be more important than the defense of human rights in a particular circumstance.
>
> (quoted in Donnelly 1991: 22)

Realists also point to the centrality of states in implementing human rights standards and the weak or non-existent enforcement machinery. As a leading representative of the US delegation at San Francisco made clear, '"We the peoples" means that the peoples of the world were speaking through their governments'.[6] Amnesty International's annual report is a constant reminder that realist thinking on human rights is part of the fabric of contemporary international society. A recent report summarized its findings against the backdrop of the war on terror as follows: 'Governments have spent billions to strengthen national security and the "war on terror". Yet for millions of people, the real sources of insecurity are corruption, repression, discrimination, extreme poverty and preventable diseases' (Amnesty International 2003). This is nothing new. Driven by expediency and self-interest, governments have long trampled on their citizens' rights in order to maintain the power and privilege of an elite few. In the language of International Relations theory, what Amnesty is describing is the problem of statism, by which is meant the idea that the state should be the sole source of loyalty and values for its citizens.[7] Amnesty claims that the majority of states routinely fail to deliver even basic rights to their citizens. Governments or agencies acting on their behalf routinely imprison without trial, torture and/or kill individuals who challenge the regime.

The Westphalian practice of statism infects international bodies such as the United Nations. Amnesty International points to the *realpolitik* in the General Assembly and the UN Commission on Human Rights that it charges as being 'almost irrelevant to the protection of victims in Burundi, Rwanda, and the Democratic Republic of Congo' (Amnesty International 1998: 68). It is not unusual to find that no state has tabled a condemnatory resolution at the UN General Assembly even after it has been presented with evidence of gross human rights violations. Consistent with the charge of statism is the argument that the UN is merely an arena for *raison d'état*, a kind of global Westphalian system where the language for the conduct of international relations has changed but the interests remain the same. Human rights in this context have represented, in the words of Norman Lewis, 'nothing more than an empty abstraction whose function was the legitimation and perpetuation of the given system of power relations, domestically and internationally' (Lewis 1998: 89).

Pluralism and the discourse of international security

Although realism was undoubtedly the dominant discourse of international politics in the post-1945 period, it was not, as the realists believed, the *only* theory to have purchase on reality. There was an alternative, other than the radical discourses; this was the so-called pluralist or legalist theory which maintains that security should be provided by international rules and norms. From this perspective, narrowly defined self-help was not a descriptively or normatively accurate depiction of international politics. States, according to Hedley Bull, form an international society because they are 'conscious of certain common interests and common values' and believe themselves to be 'bound by a common set of rules and institutions' (Bull 1977: 13). The social fact of this society is the source of states' obligations to one another; primary among these is a responsibility to maintain international order which theorists of international society take to be synonymous with the provision of international security.

The discourse of security for theorists of international society makes the *who* of security – the referent object – the security of the society of states. With respect to human rights, we have already encountered the standard critique mobilized against this view by critical security theorists, namely, that the rules of sovereignty and non-intervention issue a licence for statist elites to abuse human rights from behind the walls of sovereignty. In response, pluralists would argue that while the rules are inhospitable to the protection of human rights, making the latter the referent object for security would place in jeopardy the foundations of international order. They would further argue that it is too easy to interpret their privileging of order over human rights as an ethically bankrupt position since the moral justification for pluralist practices is their contribution to individual security. Thus, Bull believed that international order is only to be valued to the extent to which it delivers world order which he defined as the provision of the primary goals of social life to all individuals such as 'security from violence'.[8] Bull was elusive about the relationship between international order and world order, but there is no doubt that he made the latter the normative test in judging the success of the institutions of international society such as diplomacy, law and the balance of power in providing the *how* of security.

Advocates of a pluralist view of security would further argue that in the post-1945 period an important linkage has been established between the provision of human rights and wider international security. Reflecting on the terrible domestic and international consequences of the rise of Fascism in Europe, the framers of the UN Charter believed that there was a clear link between good governance at home and peace abroad. Although practice has tragically turned out very differently, it is clear from reading the UN Charter that there is no necessary or automatic conflict between the cardinal rules of sovereignty and non-intervention in Article 2 and the human rights standards set out in Articles 55 and 56. For the first time in history governments committed themselves to protect human rights, a significant retreat from the Westphalian conception of unlimited sovereignty. This was marked by the Preamble to the Charter which signalled a declaratory shift in legal thinking in favour of 'we the peoples'. As Jack Donnelly has argued, the post-1945 human rights regime represented a significant shift in the normative language of international politics. Three years after the signing of the UN Charter, the UDHR was accepted by the UN General Assembly on 10 December 1948. Although this was declaratory and non-binding, the document provided further hope to people living under governments that denied them their dignity. According to Article 28, 'Everyone is entitled to a social and international order in which the rights and freedoms set forth on this Declaration can be fully realized' (United Nations 1948: Article 28).

The manifesto for human rights and international security contained within the Charter and the Declaration represented, therefore, a considerable challenge to the traditional realist paradigm. As a consequence of these standard-setting instruments, and the UN human rights regime which developed in the years after 1945 to monitor compliance with them, the way in which a state behaved towards its own citizens became in R. J. Vincent's words 'a legitimate subject of international scrutiny and censure' (Vincent 1986: 152). While the regime can monitor and report on human rights violations, pluralists emphasize that the capacity of the society of states to 'do something' depends ultimately on interests and morality coinciding.

The failure of international society to prevent or halt the genocide in Rwanda in 1994 demonstrated the limits of this conception of the relationship between human rights and security. The mass exodus of refugees across the Rwandan border into neighbouring states clearly affected regional security, but no government in Africa was either capable or willing to intervene to end the atrocities. However, can it really be argued that the genocide in Rwanda posed a threat to western security interests that justified sacrificing soldiers' lives and scarce resources? Western governments answered this question with a resounding no, and this is why no action was taken to stop the third genocide of the twentieth century (the other two being the extermination of the Armenians and the Jews).

Whereas Rwanda highlights the ethical limitations of international society's framing of human rights and security, there have been some important successes in conjoining human rights and security. One of the most notable is the Helsinki Process in the 1970s and 1980s. This was justified on the grounds that a critical relationship existed between respect for human rights in the Eastern Bloc and improved interstate relations between East and West. The Soviet Union accepted that the price for western legitimation of the post-war status quo in Central and Eastern Europe was its signing of the human rights provisions in the 1975 Helsinki Final Act. However, what the Soviet Union and its allies interpreted as rhetorical commitments became important weapons in the struggle of human rights activists in Czechoslovakia, Poland, Hungary and the German Democratic Republic. Their courageous struggle to hold eastern governments accountable for their human rights abuses was supported by western governments who used human rights as an instrument of Cold War diplomacy. These efforts on the inside and the outside played a key role in robbing the Communist regimes of their legitimacy which led to the revolutions of 1989.[9]

The limits of traditional discourses of security

One entry point for critical security thinkers with respect to human rights is to reveal the limitations of the morality of states discourse by showing how the UN Charter system systematically fails to deliver on its promise to provide both international security and human rights. Whereas outright rejection is an appropriate critical security response to realism for normative reasons, pluralism needs to be engaged because of its immanent universalism. The fact is that if all states followed the principles and rules of the 'international bill of rights', then there would be no individuals without food, democratic governance, legal protection, education, national identity, property and an adequate standard of living. However, one major reason why this does not happen, according to proponents of critical security studies, is because states only obey the rules of international society when power and interest make it prudent for them to do so. Thus, Britain and the US carried the banner of civil and political rights against the Soviet Union because it served their power political interests, but both felt more than justified in supporting the apartheid regime in South Africa which practised racial hatred and massively violated the economic and social rights of the majority, as well as conducting campaigns against neighbours that resulted in massive casualties. The lesson is when human rights collide with the goals of either national or international security, these interests win out every time.

Western governments are particularly (although not exclusively) guilty of inconsistently complying with the human rights standards they trumpet with missionary-like enthusiasm at the various multilateral social gatherings. This argument is frequently and eloquently made by the public intellectual Noam Chomsky. From Vietnam to the Vienna Declaration on Human Rights, he castigates the US for its hypocritical approach to human rights in foreign policy. He attacked the decision of President George Bush Sr to forcibly return Haitian people seeking asylum (in contravention of Article 14 of the UDHR). Presidential candidate Bill Clinton fiercely condemned this policy, but according to Chomsky, 'his first act as President was to make the illegal blockade still harsher' (Chomsky 1998: 31). Or take the US government's persistent suspicion of economic and social rights, which UN Ambassador Jean Kirkpatrick once described as 'a letter to Santa Claus' (quoted in Chomsky 1998: 32). The US vetoed the right to development in 1992 despite Article 25 of the UDHR's commitment to 'a right to a standard of living' adequate for 'health and well-being'. Only the US and Somalia have not ratified the 1989 Convention on the Rights of the Child. For Chomsky, these practices illustrate Washington's largely rhetorical commitment to 'the universality of human rights', except as a weapon used selectively against others (Chomsky 1998: 31).

The most fundamental weakness of the pluralist discourse on security and human rights relates to what it excludes from consideration as security problems. What issues get named as 'security' ones is crucial to whether individuals survive or perish. Pluralism is silent on the politics that produces the following litany of global human wrongs:

- Every day more than 30,000 children around the world die of preventable diseases, a total of over 11 million a year.
- The richest 5 percent of the world's people have incomes 114 times those of the poorest 5 percent. The richest 1 percent receive as much income as the poorest 57 percent.
- 2.8 billion people live on less than $2 a day, with 1.2 billion of them subsisting on less than $1 a day.
- In 1997–99 an estimated 815 million people were undernourished.
- During the 1990s the number of people in extreme poverty in Sub-Saharan Africa rose from 242 million to 300 million.
- By the end of 2000 almost 22 million people (now updated by the UNDP to 24.8 million) had died of AIDS, 13 million children had lost their mother or both parents to the disease and more than 40 million people were living with HIV. Of these, 90 percent were in developing countries and 75 percent were in Sub-Saharan Africa.
- There are 100 million 'missing' women who would be alive but for infanticide, neglect and sex-selective abortion.
- Every year there are 300 million cases of malaria, 90 percent of them in Sub-Saharan Africa.
- More than 500,000 women die a year as a result of pregnancy and childbirth.

(United Nations 2002: 10–30)[10]

Even for the survivors, life can be nasty, brutish and short. What causes this production and reproduction of gross and systematic human rights abuses is strongly disputed by liberals and Marxists. But what is clear is that the massive structural inequalities generated by global capitalism have not been given sufficient attention by theorists of international society. For the last two decades, leading states in the system such as Britain and the US have promoted a neo-liberal economic ideology that centres upon the following principles that have governed the debt and aid policies of the International Monetary Fund (IMF) and World Bank in the 1980s and 1990s: free trade, deregulation, reduction of public spending and freedom of choice for individual consumers. International institutions and regimes, such as the G8 and the various International Financial Institutions (IFIs) have internalized these neo-liberal norms. From a global humanitarian perspective, the consequence of these policies has been twofold: first, a redistribution of wealth from the underdeveloped to the developed world (the 'trickle-up' effect); and second, a decline in the ability of states to provide economic and welfare rights to their population. In short, the scope for a state to deliver a system of justice which would be acceptable to the least advantaged has diminished considerably. The consequences of both these factors have been to undermine the provision of economic and social rights.

The critical theory of security advanced here opposes the pluralist conception of security on three main grounds: first, it argues that states conform to the internationalist and humanitarian rules of the UN Charter only when it is in their selfish interests; second, it argues that pluralism in its focus on the rules and norms of international society ignores most deaths by political violence; and third, the normative practices of the society of states leave untouched the structural causes of the economic and social injustice rooted in the deregulated capitalist world system.

The last two factors converge in the case of the trade in weapons, which arms the aggressors, authoritarian regimes and torturers of the world. Writing in the early 1980s, Bull described the superpowers as the 'great irresponsibles'. In the context of the post-Cold War period, there is probably no better illustration of this apt description than the arms trade. The permanent members of the Security Council, responsible for maintaining 'international peace and security', account for approximately 90 per cent of the world's arms exports, the US with a share of 49 per cent.[11]

When discussing the arms trade, it is important to bear in mind that arms sales can be justified on the grounds that all states have a legitimate right of self-defence. This right is enshrined in customary international law and codified in the UN Charter. This principle is acknowledged by human rights organizations like Amnesty International, and their opposition is to arms sales that bolster governments that repress human rights inside their borders. One of the most worrying aspects of the arms trade is the lack of concerted control exercised by exporters to ensure that weapons are used for legitimate defensive purposes. Once again, the pluralist rules regulating the trade in weapons are either weak, non-existent or ignored altogether. The wider issue raised by the arms trade concerns the degree of militarization found in the developing world in particular. Child soldiers (under 15 years of age) have been used in combat in civil conflicts in Russia, India, Cambodia, Iran, Iraq, Turkey, Afghanistan, Sudan, Ethiopia, Eritrea, Somalia, Columbia, Peru, Nicaragua, Guatemala, Burma and Vietnam. Although there has been a marked decline in the trade in major weapons, the trade in light weapons – the kind used in civil conflicts – has spiralled out of control.

Human security

A critical security approach to human rights opens with a fundamental belief in the indivisibility of security and human rights. How does this 'indivisibility' play out in practice? The human security discourse would maintain, for example, that there can be no security for the individual if their right to life is being threatened by their government. Similarly, security is absent when an individual is denied the rights to subsistence, such as food, clothing and housing. If security is defined as protection from harm, then it is clear that the infringement of fundamental rights signifies the presence of insecurity.[12]

Just as its prescriptive orientation emphasizes indivisibility, the human security discourse recognizes the multidimensionality of the sources of harm. There are military and non-military producers of harm, national and transnational, private and public. Harm can be the outcome of intentional acts (employers using child labour) as well as unreflective acts (children in the west buying a football that has been manufactured by heavily exploited workers in India). Rights may be secured by one agent while simultaneously being threatened by another. For example, the citizens of a social democratic society may have all their human rights protected by the state, but that does not necessarily mean their community has security. It could, for example, have borders that are contiguous with a predatory state committed to an expansionist foreign policy. Another threat could be transnational and unintentional, such as that posed by high levels of radioactivity caused by an accident in a nuclear power station (for example, the disaster at Chernobyl).

We would argue that the interdependence between security and human rights is at its strongest when the focus is upon what Henry Shue, and later R. J. Vincent, referred to as 'basic rights' (Shue 1989: 18–22). 'Security from violence' and 'subsistence' were defined by Shue as the key basic rights. On the surface, this might seem to rely on a narrow definition of rights but we define subsistence as covering a range of economic and social rights (such as work, property, social security) while security from violence includes many civil and political rights (protection from torture, racial hatred, slavery and asylum).

If, as we have argued earlier, the litmus test for human security is success in delivering basic rights, one challenge is to identify the agents who can bring this about. In the critical security literature, global civil society is often represented as being the crucial agent of emancipation. There are many good reasons for investing hope in transnational civil society. Groups like Amnesty International, Médecins Sans Frontières, the International Red Cross, Oxfam and Save the Children exist to raise the consciousness of the security 'haves' about the plight of the 'security have-nots'. Their success is measured in terms of membership, donations and a level of public support which enables their voice to carry weight in the corridors of power. By ordinary acts such as writing letters on behalf of prisoners of conscience, individuals living in the secure sphere of world politics keep alive the hopes of victims of human rights abuses around the world. The moral obligation or duty to assist distant strangers in need demands a commitment to action which goes beyond feelings of pity, since sentimentality is not enough by itself to produce a 'more intense moral or practical commitment' to human security.[13] What is required is the growth of a cosmopolitan moral awareness such that we come to empathize with and respond to the sacrifices made by those fighting for basic rights in repressive regimes. The annual Amnesty International report and its website are replete with references to local human rights organizations fighting for human security. One such group is the pro-democracy movement in Burma led by Daw Aung San Suu Kyi. Although Burmese civil society remains firmly locked in the steel-hard cage of the brutal government, the opposition has won enormous support from world public opinion. Moreover, leaders of human rights groups in South Asia such as Suu Kyi have taken a stand against governmental elites in the region, who as part of their attempt to keep hold of power have argued that human rights are alien to the Asian way of life.

Without transnational human rights groups like Amnesty International and Human Rights Watch monitoring human rights abuses, governments would find it even easier to evade their humanitarian responsibilities to 'we the peoples'. Indeed, one of the most significant changes in the human rights regime in recent decades has been the involvement of transnational civil society in standard-setting. For example, Amnesty International and the International Commission of Jurists had significant input into the UN Declaration and Convention against Torture. Other successes in promoting new standards for protecting human security are evident in the 1989 Convention on the Rights of the Child which owed a great deal to the lobbying of women's human rights NGOs in particular (Ashworth 1999: 270). David Beetham has also convincingly argued that NGOs can make a significant contribution to drawing the attention of world public opinion to abuses of human security in the economic and social realm; for example, their work on famine relief, refugee alert and support, and their wider contribution to promoting economic development (Beetham 1995: 1–9).

There is no doubt that global civil society is playing an increasingly important role in the standard-setting and monitoring of basic rights. Yet the post-Cold War period has given us good reasons for not investing too much hope in transnational civil society as a vehicle for providing human security. The first and most obvious problem is that, when facing supreme humanitarian emergencies, aid agencies only have at best a limited capacity to deliver food or medical supplies. When warring governments (or factions) do allow them to operate in conflict situations, NGOs often become pawns in the wider game of power politics, as was all too clearly the case with the Hutu-run refugee camps in the Great Lakes region of Africa in 1995–6. One of the difficulties here is that aid agencies generate most of their income through the response of public opinion to the kind of 'loud emergencies' they are least able to deal with. Small-scale community projects to do with promoting welfare, health and food security are rarely under the media spotlight and consequently do not rise to the top of NGO agendas.

It is also important to guard against the assumption that transnational movements necessarily promote human security. At the Cairo conference on Population and Development for example, there were groups committed to providing contraception to enhance human security for women. But there were also transnational religious groups opposed to this measure despite AIDS being a huge threat to human security in the developing world. We should not be surprised that transnational forces can be reactionary as well as emancipatory: contradictory normative tendencies are at work in all forms of social organization. The right to life entails different claims (and politics) for Catholics, secular liberals and Hindus. Like all other actors in world politics, NGOs and civil society groups are part of the conversation and struggle about the meaning and interpretation of norms in international relations.

A further concern with global civil society as an emancipatory actor relates to the construction of humanitarianism. In the liberal west, there is a tendency to treat 'security have-nots' as distant objects of our liberal sympathy. Apart from failing to see the insecurity of our neighbours, the problem with the discourse of humanitarianism is that it is ultimately *for* us and *for* some purpose, to adopt Robert Cox's aphorism. We may sometimes imagine ourselves in the shoes of the dispossessed, and we may tell our loved ones sad and sentimental stories of suffering others, but how many of us make any real sacrifices? As the late Rabbi Hugo Grin once put it in the context of the Second World War, 'we cared about the Jews, but we didn't care *enough*'.

Conclusion: agency and human security

This article has put the victims of global politics at the centre of our academic inquiry. The act of bringing together human rights and security provides an opening into a holistic and indivisible approach. At the level of theory, it is possible to make a convincing case for a Kantian synthesis; a violation of security in one part of the world ought to be a violation of security everywhere. And a violation at one level is a violation at all levels. In keeping with the spirit of Critical Security Studies, we have mobilized a case for changing the referent for thinking about security from that of states to 'we the peoples'. The reason for making this move is that all too often states have failed to act as moral trustees for their citizens, creating a situation globally where millions of people have more to fear from the violence or neglect of their own governments than they do from that of neighbouring states. Yet even in those parts of the world where citizens can place greater hope in the rule of law and the provision of basic rights, there has been a failure on the part of governments to live up to the humanitarian obligations imposed by the Charter. The pursuit of these values has been crushed by the power of realism's moral indifference, and numbed by a set of legal rules which have narrowed our moral imaginations.

Expanding humanity's moral horizons requires recognizing both the indivisibility of human rights and security, and the concomitant responsibility to rescue those trapped in situations of violence, poverty and ill-health. This might require the use of force in exceptional cases like genocide and mass murder, but the best way of avoiding such a drastic remedy is to utilize the instrument of preventive diplomacy as soon as there is evidence of abuses. Such measures applied on a concerted and international basis might prevent a deterioration of the human rights situation, avoiding recourse to more costly actions.

Since governments have manifestly failed as guardians of human rights, the question is whether they are – like Nietzsche thought – 'cold monsters'? Or, is it simply that it is too soon to tell whether states can live up to the moral vision that inspired the framing of the Charter? The argument advanced here is that statehood is not an undifferentiated political category; states can be good or bad international citizens just as individuals can be in domestic society. This leads to a rejection of the dualism of agency that pits the state against transnational civil society; we would argue that moral boundaries have frequently been widened when state actors and global civil society have pulled in the same direction. It is not our claim that state leaders are always in the vanguard of this, but as some humanitarian NGOs readily attest, big battalions – measured in military, political and economic terms – are sometimes required to promote their ends. By recognizing the interconnectedness of states *and* global civil society, the article argues for a multidimensional approach to agency in the same manner that critical thinking on security has pioneered a multidimensional conception of 'threats'. The best recent examples of this process of 'top-down' and 'bottom-up' pressures are the emergence of a new norm banning landmines[14] and the development of the International Criminal Court.[15] Enlightened state leaders were crucial in realizing the normative potential of these ideas. But without the pressure exerted by what Geoffrey Robertson calls the global 'human rights movement' (Robertson 1999), it is unlikely that these political projects would have secured the widespread support that they achieved in the society of states.

The pressures exerted on governments by agencies such as Oxfam, Amnesty International and CARE are strengthened the more that these groups can mobilize public opinion to hold governments accountable for their actions. But there has not been *enough* pressure from below to transform the foreign policy agendas of liberal governments so that human rights become as powerful a constituency as commercial and political interests. As Michael Ignatieff argues, citizens exposed to media images of ethnic cleansing and starvation, living in what he calls 'the zones of safety' (Ignatieff 1998) are quite good at reaching for their chequebooks and dropping money into collection boxes. However, this is often selective, both in terms of the proximity of the crisis and the definition of what counts as a supreme humanitarian emergency.

Liberal societies express outrage at the treatment of Kurds, Rwandans or Kosovo Albanians at the hands of state power, but accept as natural the death elsewhere of millions through poverty and malnutrition. They are good at being charitable, but they have been very bad at making even those *modest* changes to lifestyles that could lead to the eradication of global poverty and give real substance to 'we the peoples'. The west punishes those states and terrorist networks which break the rules – Iraq and al-Qaeda being obvious examples – but it has been bad at healing the deep rifts that exist between the west and the rest. Yet as the attacks on 11 September showed, it is not possible to hermetically seal liberal societies from the violent consequences of insecurity in other parts of the world. Had human rights concerns guided the west's relations with post-Soviet Afghanistan and the Taliban, that country would not have become a safe haven for al-Qaeda. Moral exhortations are important in persuading publics and governments in the west to change the *who* and the *how* of security thinking. But the next stage for a critical approach to human security is to advance and win the argument that an unjust world will be a disorderly one for all of us.

Notes

1 This is an amended reprint of '"We the Peoples": Contending Discourses of Security in Human Rights Theory and Practice', published in *International Relations*, vol. 18, no. 1 (2004).
2 Carr was of course a critical thinker but he was not a proponent of critical theory. For critical 'readings' of Carr, see Booth 1991; Linklater 1997 and Cox 2000.
3 Significantly, the phrase 'we the peoples' was used by Kofi Annan to frame his millennium report. See Annan 2000.
4 A good example of this is the UK where Prime Minister Tony Blair has argued that Britain's participation in the war on terror is compatible with liberal internationalism. See T. Blair's speech to the Labour Party Conference, 2 October 2001 and The Fifth Report (Session 2001–2) of the Foreign Affairs Committee *Human Rights Annual Report 2001*.
5 The Bush Administration has not explicitly admitted that it is declaring a strategy of preventive war. Instead, it employs the language of pre-emption, claiming that its policy is in accordance with an interpretation of international law that is suited to the changed

conditions of the world after 9/11. For a discussion of these issues, see Byers 2003: 171–90 and Hendrickson 2002.
6 Leo Pasvolsky, in the Committee on Foreign Relations, 1945. Quoted in Lewis 1998: 87–88.
7 This view of states informs much critical thinking on security. See Booth 1995: 121.
8 This is most explicitly spelt out in Bull 1977: 22.
9 For an insightful account of the human rights–security relationship within the Helsinki Process, see Kaldor 1999.
10 These figures are used by Steve Smith in his ISA 2002 address. See Smith 2004.
11 This makes something of a mockery of Warren Christopher's claim at the World Conference on Human Rights in Vienna in 1992 that 'the worst violators [of human rights] are those who encourage the spread of arms'. Quoted in Chomsky1998: 27.
12 The idea of 'human security' has been discussed in a variety of publications. See, for example, the UN *Human Development Report 1994*. According to the report, human security includes safety from 'chronic threats' such as disease, hunger and repression. See Booth, 1999: 59, and Puchula 1997: 175.
13 This critique of viewing morality as only an education of the sentiments is developed by Geras 1995.
14 For an excellent study of this process in relation to landmines, see Price 1998.
15 For an excellent discussion of this process, see Wippman 2004.

Bibliography

(URLs last accessed in 2002/3)

Amnesty International (1998) *Amnesty International Report 1998*, London: Amnesty International Publications.

—— (2003) *Amnesty International Report 2003*. Online. Available URL http://web.amnesty.org/report2003/index-eng

Annan, K. A. (2000) *We the Peoples*, United Nations. Online. Available URL http://www.un.org/millennium/sg/report/ch0.pdf

Ashworth, G. (1999) 'The Silencing of Women', in T. Dunne and N. J. Wheeler (eds), *Human Rights in Global Politics*, Cambridge: Cambridge University Press, 259–76.

Beetham, D. (1995) 'Human Rights in the Study of Politics', in D. Beetham (ed.), *Politics and Human Rights*, Oxford: Blackwell, 1–9.

Blair, T. (2001) speech to the Labour Party Conference, 2 October 2001 and The Fifth Report (Session 2001–2) of the Foreign Affairs Committee *Human Rights Annual Report 2001*. Online. Available URL http://www.parliament.uk/commons/selcom/fachome.htm

Booth, K. (1991) 'Security in Anarchy: Utopian Realism in Theory and Practice', *International Affairs* 67 (3): 527–45.

—— (1995) 'Human Wrongs and International Relations', *International Affairs* 71 (1): 121.

—— (1999) 'Three Tyrannies', in T. Dunne and N. J. Wheeler (eds), *Human Rights in Global Politics*, Cambridge: Cambridge University Press.

Bull, H. (1977) *The Anarchical Society*, London: Macmillan.

Byers, M. (2003) 'Preemptive Self-defense: Hegemony, Equality and Strategies of Legal Change', *Journal of Political Philosophy* 11 (2): 171–90.

Chomsky, N. (1998) 'The United States and the Challenge of Relativity', in T. Evans (ed.), *Human Rights Fifty Years On: A Reappraisal*, Manchester: Manchester University Press.

Crawford, B. and Lipschutz, R. D. (1997) 'Discourses of War: Security and the Case of Yugoslavia', in K. Krause and M. Williams (eds), *Critical Security Studies: Concepts and Cases*, London: UCL Press.

Cox, M. (ed.) (2000) *E.H. Carr: A Critical Appraisal*, London: Palgrave.
Donnelly, J. (1991) 'Security, Human Rights and East–West Relations: Theoretical Bases of the Linkage', in V. Mastny and J. Zielonka (eds), *Human Rights and Security: Europe on the Eve of a New Era*, Boulder, CO: Westview.
Geras, N. (1995) *Solidarity in the Conversation of Humankind: The Ungroundable Liberalism of Richard Rorty*, London: Verso.
Hendrickson, D. C. (2002) 'Toward Universal Empire: The Dangerous Quest for Absolute Security', *World Policy Journal* 19 (3): 1–10.
Ignatieff, M. (1998) *The Warriors' Honor: Ethnic War and the Modern Conscience*, London: Chatto and Windus.
—— (2002) 'Is the Human Rights Era Ending?', *The New York Times*, 5 February 2002.
Kaldor, M. (1999) 'Transnational Civil Society', in T. Dunne and N. J. Wheeler (eds), *Human Rights in Global Politics*, Cambridge: Cambridge University Press.
Lewis, N. (1998) 'Human Rights, Law and Democracy in an Unfree World', in T. Evans (ed.), *Human Rights Fifty Years On: A Reappraisal*, Manchester: Manchester University Press.
Linklater, A. (1997) 'The Transformation of Political Community: E.H. Carr, Critical Theory and International Relations', *Review of International Studies* 23 (3): 321–38.
Lippmann, W. (1943) *US Foreign Policy: Shield of the Republic*, Boston: Little Brown, quoted in Ayoob, M. (1997) 'Defining Security: A Subaltern Realist Perspective', in K. Krause and M. C. Williams (eds), *Critical Security Studies*, Minneapolis, MN: University of Minnesota Press, 121–46.
Price, R. (1998) 'Reversing the Gun Sights: Transnational Civil Society Targets Land Mines', *International Organization* 52 (3): 613–44.
Puchula, D. J. (1997) 'The United Nations and the Myth of the Unity of Mankind', in Y. S. Choue and J. Shik Sohn (eds), *Peace Strategies for Global Community and the Role of the UN in the 21st Century*, Seoul: Institute of International Peace Studies.
Robertson, G. (1999) *Crimes Against Humanity: The Struggle for Global Justice*, London: Allen Lane.
Shue, H. (1989) *Basic Rights: Subsistence, Affluence, and US Foreign Policy*, Princeton, NJ: Princeton University Press.
Smith, S. (2004) 'Singing Our World into Existence: International Relations and September 11', *International Studies Quarterly* 48: 499–515.
United Nations (1948) *Universal Declaration of Human Rights*, Article 28.
—— (1994) *Human Development Report 1994*, Oxford: Oxford University Press.
—— (2002) *Human Development Report 2002*, Oxford: Oxford University Press.
Vincent, R. J. (1986) *Human Rights and International Relations*, Cambridge: Cambridge University Press.
Wippman, D. (2004) 'The International Criminal Court', in C. Reus-Smit (ed.), *The Politics of International Law*, Cambridge: Cambridge University Press.
Wyn Jones, R. (1995) '"Message in a Bottle?" Theory and Praxis in Critical Security Studies', *Contemporary Security Policy* 16 (3): 299–319.

3 Development of the human security field
A critical examination

David Bosold

'History', Alexis de Tocqueville once stated, 'is a gallery of pictures in which there are few originals and many copies.' Some 150 years later, this metaphor is an apt description of the recent history of human security which has seen a rapid integration into the academic canon. Newly published textbooks in IR and security studies now regularly feature a chapter on human security (e.g. Kerr 2007; Hampson 2008; Fierke 2007: 144–66; Sheehan 2005: 75–81; Lawson 2003: 89–92; Dannreuther 2007: 46–49; Acharya 2008) and articles on human security in academic journals proliferate.[1] Yet, despite the sheer number of publications, most analyses and academic debates on human security have been surprisingly superficial and often unfruitful. It thus seems that there are simply too many copies of the 1994 UNDP report and Roland Paris' 2001 article in *International Security* and too little additional originals. It would be presumptuous to suggest that this chapter equals a new collection of original insights but it is nonetheless my attempt to add an additional spotlight to illuminate the existing human security gallery.

Analysing human security

Most accounts of human security still refer to the publication of the 1994 UNDP Human Development report as the origin of this seemingly new, innovative and radical form of security thinking (e.g. Fierke 2007: 144; Kerr 2007: 92; Kaldor 2007: 182; Thomas 2000: 7). In the mid-1990s, academic discussions revolved around the 'broadening' and 'deepening' of security and the addition of new referent objects (see, among others, Walt 1991; Booth 1991; Krause and Williams 1996), while political debates at the time often centred around a broad and a narrow understanding of human security. The perception of analysts that the old national security thinking had become anachronistic was essentially mirrored by policy-makers who complemented their security lexicon beyond earlier catch phrases of deterrence, military capabilities and national security. Unsurprisingly, there is now little contention that we are living in an era (of an inflationary use) of 'new' forms of security – be it human, environmental, economic, energy, networked or comprehensive, to name but the most prominent. Yet, a satisfactory answer as to how we have come there in the first place or how we could move beyond the level of semantics in the analysis of human security have been scarce until recently (see e.g. Shani *et al.* 2007; Chandler 2008; Hynek 2008a).

Investigating the profound societal, political and economic changes of the past two decades, which have been associated with the changed rhetoric does however still remain a fruitful research agenda, for human security cannot be properly understood, or rather must not be understood, as a mere semantic re-branding of security. On the contrary, the concept has not come out of nowhere but has been based on earlier thoughts and critiques of existing (security) policies and is now embedded in a number of changed political practices, such as nation-building, and ways to make sense of our contemporary world, e.g. in discussions about the security–development nexus. It is not my intention to analyse these political changes which have occurred over the last decades since the authors of the following chapters will do so in a more sophisticated way.

A critical history of human security

Still, it is the starting point of my analysis, to present the historic development of the human security field from an angle that eschews the discussions of the 'right' definition of human security, attempts to 'measure' human security, to juxtapose national and human security and to investigate human security policies through the lens of the 'freedom from fear' and 'freedom from want' labels. Some exceptions left aside, these four aspects – definition(s), measurement, national vs human security and the quest for the 'correct' list of core issues – do still dominate contemporary debates. While I won't be able to remedy this situation in the sense of presenting the 'correct' or 'right' interpretation of the current human security discourse, I attempt to re-contextualise these debates in three different ways. I will do so by first addressing the myth that the year 1994 has been the magic date of the invention of the term 'human security'. In a second step, I will move beyond the semantic label and briefly juxtapose the essence of the 1994 UNDP report with debates in the UN framework that took place some one or two decades earlier. In doing so, I will substantiate my argument that its added value in the sense of broadening the understanding of security has been negligible. Still, taking a closer look at the UNDP report will make possible the illustration that its progressive ideas have been silenced and that a specific, interventionist interpretation of it has become hegemonic. I will close with some thoughts on what I perceive to be the main hurdles and pitfalls that have so far thwarted a more fruitful debate on human security by providing a brief sketch of the development of the academic discourse of the last one and a half decades. This will then, hopefully, provide a more fertile ground to contextualise the ensuing chapters which will examine the deeper structural changes that have been associated with the emergence of human security as it has come to be understood in today's politics.

The semantic dimension of human security

As already noted, it has become an almost uncontested fashion to read and write the history of human security by maintaining that its origins are to be found in the publication of the 1994 UNDP report. Such a caveat also refers to those scholars who simply date back the origin of the concept to the beginning of the 1990s when the Pakistani scholar and politician Mahbub ul Haq was in charge of the conceptualisation and publication of the UNDP report. These scholars argue that human security had been ul Haq's brainchild and that it was him who made the concept available to a wider public with the publication of the 1994 UNDP report. The roots of the concept, according to this strand of the literature, are thus to be linked with his person (Thomas 2000: 7; Tehranian 1999: xiii; MacFarlane and Khong 2006: 144). Still, no matter how strong ul Haq's imprint on the UNDP report actually may have been, he, too, had been influenced by other scholars and colleagues in the UN. In addition, there is no doubt that the term 'human security' as such was already coined and used much earlier. For instance, one can find the warnings of a nuclear physicist in an open letter to the UN, who argued as early as 1945, that the potential of 'active atomic materials' represented a 'perpetual menace to human security' (Bohr 1950: 2). And it was in the early 1970s when the UN Secretary-General at the time, Sithu U Thant, stated that 'the massive sums devoted to armaments do not increase international or national or human security or happiness' (U Thant 1971: 317). Of course, it would be naïve to suggest that these earlier uses were either in any way linked to the contemporary human security discourse or that they represented its 'true' origin. At the same time, though, these examples reveal that a number of scholars have been, at least in the not-so-distant past, too attentive of the semantic label and the 'magic' year 1994. Against this backdrop, it seems that the defining feature of human security for many has been the act of labelling a specific policy in such a way.

Existing histories of human security

Admittedly, there have also been some historically informed analyses of human security. Most scholars investigating the antecedents of 'human security', however, have so far focussed on but two aspects that are not linked to the semantic dimension of it. These authors have paid little attention as to how the laundry list of human security threats came to dominate the political discourse in the last two decades.

The human/citizen vis-à-vis the state

One strand has been highlighting the historical debates in political philosophy, dating back to the early modern era, revolving around the relationship between the individual – in its quality as a human and a citizen – vis-à-vis the state (MacFarlane and Khong 2006: 23–60; MacFarlane 2005; Hampson and Penny 2007: 540–54; Hampson *et al.* 2002: 23–26; Kaldor 2007: 37–38). Conceiving of this relationship in a contractual manner, the discussion has been highlighting the understanding that the state's survival has so far taken precedence over that of its citizens. This relationship has been scrutinised further with regard to the global realm, exemplified by the international legal frameworks that, broadly speaking, have been put in place since the mid-nineteenth century in order to protect people (Debiel and

Franke 2008: 69–73; Colard 2001; Stoett 1999: 17–18; Hampson *et al.* 2002: 18–21; Neack 2007: 199–200).

The history of human security within the UN system post-1945

In addition to such politico-philosophical or politico-legal conceptions, another strand in the literature has been studying the institutional embeddedness of 'human security' in terms of its emergence within and its transformation by the United Nations system (MacFarlane and Khong 2006). According to the two authors human security is about the 'freedom from threat to the core values of human beings, including physical survival, welfare, and identity' (MacFarlane and Khong 2006: 14). It is clear that such a broad definition easily allows for a retroactive appraisal of the UN's efforts to provide and strive for human security since its inception in 1945. At the same time, however, such an approach makes it difficult to illustrate the inconsistency of the different human security understandings that emerged within the United Nations in the three years after 1992. It is thus no surprise that the starting point for an analysis of human security in MacFarlane and Khong's work as well as most other studies has been based on the distinction between 'freedom from fear' and 'freedom from want'. The latter two expressions were expressed by the former US Secretary of State Edward R. Stettinius when briefing the government about the results of the founding conference of the UN in San Francisco in 1945 (UNDP 1994: 24). However, these two freedoms had been previously part of the influential so-called 'four freedoms' speech by President Roosevelt in 1941 including, in addition, freedom of religion and freedom of speech (Donohue 2006: 1). Notwithstanding its US origins, the contemporary human security debate has taken up the definition of human security as 'freedom from fear' and/or 'freedom from want' in order to distinguish between a narrow and a broad definition of human security (Gasper 2005; Newman 2001). This distinction has been of little, if any, analytic value because its essence was neither reflected in any specific understanding nor in any characteristic form of policy. Essentially, it allowed for making available an argument to which degree policy-makers were to devote resources to any of the seven categories that are said to define human security.[2]

Human security and the UN in the late 1980s and early 1990s

Looking at the list of issues covered by the UNDP – economic, food, health, environmental, personal, community and political security – and bearing in mind the work of a series of UN commissions in the late Cold War years, it becomes obvious that the human security concept of the UNDP report has been based on the merging of two complementary strategies: first, the reaffirmation of previous calls for a broader understanding of security that originated from within the UN system, e.g. the Brandt, Palme, Brundtland, and Nyerere commissions (ICIDI 1980, 1983; ICDSI 1982; WCED 1987; ICSDI 1990) and, second, new ways to tap sources of funding for former areas of 'low politics' such as the developmental agenda.

This becomes all too evident when taking a look at the press release of the UNDP on the occasion of the publication of the organisation's 1993 report. Based on a list of 'five new pillars of a people-centred world order', the report calls for:

> New concepts of human security that stress security of the people, not just of nations and territory. This means accelerated disarmament, using defence cuts to boost human development. It means a new role for the United Nations, increasingly intervening to provide human security in areas such as the former Yugoslavia and in Somalia, where people are fighting within countries rather than between countries.
>
> (UNDP 1993a: 487)

UNDP's and ul Haq's indebtedness to the ideas and reflections of the aforementioned commissions is, in addition, amply demonstrated by the references and comments in his 1995 book on human security. In *Reflections on Human Development* he repeatedly quotes the Brundtland report (ul Haq 1995a: 77–78, 252), talks about his personal encounters with Julius Nyerere (ibid: 9) and mentions his participation in some of the meetings of the Brandt commission (ibid: 253, ICIDI 1980: 298). Even if he does not mention the Palme report explicitly, he also must have been aware of his writings because Palme himself had been a member of the Brandt commission. In that respect, some form of influence of these more sectoral and narrow ways of broadening the concept of security on ul Haq is evident. What is more is that the key dimensions of these reports, a broadened understanding of security (ICDSI 1982), the environmental aspects of security (WCED 1987) and the developmental aspects of security (ICIDI 1980), are key pillars of the broader UNDP line of reasoning.

Moreover, the aforementioned quote reveals that the breadth of UNDP's human security concept had never been carved in stone as most of the advocates of the 'broad' understanding of human security like to suggest. It is, on the contrary, quite remarkable that there is a considerable discrepancy between the more narrow understanding of human security in the UNDP report of 1993 and that of the more broadly conceptualised one of 1994. This is even reflected on the semantic level where the 'five new pillars of a people-centred world order' comprise 'new concepts [sic] of human security' (UNDP 1993b: 2) while the 'new concept for human security' (UNDP 1994: 3ff.) a year later attempts to attach the human security label to an even greater number of issues.

Arbitrary meaning(s)

One explanation for that may be found in the fact that the use of the term 'human security' in UN documents shortly before 1994 had already occurred in different contexts. In addition, the lack of the term in all human development reports prior to 1993 (and the use of 'personal security' in the 1990 report, cf. UNDP 1990: 3) suggest that the internal consistency of what constituted human security beyond being a catchphrase was not only contested within the UN as such but also within the UNDP department putting together the human development report. Against this background it seems rather odd that a number of authors (e.g. Bosold and Werthes 2005; Burgess *et al.* 2004) have so persistently debated the question whether for human security to gain practical importance it needed to be conceived of in the broad UNDP fashion or in the supposedly narrower Canadian way (Axworthy 1997; DFAIT 1999). Given that the understanding of what constitutes human security has been incoherent within the UNDP itself illustrates that this question scratches too much on the surface to be a valuable departure for research. This is even more so, if one looks into other UN documents of the early 1990s such as the 'Agenda for Peace' (UN 1992), the 'Supplement to an Agenda for Peace' (UN 1995) or the 'Agenda for Development' (UN 1994). Here, human security is void of any specific character beyond what the editors, in the Introduction, have already referred to as 'empty signifier'.

That the term does not have any inherent meaning and that there was no strategic or conceptually stringent use of it, is again highlighted by the statement that 'national budgets which focus directly on development better serve the cause of peace and human security' (UN 1994: 19). This is insofar puzzling as it seems to suggest that human security with its link to development (and, hence, an economic dimension) is much more than the UN's 'security arm [that] has emerged as a central instrument for the prevention and resolution of conflicts and for the preservation of peace' mentioned in the Agenda for Peace in which 'all functional elements' of the UN have a 'role to play in an integrated approach to human security' (UN 1992: 15–16, UN 1995: 81).

Human security as a strategy to push for UN reform

At the same time, however, a common denominator of the use of human security in UN (and UNDP) documents at the beginning of the early 1990s is its dual function of defining security threats beyond the military dimension and providing an impetus for institutional reform within the UN system for the organisation to gain additional clout as a global security provider. These thoughts are already clearly addressed in the final report of a 1988 UN reform commission which may have served as one source of inspiration for the authors of the later documents. The report does at least use a jargon that is reminiscent of those published some five years later by calling for new ways of 'consensus-building' in addressing issues of converging interests in the field of 'equity-security' where: '[l]inks between economic equity and security (in the broadest sense of *human* security) are increasingly direct, and future consensus-building efforts, particularly as they relate to the crossover between economic, technological, and environmental concerns, must reflect this linkage' (Fromuth 1988: xvii).

For that reason, the commission calls for a 'global watch' function that is not 'within the jurisdiction of the Security Council' (Fromuth 1988: xviii) and that is supposed to perform the 'proposal of global human security agendas by tagging issues that fit the sovereignty-gap criteria' examples of which include 'natural disasters', 'global biosphere', 'least-developed countries', 'international debt', 'disease control', 'international capital flight', 'international narcotics trafficking', 'cross-border population movements' and 'urban overpopulation' (Fromuth 1988: 44–47). Bearing in mind that the common denominator of all uses of the term 'human security' within the UN system was its strategic use to extend the UN's reach and making it a key player in discussions of global non-military issues suggests that invoking the term was never intended to provide for an internally consistent agenda and definition. The main intention by all promoters within the UN, be it Boutros-Ghali, ul Haq or others, was instead a push for subscribing to new tasks and to open up new forms of funding. This seemed all the more feasible against the background of a global decrease in military budgets which seemed to allow for cashing in on a 'peace dividend'. Talking about human security in this respect ul Haq, who also explicitly made reference to Boutros-Ghali's Agenda for Peace and Agenda for Development (ul Haq 1995b: 8), considered such a move as reviving the initial idea of the UN since:

> Two major issues dominated the creative period of international rethinking during and just after the Second World War. One was to avoid another catastrophic war. The other was to avoid another global economic depression and to ensure universal economic and social well-being. The first preoccupations was with military security, the second with human security – and the link between the two was never forgotten. Unfortunately, with the start of the cold war between the superpowers, the first component of security often dominated the second.
>
> (ul Haq 1995b: 3)

That the lack of any inherent meaning of 'human security' was simultaneously powerful in providing legitimacy for other national and multilateral agendas by (a) silencing a number of suggested policies of the UNDP report and by (b) pursuing a militarised (and, in that sense, 'narrow') agenda became clear soon afterwards.

Silencing innovative ideas and pursuing old policies

As noted earlier, the 1994 UNDP report included more than the rather erratic definitions of seven human security dimensions. Unnoticed by many, it contained a number of innovative or even radical ideas for new human security practices and a critical depiction of the state of human security in the industrialised societies of the west. Yet, most or even all of these progressive parts of the report soon fell into oblivion. That the 'West', at the time, experienced situations of human insecurity was passionately put forward in the report by making reference to the number of homeless people in New York City, London and Paris, people living below the poverty line in Germany and Austria, the impact of smog on the health conditions of Los Angeles inhabitants, of air pollution on Scandinavians and the increase of drug-related crimes in Canada and Japan (UNDP 1994: 26–27). Interestingly, all recent documents calling for new human security policies, although to a different degree, locate the sources and spots of human insecurity within the global South

(CHS 2003: 4–12; DFAIT 1999; HPTRHS 2005: 5–6; ICISS 2001: 6–7, 12; also see Duffield 2007). More importantly, however, all of these follow-up commissions and reports, except for the CHS, have failed to generate or propose a source of funding for human security policies that are not based on national budgets. The creation of such a budget (human security fund) was supposed to be the key instrument of the UNDP report to pursue its human security agenda. It was intended to equal a total of US$ 1,500 billion generated over five years (1995–2000) and was based on four prospective sources of funding:

(1) a tax of 0.05 per cent on speculative international capital movements (the so-called 'Tobin tax')
(2) a proportion of the global peace dividend derived from a total 3 per cent reduction in military spending
(3) a tax on non-renewable energy equalling 1US-$ per barrel of oil and, eventually a
(4) share of one third of the existing Official Development Assistance (ODA).

The major share (> 85 per cent) was expected to be derived from the Tobin tax and the energy tax (UNDP 1994: 68). Given that the ODA target of 0.7 per cent of national GNP is still not being met by most of the member-states of the Organisation for Economic Cooperation and Development (OECD), that the less ambitious Millennium Development Goals were put forward some five years later and are as of now bound to fail, illustrates that there was never the political will to follow up on the core institutional ideas of the human development report. This even holds true for the creation of the Japanese Trust Fund for Human Security (TFHS). Although it was established in 1999, the fund currently administered by the UN's Office for the Coordination of Humanitarian Affairs (OCHA) has almost exclusively been supported by the Japanese government. What is more is that its US$ 300 million budget from 1999 to 2008 has been but a fraction of the budget proposed by the UNDP (Edström 2008: 155–63, Bosold 2008: 129).

An interventionist understanding of human security emerges

That being said, one can observe one aspect of the UN human security documents becoming increasingly hegemonic, namely the extended peacekeeping, peace-building and prevention agenda. Rooted in the Agenda for Peace (UN 1992), the human development report inter alia supported such a broader way of engagement of the international community (UNDP 1994: 11). The plea was also supported by other supporters of the human security concept such as Australian foreign minister Gareth Evans, who, reflecting upon the Rwandan genocide, stated in late 1994 that:

> Two approaches seem particularly worthy of further exploration. The first is to develop the notion that 'security,' as it appears in the Charter, is as much about the protection of individuals as it is about the defense of the territorial integrity

of states. 'Human security,' thus understood, is at least as much prejudiced by major intrastate conflict as it is by interstate conflict. [. . .] A second approach, which could either stand alone or be seen as reinforcing the 'human security' reading just described, would pursue to its logical limits the international community's obligations, under the U.N. Charter, to protect basic human rights, bearing in mind that the most basic human right of all, that of life, is violated on a very large scale in intrastate conflicts.

(Evans 1994: 9–10)

In a similar vein, two scholars analysing El Salvador's turbulent transition to peace concluded in the same year that:

El Salvador's dilemma offers a stark example of the need for the 'integrated approach to human security' to which U.N. secretary-general Boutros Boutros-Ghali referred in his Agenda for Peace. Under such an approach, military, political, economic, social, and environmental problems should be addressed jointly and coherently rather than separately as has traditionally been the case.

(de Soto and del Castillo 1994: 71)

Furthermore, support for a stronger involvement in the internal affairs of other states was voiced by the members of the Commission on Global Governance which, in 1995, presented its findings in a final report entitled 'our global neighborhood'. Although the CGG mentioned the term 'human security' and the 1994 UNDP report, it proposed the two-pronged 'security of the planet' and 'security of people' as a more viable and fruitful alternative (CGG 1995: 80–84). Referring to the latter, the report's call for a more interventionist policy in line with the Agenda for Peace read:

The principle of non-intervention in domestic affairs should not be taken lightly. But it is necessary to assert as well the rights and interest of the international community in situations within individual states in which the security of people is extensively endangered.

(CGG 1995: 339)

It is certainly too far-fetched to suggest that the key human security documents of the Canadian foreign ministry published after Kosovo (DFAIT 1999, 2002) and the International Commission on Intervention and State Sovereignty (ICISS 2001) have been influenced by the quoted documents. Yet, an understanding of human security that is detached from any developmental and/or welfare dimension besides these three documents has clearly been characteristic of most recent international human security commissions or reports such as the Study Group on Europe's Security Capabilities 'Human Security Doctrine', the Helsinki Process Track Report on 'Human Security' conducted in preparation for the Finnish EU presidency (HPTRHS 2005) or the UN's High-level Panel on Threats, Challenges and Change report 'A More Secure World' (HLPTCC 2004). This common thrust notwithstanding, one should still be careful to employ but the 'narrow' label for this kind of policy since such a search for a common denominator will most likely obliterate more important differences *between* these approaches than highlight similarities *among* them.

Japan – the notable exception?

It is therefore only on a more superficial level that Japan seems to be the only exception to the aforementioned rule, not least because it has been the main sponsor of the *Commission on Human Security* whose report 'Human Security Now' (CHS 2003) put forward an understanding of human security encapsulated in the idea of 'protection from downside risks' and, hence, a broader developmental agenda. In addition, as has been outlined in more detail previously, the country brought the TFHS into being. This policy, however, has not been surprising given that Japan had, up to this date, been the most generous ODA donor for more than a decade (in total numbers, not percentage of GNP, cf. Edström 2003: 218–21). Taking into account Japan's (formerly) pacifist foreign policy, enshrined in the Yoshida doctrine which aimed to exert influence through economic rather than military power, serves as the most striking explanation why the country has not been supportive of the more interventionist approach (Hynek 2008b: 39–40, Edström 2008: 45–48). According to the Japanese Ministry of Foreign Affairs:

> [. . .] in addition to protection by the state and the international community, it is necessary for the international community to put the focus on individuals and endeavor to empower people and societies through cooperation by countries, international organisations, non-governmental organisations (NGOs), and civil society so that people can lead self-sufficient lives. This is the thinking behind the concept of 'human security'.
>
> (MOFA 2006: 183)

Although some scholars still believe in the heuristic usefulness of distinguishing the 'narrow' Canadian or 'PoC' ('protection of civilians', Muggah and Krause 2006: 115) and the 'broad' Japanese agenda, the fact that both countries have based the focus of their human security policy primarily on their existing foreign policy expertise – Japan: ODA, Canada: peacekeeping (Edström 2003; Thomsen and Hynek 2006) – suggests that what really constitutes the specificity of human security in the contemporary world is actually not analysed. This seems to be further reflected in the attempts to apply the 'broad' and 'narrow' level with regard to the multilateral ad hoc groups of the Canadian-led 'Human Security Network' (Krause 2008) and the Japanese-founded 'Group of Friends of Human Security' (Ho 2008). Since the attempts of both networks to influencing global agenda-setting have proven to be unsuccessful and other countries, such as the UK, not belonging to one of the two networks claiming to pursue the very same policy (Kaldor *et al.* 2007: 274), future analyses will have to be based on different categorisations to yield promising new insights.

Failing to measure human security

The absence of any inherent essence of human security (beyond the semantic label) has also indirectly been demonstrated by those scholars who have attempted to measure human (in)security. While most of the utilised methodologies are doubtlessly innovative and sophisticated, the striking commonality among the authors of these indexes is their failure to acknowledge the subjective nature of their categorisation and the political implications of their research. The latter is insofar uncritical as it reifies the current hegemonic understanding of human security as a bifurcated policy of a generous 'West' attempting to alleviate the failures and misery in the global South by employing an essentialist understanding of the 'human'. It is this depoliticised understanding of human security as a universal, quantifiable state of a person that is at the centre of all of the five indexes that have come up with ways to measure 'human security'. These include the index of *Harvard's Program on Humanitarian Policy and Conflict Research* (King and Murray 2001), Bajpai's as well as the Human Security Centre's *Human Security Audit* (Bajpai 2000; HSC 2005) and Owen's *Human Security Mapping* (Owen 2003). Yet, it is but the AVISO GECHS Index on *Global Environmental Change and Human Security* that explicitly addresses the arbitrariness in the measurement process and coding of the indicators that make up the respective human security index. According to the authors:

> [t]hese categories are not natural, nor are they universal; rather, they are historically and spatially unique, and they are constructed according to sets of social, economic, and political relations. These concepts, in and of themselves, possess no value or meaning; human interaction endows them with value and meaning. The use of terms such as environment, global environmental change, and human security, and related terms such as sustainable development, mobilises certain, often competing, assumptions about, for example, what is desirable (or not), what needs to be done (or not done), who decides (and who does not), and so on.
>
> (GECHS 2007)

It is surprising, given the self-reflective nature of the earlier statement, that the GECHS programme has eventually continued its work on setting up an index that measures human security. And it is even more so, if one takes into account that three of the other four projects have been abandoned. At this stage it is but the Human Security Centre that has continued to publish yearly updates on the global human security situation.

Conclusion

Fifteen years after the UNDP put forward its understanding of human security, scholars still seem to struggle as to how one should best study it. Cursory readings of the 1994 UNDP report suggesting a consistent and quasi-iconic new way of conceptualising security and research on 'broad' and 'narrow' understandings of human security have dominated the scholarly landscape. Yet these approaches have by now come to a point where they are insufficient to capture the essence of the contemporary human security discourse and the new practices in security policy that have evolved over the last decade. In the same vein, the added value of projects seeking to measure human security has now been called into question and the silent death of the majority of these advances suggests that most policy-makers who funded these programmes in the first place do now share this perception. In addition, claims that the emancipatory potential of human security is reflected in the latter taking precedence over national security are insofar grossly exaggerated as the last decade saw an even stronger division of the community of states into strong and failed states. Worse still, human security policies such as post-conflict peacebuilding in places like Haiti or Kosovo have actually not significantly reduced the insecurity of people while, simultaneously, apologists of realism have gained the upper hand by acquiescing in accepting human insecurity for geopolitical gains. Although this normative arbitrariness should come as no surprise, it does question most of the beliefs and assumptions of the contemporary human security literature. Moving beyond the established labels to address the current conundrum of normative rhetoric and pragmatic policies is therefore in order.

Notes

1 A search on Google scholar finds 1,340 articles and books published between 1994–1999, 6,110 for the period between 1999–2004 and 10,800 for 2004–2009.
2 The UNDP report stated that '[t]he list of threats to human security is long, but most can be considered under seven main categories: Economic security, food security, health security, environmental security, personal security, community security, political security' (UNDP 1994: 24).

Bibliography

Acharya, A. (2008) 'Human Security', in J. Baylis, S. Smith and P. Owens (eds), *The Globalisation of World Politics: An Introduction to International Relations*, Oxford: Oxford University Press, 490–505.
Axworthy, L. (1997) 'Canada and Human Security: The Need For Leadership', *International Journal* 52 (2): 183–84.
Bajpai, K. (2000) 'Human Security: Concept and Measurement', *Kroc Institute Occasional Paper No. 19*, Notre Dame, IN: University of Notre Dame.
Bohr, N. (1950) 'Open Letter to the United Nations', *Science* 112 (2897): 1–6.
Booth, K. (1991) 'Security and Emancipation', *Review of International Studies* 17 (4): 313–26.
Bosold, D. (2008) 'Menschliche Sicherheit in der Praxis: Der institutionelle Kontext zur globalen und regionalen Umsetzung von menschlicher Sicherheit', in C. Ulbert and S. Werthes (eds) *Menschliche Sicherheit*, Baden-Baden: Nomos, 123–34.
Bosold, D. and Werthes, S. (2005) 'Human Security in Practice: Canadian and Japanese Experiences', *International Politics and Society* 1 (Spring): 84–101.
Burgess, J. Peter *et al.* (2004) 'Special Section: What is "Human Security"?', *Security Dialogue* 35 (3): 345–71.
Chandler, D. (2008) 'The Dog That Didn't Bark', *Security Dialogue* 39 (4): 427–38.

Colard, D. (2001) 'La doctrine de la "securité humaine": le point de vue d'un juriste', in J. F. Rioux (ed.) *La sécurité humaine. Une nouvelle conception des relations internationales*, Paris: L'Harmattan, 31–56.

Commission on Global Governance (CGG) (1995) *Our Global Neighbourhood*, Oxford: Oxford University Press.

Commission on Human Security (CHS) (2003) *Human Security Now*, New York: United Nations Publications.

Dannreuther, R. (2007) *International Security. The Contemporary Agenda*, Cambridge: Polity Press.

Debiel, T. and Franke, V. (2008) 'Auf tönernen Füßen? Zur normativen Begründbarkeit menschlicher Sicherheit', in C. Ulbert and S. Werthes (eds) *Menschliche Sicherheit. Globale Herausforderungen und regionale Perspektiven*, Baden-Baden: Nomos, 66–80.

Department of Foreign Affairs and International Trade (DFAIT) (1999) *Human Security: Safety for People in a Changing World*, Ottawa: DFAIT.

Department of Foreign Affairs and International Trade (DFAIT) (2002). *Freedom from Fear: Canada's Foreign Policy for Human Security*, Ottawa: DFAIT.

de Soto, A. and del Castillo, G. (1994) 'Obstacles to Peacebuilding', *Foreign Policy* 94 (Spring): 69–83.

Donohue, K. G. (2006) *Freedom from Want: American Liberalism and the Idea of the Consumer*, Baltimore, MD: Johns Hopkins University Press.

Duffield, M. (2007) *Development, Security and Unending War. Governing the World of Peoples*. Cambridge: Polity Press.

Edström, B. (2003) 'Japan's Foreign Policy and Human Security', *Japan Forum* 15 (2): 209–25.

—— (2008) *Japan and the Challenge of Human Security. The Founding of a New Policy 1995–2003*, Stockholm: Institute for Security and Development Policy.

Evans, G. (1994) 'Cooperative Security and Intrastate Conflict', *Foreign Policy* 96 (Fall): 3–20.

Fierke, K. M. (2007) *Critical Approaches to International Security*, Cambridge: Polity Press.

Frohmuth, P. (ed.) (1988) *A Successor Vision. The United Nations of Tomorrow*, Lanham, MD: University Press of America.

Gasper, D. (2005) 'Securing Humanity: Situating "Human Security" as Concept and Discourse', *Journal of Human Development*, 6 (2): 221–45.

Global Environmental Change and Human Security (GECHS) (2007) *IHDP Report No. 11: GECHS Science Plan*. Online. Available URL: www.ihdp.uni-bonn.de/html/publications/reports/report11/gehssp.htm (accessed 9 January 2008).

Hampson, F. O. (2008) 'Human Security', in P. D. Williams (ed.) *Security Studies: An Introduction*, New York: Routledge, 229–43.

Hampson, F. O. and Penny, C. K. (2007) 'Human Security', in T. G. Weiss and S. Daws (eds) *The Oxford Handbook on the United Nations*, Oxford: Oxford University Press, 539–57.

Hampson, F. O., Daudelin, J., Hay, J. B. and Reid, H. (2002) *Madness in the Multitude. Human Security and World Disorder*, Don Mills: Oxford University Press.

ul Haq, M. (1995a) *Reflections on Human Development*, Oxford: Oxford University Press.

ul Haq, M., Jolly, R., Streeten, P. and Haq, K. (eds) (1995b) *The UN and the Bretton Woods Institutions*, Houndmills, Basingstoke: Macmillan.

Helsinki Process Track Report on Human Security (HPTRHS) (2005) *Empowering People at Risk: Human Security Priorities for the 21st Century*, Helsinki: Helsinki Process Secretariat.

High-Level Panel on Threats, Challenges and Change (HLPTCC) (2004) *A More Secure World: Our Shared Responsibility*, New York: United Nations.

Ho, S. (2008) 'Japan's Human Security Policy: A Critical Review of its Limits and Failures', *Japanese Studies* 28 (1): 101–12.

Human Security Centre (HSC) (2005) *Human Security Report 2005. War and Peace in the 21st Century*, Oxford: Oxford University Press.

Hynek, N. (2008a) 'Conditions of Emergence and Their (Bio)Political Effects: Political Rationalities, Governmental Programmes and Technologies of Power in the Landmine Case', *Journal of International Relations and Development* 11 (2): 93–120.

—— (2008b) 'Japan's Human Security: A Conceptual and Institutional Analysis', *Ritsumeikan Annual Review of International Studies* 7 (1): 35–54.

Independent Commission on Disarmament and Security Issues (ICDSI) (1982) *Common Security. A Blueprint for Survival*, New York: Simon and Schuster.

Independent Commission on International Development Issues (ICIDI) (1980) *North-South. A Program for Survival*, Cambridge, MA: MIT Press.

—— (1983) *Common Crisis North-South. Cooperation for World Recovery*, Cambridge, MA: MIT Press.

International Commission on Intervention and State Sovereignty (ICISS) (2001) *The Responsibility to Protect*, Ottawa: International Development Research Centre.

Independent Commission of the South on Development Issues (ICSDI) (1990) *The Challenge to the South: The Report of the South Commission*, Oxford: Clarendon.

Kaldor, M. (2007) *Human Security*, Cambridge: Polity Press.

Kaldor, M., Martin M. and Selchow, S. (2007) 'Human security: a new strategic narrative for Europe', *International Affairs* 83 (2): 273–88.

Kerr, P. (2007) 'Human Security', in A. Collins (ed.) *Contemporary Security Studies*, Oxford: Oxford University Press, 99–108.

King, G. and Murray, C. J. L. (2001) 'Rethinking Human Security', *Political Science Quarterly* 116 (4): 585–610.

Krause, K. (2008) 'Building the Agenda of Human Security: Policy and Practice within the Human Security Network', *International Social Science Journal* 59 (1): 65–79.

Krause, K. and Williams, M. C. (1996) 'Broadening the Agenda of Security Studies: Politics and Methods', *Mershon International Studies Review* 40 (2): 229–54.

Lawson, S. (2003) *International Relations*, Cambridge: Polity Press.

MacFarlane, S. N. (2005) 'The Pre-History of Human Security', *St Antony's International Review* 1 (2): 43–65.

MacFarlane, S. N. and Khong, Y. F. (2006) *Human Security and the UN. A Critical History*, Bloomington, IN: Indiana University Press.

Ministry of Foreign Affairs (MOFA) (2006) *Diplomatic Bluebook*, Tokyo: Ministry of Foreign Affairs.

Muggah, R. and Krause, K. (2006) 'A True Measure of Success? The Discourse and Practice of Human Security in Haiti', in S. J. MacLean, D. R. Black and T. M. Shaw (eds) *A Decade of Human Security. Global Governance and New Multilateralisms*, Aldershot: Ashgate, 113–26.

Neack, L. (2007) *Elusive Security. States First, People Last*, Lanham, MD: Rowman and Littlefield.

Newman, E. (2001) 'Human Security and Constructivism', *International Studies Perspectives* 2 (3): 239–51.

Owen, T. (2003) *Measuring Human Security. A New View of Cambodian Vulnerability*, unpublished M.A. thesis, Vancouver: University of British Columbia.

Paris, R. (2001) 'Human Security. Paradigm Shift or Hot Air?', *International Security* 26 (2): 87–102.

Shani, G., Sato, M. and Pasha, M. K. (eds) (2007) *Protecting Human Security in a Post 9/11 World. Critical and Global Insights*, Houndmills, Basingstoke: Routledge.

Sheehan, M. (2005) *International Security. An Analytical Survey*, Boulder, CO: Lynne Rienner.

Stoett, P. (1999) *Human and Global Security. An Exploration of Terms*, Toronto: University of Toronto Press.
Tehranian, M. (1999) 'Preface', in M. Tehranian (ed.) *Worlds Apart. Human Security and Global Governance*, London: IB Tauris, xi–xiii.
Thomas, C. (2000) *Global Governance, Development and Human Security. The Challenge of Poverty and Inequality*, London: Pluto Press.
Thomsen, R. and Hynek, N. (2006) 'Keeping the Peace and National Unity: Canada's National and International Identity Nexus', *International Journal* 61 (4): 845–58.
United Nations (UN) (1992) *An Agenda for Peace* A/47/277–S/24111, 17 June 1992, New York.
—— (1994) *An Agenda for Development* A/48/935, 6 May 1994, New York.
—— (1995) *Supplement to An Agenda for Peace* A/50/60–S/1995/1, 3 January 1995, New York.
United Nations Development Programme (UNDP) (1990) Human Development Report: *Concept and Measurement of Human Development*, New York: Oxford University Press.
—— (1993a) 'United Nations Development Programme Press Release 1993', *American Journal of Economics and Sociology* 52 (4): 486–91.
—— (1993b) *Human Development Report: People's Participation*, New York: Oxford University Press.
—— (1994) *Human Development Report: New Dimensions of Human Security*, New York: Oxford University Press.
U Thant, S. (1971) 'People are asking "Why". Address to the Council on Foreign Relations in Chicago', *Bulletin of Peace Proposals* 2 (4): 317.
Walt, S. M. (1991) 'The Renaissance of Security Studies', *International Studies Quarterly* 35 (2): 211–39.
World Commission on Environment and Development (WCED) (1987) *Our Common Future*, Oxford: Oxford University Press.

4 Post-colonial hybridity and the return of human security

Oliver P. Richmond[1]

Introduction

In the early 1990s human security (HS) appeared to be part of a major reform of the underlying philosophy, interests, material capacities and institutions of International Relations, particularly in a move towards consolidating a liberal peace (UNDP 1994: 24). It has drawn together an international range of actors and analysts in a common research project spanning a range of cultures and political ideologies (Ponzio 2005: 69). Yet by the 2000s, and from where we stand today, the associated international community of actors which had adopted this new version of security now seem to have turned it into an empty concept, paradoxically not redolent of a social contract, and international contract, responsibility towards others, intellectual and policy openness, or concerned with the very being and situation of individuals and communities caught up in violence. This apparent collapse of HS is far more important than the initial conservative complaints that it was simply too broad to be operationalised in the 1990s. The contestation of HS remains an ongoing debate.

By the 2000s, it became clear that HS had partially collapsed because, like many concepts and theories associated with conflict management, resolution, peacebuilding, development, political stabilisation and reconciliation (and indeed orthodox IR itself), it had been captured by the conservative wing of liberalism (which itself has been partially co-opted by political realism).[2] This saw it deployed as a cover for social engineering, institutionalisation and statebuilding as well as military/humanitarian intervention since the mid-1990s, in order to provide a veneer of legitimacy for interventionary projects (which are often more focused on regional order and state institutions than they are on HS as it was critically envisaged).

Predictably, the liberal peace and statebuilding project itself has now more or less been reduced in ambition in terms of their aspirations to universal legitimacy, or in terms of local perceptions of its legitimacy.[3] Yet, some scholars see the critiques, radical, post-colonial or otherwise, of liberal peace as being answerable by the remounting of the HS concept, both in theoretical and policy terms (Begby and Burgess 2009). This appeal to the emancipatory aspect of HS present in its earlier conceptualisations in my view, rather than its conservative co-option (focused on its provision by international institutions, distant and technologically 'advanced', and ultimately depoliticising and capacity-destroying), offers some hope for the concept's revitalisation in an international system (or western-oriented international community) that remains concerned with helping or 'saving' others.

But, some significant obstacles remain if this re-emerging emancipatory version of HS is to be, or remains, framed by the liberal peace, by liberal statebuilding, and by the western international communities' capacities (or lack thereof), interests, norms, policies and theories. If this community is to determine and provide for its others in conflict settings, emancipatory HS should not operate as if its subjects are helpless and incapacitated would-be liberals, but instead should help determine an approach to security on post-liberal terms and which enables local autonomous agencies (self-government and self-determination) in negotiation with international norms. A post-colonial version of HS should emerge, in other words, capable of organising hybrid understandings of security in relation to the human subjects they produce and are constituted by rather than falling back on the often empty securitisation of western forms of liberalism and realism. It should be remembered that there was a post-colonial dynamic behind the earlier emergence of the concept.

For HS to overcome such problems and reach its potential – an emancipatory version of HS – as I argued for in a previous paper (Richmond 2007), it needs to engage with 'local-local' understandings of security, and to recognise difference, enable agency and to respect autonomy as far as possible. This may form the basis for a post-colonial renegotiation of liberalism and of local context in their 'local-local', transversal, transnational forms. Post-liberal versions[4] of HS, conservative, institutional or emancipatory, would seek to enable local autonomous agency, whether liberal or non-liberal, individual, community or institutional, while also respecting international norms, rights and institutional frameworks. This would see HS as a basis for the emergence of hybrid agencies for peacebuilding, both local and international, and point towards self and mutual emancipations, which are representative of fairly autonomous localised agencies as well as – and not just – international agencies. This will, as in the current debate over 'reaching out' to the Taliban in Afghanistan (Schmeidl and Karokhail 2009), or the incorporation of customary forms of governance into the 'modern' states in Timor Leste or the Solomon Islands (Boege *et al.* 2008; Richmond forthcoming) often be very uncomfortable, but ultimately both locally and internationally resonant (rather than mainly resonant from a western perspective). This approach would be opposed to the view that HS might be used as a way of converting 'others' to political liberalism and its attendant institutions. Here may also lie the roots of an international-social contract for peacebuilding, which scholars have called for in several forms. This essay examines the dynamics of the initial two main forms of HS which emerged in the 1990s, and the current possibilities of a return of HS in a third, post-liberal and hybrid form.

HS And liberal peacebuilding

When the concept of HS was first articulated as an alternative to territorial and military security through a focus on individual security and sustainable development, it drew upon a range of antecedents that had long been critical of mainstream orthodoxies (UNDP 1994: 24). There was a clear concern that it might undermine sovereignty, however (Tadjbakhsh 2005: 10). Yet, HS became a central concept in the development of a liberal international system after the end of the Cold War, and is visible in documentation such as the *Responsibility to Protect* and the subsequent *High Level Panel Report* (Canadian International Commission on Intervention and State Sovereignty 2004). Yet, predictably perhaps during the 'war on terror' many states and actors began to abandon the concept, arguing that it was too ambitious and had become somewhat 'hollow', and that what was needed in general terms was not a focus on HS but on statebuilding. Still, human security remains a recognised concept across much of the UN system and in many member states and donors (MacFarlane and Khong 2006: 10).

In its broadest incarnation, HS was defined as 'freedom from want' and 'freedom from fear': positive and negative freedoms and rights. HS became a validating concept of the overall liberal peace project's goals, even though many international actors working in non-civil society oriented areas may not use this term to describe their work. Because HS is constructed within the context of democratisation, the rule of law, human rights, free trade, globalised markets and neo-liberal economic development, it is most strongly characterised by an institutional approach, but of course this is legitimated by its emancipatory claims. The actors generally associated with HS are foreign state donors, state donor funded non-governmental organisations (NGOs), international organisations (IOs), international agencies, international financial institutions (IFIs) and regional organisations, all of which have tended to present HS as a universal set of very basic security needs constructed within a liberal state. This is then extended to reflect the right of such 'internationals' to bypass state sovereignty and officialdom, and to intervene in areas that are normally reserved for domestic, sub-regional, community or familial competency. The definitions, associated rights, needs and limits of HS are constructed according to an external liberal consensus with the automatic assumption that what translates into a merging of military security and humanitarian provisions conforms to local expectations and needs, while serving as a universally liberal normative regime. Such processes are conducted by donor states and IOs, such as the UN and its agencies, the World Trade Organization and the World Bank, in association with civil society (Keane 2003: 2). While it is odd that HS can be framed in this way, without any real engagement with 'local' issues, needs, sources of identity or authority, HS has also provided a basis by which these have increasingly become a factor in top-down versions of liberal peacebuilding.

The discourses and practices associated with HS-oriented approaches involve a normative commitment to the just settlement of conflict, the reframing of security debates and the involvement of either external non-state actors with access to conflict zones, or domestic non-state actors. This is connected to the role and status that civil society now has in the construction of peace, producing a range of complex tensions in the operationalisation of the concept. Civil society focused intervention has been important in the wider legitimisation of the liberal peace.[5] This is aimed at constructing a future social contract as a way of balancing elite governance with the emancipation of citizens in a civil society.

Thus, HS is strongly connected to the liberal peace, which has four main strands including the victor's peace, the institutional peace, the constitutional peace and the civil peace. These strands of liberal peacebuilding, leading to a conservative or institutionally focused process or outcome, are often legitimised by appeals for a future emancipatory graduation of the liberal peace. This incorporates in particular the following: an institutional strand, resting upon the attempts to anchor states within a normative and legal context in which states agree multilaterally how to behave and how to enforce or determine their respective behaviour; a constitutional strand, resting upon the Kantian argument that peace rests upon democracy, trade and a set of cosmopolitan values that begin from the notion that individuals are ends in themselves, rather than means to an end; and a civil strand, derived from the phenomena of direct action, of citizen advocacy and mobilisation, in the attainment or defence of basic human rights and values.[6] Without a civil peace and HS, an institutional and constitutional peace is unlikely to be legitimate, and the resulting conservative focus merely resembles a colonial praxis of intervention. Without legitimacy and consensus – via a social contract and a civil society – the liberal peace veers towards the unsustainable, conservative end of the spectrum where peace is top-down, based upon coercion or force, and focuses on constraints rather than emancipation.

In this context, HS is assumed to enable the implementation of an emancipatory civil peace and a social contract, contributing to the construction of a constitutional peace in a broader international context. This reflects both institutional and emancipatory strands of HS. At the same time states, international institutions and IOs are provided with legitimate access to the norms, regimes and institutions of civil society and the HS discourses they deploy. Partly because of this, the liberal peace has become an end that appears to legitimise the means, giving rise to some significant contradictions in contemporary non-state practices designed to construct a liberal peace from the bottom up.

HS's initial acceptance in policy circles was mainly because liberal-state and international-organisation objectives shifted from status quo management to the multidimensional approaches towards peacebuilding in which strategies are applied that aim to transform conflict 'into peaceful non-violent process of social and political change' (Miall *et al.* 1999: 22). Yet, at the same time, and more subversively, the version of HS that was being expounded was a liberal one focusing on legitimating the governance of post-conflict zones by external actors which would make their interactions with local actors conditional upon the liberal peace. These developments can be observed in the context of the UN 'Agenda reports' for the reform of international approaches to peace, published throughout the 1990s, in which it is clear that the envisioned notion of peace depended significantly on international agencies and on non-governmental actors due to their unparalleled access to conflict zones.[7] Yet, it still rested upon a conception of governance by liberal actors and their institutions rather than empowerment and emancipation, though of course these were deemed to be a product of HS-oriented strategies.

HS developed to allow such a move (Newman and Richmond 2002: Introduction). Broadening security to include a range of political, social and economic factors allowed for the consideration of security in the context of everyday life, though this was soon attacked and labelled as implausible and unable to be operationalised.[8] As it was widely adopted by various states and international organisations, HS developed into a liberal institutionalist form, rather than the emancipatory form that was often envisaged (Richmond 2007; Newman 2010). While it is likely that actors engaged in HS practices often replicate state practices (particularly through their conditional relationship with their state donors), this tends to overlook the independent capacity of some HS actors that has also emerged, which enables them to act relatively independently of institutional and state control. Yet, there is a broad concurrence between HS-oriented agents and their actions, and that of states and their organisations within the liberal peace context. While this concept and these types of actors seem to provide a challenge to the traditional foundations of the international system, most non-state actors must work within the confines of the dominant institutions and regimes of the state to preserve their very existence. In a sense, this reduces their role in the negotiation and renegotiation of the liberal peacebuilding consensus (representing the common agreement between liberal states, donors, IOs, IFIs and NGOs, that the liberal peace is the objective of all HS-oriented interventions) as subservient to that of states. However, most commentators agree that non-state actors are a vital and key part of peacebuilding, and indeed that global governance is not possible without their cooperation (Reinicke 1998: 259). They have become integral to the overall project of the liberal peace because the many different actors involved in, and many approaches to, peacebuilding have been used to provide avenues of legitimate intervention for the broader state-led liberal peace project. These ever-deeper forms of intervention involve structural policies whereby social, political, economic and cultural frameworks are altered or introduced to contribute to the creation of the liberal peace.

The implication of this is that both interveners and domestic actors effectively need to agree on what constitutes the peace to be installed, and how this is to be carried out. HS effectively provides a response to these concerns: the peace to be created protects the individual, and a mixture of international, local, official and unofficial actors can take part in its provision. The *Brahimi*, *High Level Panel* and R2P reports developed familiar contradictions in this respect by declaring clear aspirations towards human security, but accepting their delegation to state provisions for peacebuilding, through NGOs and other actors.[9] What was characteristic of these developments was the emergence of democratisation as a key objective in which civil society could be stabilised in a sustainable manner and HS could be guaranteed (Annan 2002: 135). What this indicated was that any form of intervention in a conflict, whether state, IO or NGO, became implicitly contingent upon the actor's contribution to democratisation processes. Similarly, this was also associated with arguments about the need for development, which is itself linked to the entry of the conflict zone into the globalised economy. As can be seen from El Salvador to Angola, Mozambique and Cambodia, democratisation provided an umbrella for liberal constructions that are seen as integral to the creation of long-term sustainable conditions of peace. From Bosnia, to Kosovo and East Timor, international institutions and transitional administrations tried to take control of democratisation and induce parallel neo-liberal development process. Aid and its provision, often through NGOs and UN and government agencies, became linked to governance (Duffield 2002: 83). The agendas established for creating human security meant that civil society became intricately entwined with official actors and transitional administrations through conditionalities relating to the construction of the liberal peace by donors vis-à-vis NGOs and their target populations. If HS had been mainly about substituting absent agency for freedom from fear and want, it now began to look like it was being used to marginalise those local agencies in favour of security for states rather than citizens.

The HS framework is susceptible to the accusation that it operates as a liberal and neo-liberal form of biopower, through which intervention is designed to impact upon the most intimate aspects of human life. This is aimed at domesticating and normalising mainly non-western societies and communities caught up in humanitarian crises, bringing their political structures and socioeconomic interactions into a liberal peace and governance framework. It is in this bottom-up guise that liberal peacebuilding and its statebuilding wing appear from a local perspective to take on neocolonial perspectives via the importation of 'expert' – albeit not locally grounded in historical, cultural, linguistic or political terms – knowledge into conflict zones, both for the many tasks associated with humanitarianism and security, and to establish 'governmentality' in which top-down or external control takes over most political, social, economic and identity functions of groups involved in conflict and in the construction of peace at the level of civil society. This governmentality actually depends upon the maintenance of a space between the local and the state/ international, in order to maintain authority, even though this may undermine local consent. Both the community and the individual are governed in a manner in which external actors hope will create peace (Foucault 1991). These practices and discourses have rapidly become a normalised part of our understanding of the liberal peace (Foucault 1976: 1990). Essentially, from this bottom-up analysis, the liberal peace can be said to be a hegemonic peace, broadly consensual and legitimate from the perspective of the coalition of external actors involved in it. But, its consensuality also depends on the incentives provided by, or conditionality of, such forms of intervention. What this indicates is that the privatisation of peace and the increasing subcontracting of peace activities to private actors also masks a tendency for 'bottom-up' peacebuilding to represent international rather than local consensus, and to overwhelm the voices of local actors involved in civil society efforts regarding the liberal peace. In other words it is not really bottom-up.

The question of intervention on the part of non-state actors, and whether they intervene on a rights or needs basis, is an important step towards identifying the type of peace they are attempting to construct. Intervention on a rights basis generally follows liberal state norms, whereas intervention on a needs basis often bypasses state sovereignty. There is a debate to be had about which approach gives citizens a concrete stake in peace and their states. In either case, NGOs form intimate, conditional relationships involving sponsors and recipients. This points to a civil notion of peace that incorporates a broader programme of social, political, economic, humanitarian and developmental engineering according to the liberal peace which is propagated by major donor states, agencies and IFIs. This indicates that the liberal peace is actually contested, to a large degree, by local recipients and NGOs.

Beyond this artificial civil society, contestations also occur in the 'local-local' beneath civil society, in social, religious, customary and labour movements. This is in emancipatory liberal terms, rather than in the institutional terms described previously, concerned with the construction of the civil peace in ways which resonate with local populations. But beyond these liberal terms, from the perspective of the local and its many voices, opportunities arise for its contestation and the translation of the civil peace into a more contextual version driven by localised peacebuilding agencies. Herein lies the possibility of a new approach to HS, which evades its tendency to be drawn towards biopolitical forms of governmentalism. It offers a post-colonial response (Bhabha 1994: 330; Spivak 1988: 95) in post-liberal terms to the perspective from contextual locations that liberal peacebuilding and HS have unfortunately become the praxis of a new colonialism.

Towards a third version of HS

In liberal terms, to recap then, there are two key versions of HS – the institutional approach and the emancipatory approach. The institutional approach is often fairly conservative in its aims in that it focuses on the provision of very basic versions of security, often through institutional building (via programmes such as Security Sector Reform or Disarmament, Demobilisation and Reintegration) which often extend into building the basic institutions of state (such as in Kosovo, Sierra Leone, Bosnia or Timor Leste, where such programmes have been integral to statebuilding). While one sees the creation of basic liberal institutions to provide HS as paramount, the emancipatory approach aims at the empowerment of individuals and the removal of unnecessary constraints over their lives. Within the liberal normative system it has ambitions to enable autonomous agency, though it assumes mistakenly that such agency will necessarily concur with the liberal peace framework. Both versions have failed to recognise the complexity of the environments in which they are deployed.

Despite the tendency to be pulled back to narrow and conservative versions, HS was designed and constructed with the notion of 'others' in mind, and its provision is dependent upon an external act of definition as well as the capacity of local actors. This is perhaps one of the reasons why the concept, even in its narrower forms, has been so resonant in the UN General Assembly, amongst donors and development agencies such as UNDP. The institutionalist approach is derived from the intersection between realist and liberal thinking in IR and in policy more recently, and in particular is associated with a peacebuilding consensus on the liberal peace (though this may now be more accurately called a 'neo-liberal peace'). This certainly aspires rhetorically to HS in its broader forms, but in fact focuses narrowly and in problem-solving terms on basic security plus the construction of effective institutions of governance though which HS can be imported into post-conflict development settings. This top-down perspective takes HS to be dependent upon security and strong states and international intervention driven by hegemonic states, which establish the necessary institutions in order to provide for very basic forms of HS – mainly physical security. Statebuilding might be seen to be its platform.

Clearly, the ideological position that liberal peacebuilding indicates for HS and the nature of the role of many non-state actors and NGOs in conflict zones in reproducing these types of dependencies mean that they are complicit in the reproduction of the liberal peace as the dominant form of conflict settlement. But this has led to a virtual peace, empty states and a lack of reconciliation in most contexts. Because of the relationship of conditionality, this means that the civil peace generally reflects the dominant concerns of states and donors (governance, capacity building and ownership are often mentioned in this context) and therefore is actually very close to the constitutional and institutional discourses of peace. Some actors happily accept this concurrence as inevitable in the context of the peacebuilding consensus, while others, perhaps more focused on issues of social justice, may resist it. Yet, comfortable, perhaps verging upon the hegemonic, assumptions about HS and the liberal peace may obscure some of their important problems, particularly as they have been experienced by local actors in places like Kosovo or East Timor.[10] In the context of capacity building via the peacebuilding consensus, the problem has been not that a limited capacity is being built but that institutional and local capacity is being destroyed in target conflict environments. In this, it may well be that HS approaches and broader approaches to liberal peacebuilding need a more careful appraisal: clearly making the human being a referent for security laudable, but the liberal peace framework is far more heavily weighted towards statebuilding than towards civil society (Fukuyama 2004: 53).

Producing an emancipatory version of liberal HS, which empowers a local renegotiation of the liberal peace through the statebuilding process, which does not distort the structure of the state in favour of vested interests, and which reflects the needs of everyday life in post-conflict, development settings, is the next stage in this project. Welfare, local ownership, accountability, feedback for internationally-driven projects from local actors and the 'local-local', and the realisation of the inalienable connection of work, welfare, culture and the local with democratic and stable states, are crucial if a self-sustaining, emancipatory peace, not merely an externally sustaining conservative peace, is to be constructed (Pugh *et al.* 2008).

The emancipatory approach derives from the Critical impulse in political theory and IR, and underlying conflict resolution and peacebuilding. It offers a focus on emancipation as the aim of HS. This bottom-up approach means that individuals are empowered to negotiate and develop a form of HS that is fitted to their needs – political, economic and social, but also provides them with the necessary tools to do so. This is by necessity focused on a broad notion of HS, on external providers of HS, but aims at local agency as its ultimate expression. HS is therefore focused upon emancipation from oppression, domination, hegemony, as well as want. It is thought of as a universal project, but one that is capable of being shaped and reflecting local interests and particularities. The trouble with this version of HS has been that it has been unable to transcend its liberal and neo-liberal strait-jacket.

These variants of HS underpin the modern liberal state in its orthodox, politically liberal and economically neo-liberal form in that they provide a security space in which civil society and a social contract may emerge. In modern statebuilding terms, however, this civil society and social contract have been elusive, and from Afghanistan to Timor Leste, such states have tended to be 'weak' and survive because of an elite and international bargain. All too often this has been at the expense of the social contract and civil society (Richmond 2005: conclusion). This has meant that HS has not been achieved in its emancipatory form because this would indicate the achievement of the relatively autonomous agency of citizens in their state context, incorporating democracy, human rights, rule of law and development. Given the scale of political, social and economic problems in many post-conflict settings, a conservative version of HS has mainly been achieved, which has enabled a limited form of security rather than undoing structural violence and providing for social justice.

It has become clear that liberal peacebuilding cannot succeed either in building a viable state, a civil society, or a social contract, or indeed reconciliation, unless it carries a large proportion of its target population with it via a broad consensus. Creating institutions without legitimacy or local participation has not so far succeeded anywhere since the end of the Cold War. Basic security might have been achieved in some post-conflict zones, but this has not been seen as enough on the ground by its recipients, who were often engaged in conflicts which expressed their claim for social justice, self-determination or a fairer distribution of resources from their own perspectives. Any international intervention which actively supports or implies a direction which did not acknowledge these realities has been seen as neo-colonial and ill-suited to, or even disdainful of, local contextual forms of agency, politics, society, cultures, identity and economics. So a conservative version of HS has been locally unattractive, and effectively appeals for a more emancipatory version of HS has become a rallying cry in many locales, albeit translated as such by local actors, whether civil society actors, social movements, chiefs, religious or other customary institutions, into such language so internationals can understand them. This has also held international interventions to account in local terms for the failures of the liberal peacebuilding project so far. But while the emancipatory version of HS might be attractive in this translated context, and in juxtaposition to the failure of liberal peacebuilding or institutional versions of HS, it is also something of an illusion.

To resonate more with everyday life in a range of different contexts, HS needs to be contextually mediated in every application. It is in this latter process of the local renegotiation of liberal peacebuilding, now underway in many post-conflict zones where a third, and perhaps most significant, evolution of HS may now be found. Local agencies have been deployed in a wide variety of political, customary, social and discursive ways in order to reframe international peacebuilding in more locally suited ways, as appears to be occurring from Kosovo to Timor Leste in a variety of ways.[11] This may be thought of as an unanticipated achievement of local agency, often through resistance to the limited HS capacities of international peacebuilders, and in such agency might also be found both a nascent social and an international contract. This process has aimed at ensuring human life in ways very similar to those envisaged in broader and more emancipatory versions of HS, albeit without the exclusive approaches to needs, rights and norms envisaged in the emancipatory liberal project (i.e. not necessarily in democratic, secular, meritocratic, gender equal, non-discriminatory, law-abiding and market-oriented terms). This potentially very uncomfortable third evolution of HS can be seen, at least in initial terms as both post-liberal and post-colonial.

HS remains a crucial concept. Its institutional version is clearly a basis for the emancipatory version, and this may provide a bridge into a third, post-colonial and post-liberal version. Yet, both the institutional and emancipatory versions have become part of a liberal institutional debate about social engineering (i.e. embedded liberal institutionalism). Even so they link to the question of local legitimacy and reflect more closely the indigenous facilities of local communities within changing polities than are committed to a perceived form of peace. It has been through this process that local agencies have offered a translated and post-liberal form of HS for international actors and scholars to engage with. If the crisis of the liberal peace is to be responded to and a sustainable peace developed in many of these post-conflict zones, this autonomous agency and translation needs to be mediated with the norms of the liberal peace, requiring a degree of international flexibility that has not so far been apparent.

A post-liberal, post-colonial HS?

HS is not just a policy tool or an ambitious but superficial theory, as is often thought, but has become the site of a significant debate about how liberal peacebuilding and international intervention more generally can achieve a sustainable form of peace with the sorts of capacities and characteristics that have been laid out in a range of documents from the original UN Charter to the more recent *High Level Panel Report*. HS, and its associated concepts and frameworks, is developing at several levels. Non-state actors, and especially NGOs, are engaged in constructing an emancipatory version of the liberal peace at the grass roots level. IOs and states, on the other hand, have a role that impinges upon both the grass roots and the state levels, in security and institutional terms. Local-local actors increasingly are pushing HS into areas that recognise their everyday needs, ownership, culture and identities. Rather than attempting to supplant or substitute for customary support mechanisms, social or labour movements, HS needs to reposition itself in recognition of these. Such tensions and differences have and are still shaping debates on HS' conceptualisation. Given that HS signalled in both institutional and emancipatory form a deeper engagement with the lives of others in order to assist their development of liberal agencies (some would argue it means ever-deeper intervention and social engineering), even if this has overstepped the mark into perceived neocolonialism in some cases, this has also engendered a productive confrontation between liberal politics and institutions and their 'non-liberal' others and counterparts.

It is in this agonistic confrontation that HS offers the possibility of a fascinating exchange between its emancipatory goals and local patterns of politics, society, community, interests, in customary, religious, economic and political terms. In this way, it might be said that HS is partially responsible for producing a post-colonial version of peacebuilding and removing some of the blind spots of the liberal peacebuilding paradigm. The consequences of this confrontation are only now becoming clear in the production of post-liberal hybridities in which reaction, resistance, co-option, tolerance and acceptance interact to form a new post-liberal peace, meaning a pragmatic recognition of what is, and its hard choices on the ground, and a local-liberal hybridity. The post-liberal form of HS would encounter and engages with such dynamics.

Conclusion

A few thoughts on how this post-liberal form of HS may be constituted follow. First, it would have to be contextually driven and negotiated rather than centrally or institutionally dependent on a general blueprint for peacebuilding. This means that it would offer the basis to develop an understanding of how individuals and communities situate themselves vis-à-vis their own understandings of security and peace and attempt to assist in developing how they envisage their own agencies. This means responding to how civil society and local-local voices define the problems they face in terms of the direct and most debilitating forms of violence they encounter, as well as structural violence and materially related issues. Second, it also will represent to such contexts the range of international positions on security and on the liberal peace/statebuilding frameworks, including norms and practices related to democracy, human rights, the market, development and needs. International agencies for the provision of narrow and emancipatory forms of HS must therefore create a modified process of engagement in the light of the broadest and deepest range of local voices they may engage with – from customary to transnational local actors – under the circumstances, avoiding a sole reliance on diplomatic, UN or World Bank contacts, for example. This means that new understandings of relationships, priorities, norms and best practices must be invited in an attempt to building a 'peacebuilding contract'. International interests, norms and institutions would be secondary but informative for this form of HS. This would maintain its institutional aspect, assist its emancipatory goals, and engage with its hybrid implications.

HS may have to substitute for the lack of local security capacity, but it must also be responsive to expressions of agency even in translation from acute contexts of acute alterity (say in Afghanistan, for example), and even – or especially – those that are expressive of resistance to the norms of the liberal peace. As a basis for a post-liberal form of peace, HS becomes in these terms, not a concept which is fixed and predetermined, but a process of negotiation between local and liberal, between internationals and context over what exactly constitutes HS. This may be uncomfortable but it is likely to have more durability than imagining that HS provides a platform to convert local actors to political liberalism, or liberal internationalism, or neo-liberal-framed modernisation strategies. Such focii have evaded the crucial issues of root causes and reconciliation after conflict through its faith in institutions and markets. A more contextual form of HS builds on existing institutional and security capacities and processes, including on the existing UN system, but sensitises it further in the context of local alterity, resistance and accommodation, norms, customs, culture and identity, and an international social contract as the basis for HS and peacebuilding. This is a basis for the 'return' of HS, if it ever went away in the first place.

Notes

1 Oliver Richmond is a Professor and Director of the Centre of Peace and Conflict Studies, in the School of IR, University of St. Andrews, UK. His publications include *Liberal Peace Transitions* (Edinburgh University Press, 2009, with Jason Franks), *The Transformation of Peace* (Palgrave 2005/7), *Maintaining Order, Making Peace* (Palgrave 2002), *Mediating in Cyprus* (Frank Cass 1998). He has published many articles on aspects of peace and conflict theory. This chapter refers to, and extends, an earlier paper on the topic of HS: See Richmond 2007.
2 For a discussion of how liberal peace discourses captured HS (to its detriment), and a genealogy of its intellectual development, see among others, Richmond 2009b.
3 See for example, Richmond and Franks 2009.
4 See Richmond 2009a.
5 For more on this, see Richmond 2005, esp. Conclusion.
6 For more on these contributory strands, see Richmond 2005, esp. Chapter 1 and 2.
7 Paris argues that the inclusion of development means that peacebuilding is effectively a new era in developed-developing world relations (Paris 2002: 638).
8 For conflicting views, see Paris 2001: 87–102; Tadjbakhsh 2005.
9 See United Nations 2000.
10 For an elaboration of these two case studies, see Richmond and Franks 2009.
11 See for example, Boege *et al.* 2008.

Bibliography

Annan, K. A. (2002) 'Democracy as an International Issue', *Global Governance* 8 (2): 135.
Begby, E. and Burgess, J. P. (2009) 'Human Security and Liberal Peace', *Public Reason* 1 (1): 45–57.
Bhabha, H. (1994) *The Location of Culture*, London: Routledge.
Boege, V., Brown, M. A., Clements, K. P. and Nolan, A. (2008) 'States Emerging from Hybrid Political Orders – Pacific Experiences', *The Australian Centre for Peace and Conflict Studies (ACPACS) Occasional Papers Series*, Brisbane.
Canadian International Commission on Intervention and State Sovereignty (2004) *The Responsibility to Protect*, Report of the International Commission on Intervention and State Sovereignty, IDRC, 2001, High Level Panel on Threats, Challenges, and Change, New York: UN.
Duffield, M. (2002) 'Aid and Complicity', *Journal of Modern African Studies* 40 (1): 83–104.
Foucault, M. (1976; 1990) *The History of Sexuality*, Vol.1, London: Penguin.
—— (1991) 'Governmentality', in G. Burchell, C. Gordon and P. Miller (eds) *The Foucault Effect: Studies in Governmentality*, Hemel Hempstead: Harvester Wheatsheaf, 87–104.
Fukuyama, F. (2004) *State Building: Governance and Order in the Twenty First Century*, London: Profile.
Keane, J. (2003) *Global Civil Society*, Cambridge: CUP.

MacFarlane, S. N. and Khong, Y. F. (2006) *Human Security and the UN*, Bloomington: Indiana University Press.
Miall H., Ramsbotham, O. and Woodhouse,T. (1999) *Contemporary Conflict Resolution*, Oxford: Polity.
Newman, E. (2010) 'Critical Human Security Studies', *Review of International Studies*, 36 (1): 77–94.
Newman, E. and Richmond, O. P. (eds) (2002) *The United Nations and Human Security*, London: Macmillan.
Paris, R. (2001) 'Human Security: Paradigm Shift or Hot Air?', *International Security* 26 (2): 87–102.
—— (2002) 'International Peacebuilding and the "Mission Civilisatrice"', *Review of International Studies* 28 (4): 637–56.
Ponzio, R. (2005) 'Why Human Security is a New Concept with Global Origins', *St Antony's Review* 1 (2): 66–71.
Pugh, M., Cooper, N. and Turner, M. (2008) *The Political Economy of Peacebuilding*, London: Palgrave.
Reinicke, W. (1998) *Global Public Policy*, Washington DC: Brookings.
Richmond, O. P. (1998) *Mediating in Cyprus: The Cypriot Communities and the United Nations*, London: Frank Cass.
—— (2002) *Maintaining Order, Making Peace*, London: Palgrave.
—— (2005) *The Transformation of Peace*, London: Palgrave.
—— (2007) 'Emancipatory Forms of Human Security and Liberal Peacebuilding', *International Journal* 62 (3): 459–478.
—— (2009a) 'A *post-liberal peace*: *Eirenism* and the everyday', *Review of International Studies* 35 (3): 557–580.
—— (2009b) 'The Intellectual History of Human Security', in S. Peou (ed.) *Human Security in East Asia*, London: Routledge.
—— (forthcoming) *De-romanticising the Local, De-mystifying the International: Aspects of the Local-Liberal Hybrid in Timor Leste and the Solomon Islands*.
Richmond, O. P. and Franks, J. (2009) *Liberal Peace Transitions*, Edinburgh: Edinburgh University Press.
Schmeidl, S. and Karokhail, M. (2009) '"Prêt-a-Porter States": How the McDonaldization of State-Building Misses the Mark in Afghanistan', in M. Fischer and B. Schmelzle (eds) *Peace in the Absence of States: Challenging the Discourse on State Failure*, Berghof Research Center, Berlin: Berghof Handbook for Conflict Transformation Dialogue Series Issue 8.
Spivak, G. C. (1988) 'Can the Subaltern Speak?', in C. Nelson and L. Grossberg (eds) *Marxism and the Interpretation of Culture*, Basingstoke: Macmillan.
Tadjbakhsh, S. (2005) 'Human Security: Concepts and Implications', *Les Etudes du CERI CERI/*Sciences Po, Paris, France, 117–18 (September).
UNDP (1994) *Human Development Report 1994*, Oxford: Oxford University Press.
United Nations (2000) 'Letters from the Secretary General to the President of the General Assembly and the President of the Security Council, Report of the Panel on UN Peace Operations', A/55/305-S/2000/809, New York, 21 August 2000.

5 Securitizing 'bare life'

Critical perspectives on human security discourse[1]

Giorgio Shani

As is well known by now, 'human' security differs from conventional approaches to security because it prioritizes the needs and well-being of people rather than states (UNDP 1994). Generally speaking, conventional security studies remain mired in the quicksand of realist assumptions which conflate state and people. The state, as the *only* legitimate representative of the collective will of the 'people' it controls, is empowered through the doctrine of national security to define and defend the long-term, 'national interest' of *its* people from external aggression. The interests of the 'people', the national community, are equated with those of the state and consequently any threat, real or imagined, to the state's boundaries, institutions, subjects and values from outside, even if these threats come from within the state's borders by dissident and minority groups, is regarded as external aggression. Thus, conventional security approaches have been complicit in the legitimization of the state as a 'natural' and unchanging unit of international relations and also the extension of its coercive power over 'its' people. As the authors of the *Human Security Report* point out, far more people have been killed by their own states than by foreign armies (HSC 2005: viii). Furthermore, the hegemonic doctrine of national security is unable to account for the myriad of security threats posed by the capricious nature of neo-liberal globalization. These include threats to economic, food, health, environmental, personal, community and political security as documented by the UNDP in their ground-breaking *Human Development Report 1994* which helped introduce the concept of 'human security' to an audience of international policy-makers, NGOs and academics (UNDP 1994: 24–25).

At the heart of conventional discourses on human security is a concern with the individual: the claims of all other referents derive from the sovereignty of the individual and the individual's right to dignity (MacFarlane and Khong 2006). Whereas the traditional goal of 'national security' has been the defence of the state from external threats, the focus of human security, by contrast, is the protection of *individuals* (HSC 2005: viii). The individual is viewed as 'unencumbered' (Hopgood 2000), abstracted from the social and cultural mores of his or her community, and invested with formal political equality. While the 'narrow approach' favoured by the Human Security Network seeks to 'protect' the individual from external threats to their '*physical* security or safety', (HSC 2005), the 'broader approach' seeks both to protect 'the vital core of all human lives in ways that enhance human freedoms and human fulfilment' and 'to *empower* them to act on their own behalf' (CHS 2003: 2, 4). However, the cultural context within which the individual realizes his/her self-consciousness or is 'empowered' is either ignored or downplayed. The de-historicized and deracinated individual – it is argued – is consequently reduced to 'bare life' (Agamben 2002).

This chapter will seek to further contribute to the development of a 'Critical Human Security Paradigm' or 'perspective' (Shani and Pasha 2007) by arguing that human dignity remains, despite the homogenizing impulses of neo-liberal globalization, embedded in the 'thick' values of cultural and religious communities. A major source of human insecurity, it is claimed, comes from the failure of states, in the North as well as the South, to recognize the increasing cultural diversity of their populations which has resulted from globalization. This will be illustrated by highlighting the difficulties faced by Sikhs in France in gaining recognition of their culturally distinct way of life from an assimilationist state committed to *laïcité*.

Human security: 'narrow' and 'broad' definitions[2]

The notion of human security is premised on the assumption that the individual human being is the only irreducible focus for discourse on security. Consequently, the claims of all other referents, including the nation-state, derive from the *sovereignty* of the individual (MacFarlane and Khong 2006: 2). While most advocates of human security agree that its primary goal should be the *protection* of individual human lives, they differ as to what the individual should be protected from. Although multiple dimensions and conceptions of human security have been identified,[3] conventionally a distinction, or rather an antinomy, is made between 'narrow' and 'broad' definitions.

The 'narrow' approach, which has been adopted by the pre-Harper Canadian government and institutionalized through the formation of the Human Security Network (HSN),[4] conceives of human security negatively in terms of the absence of threats to the *physical* security or safety of individuals. It is exemplified in the publication of the *Human Security Report* by the Human Security Centre which, for the sake of methodological clarity, defines human security as the protection of individuals from 'violent threats' (HSR 2005). In contrast to the 'negative' conception of Human Security favoured by the authors of the *Human Security Report*, the Final Report of the Commission on Human Security (CHS), headed by Amartya Sen and Sadako Ogata, provides a more 'positive' definition of human security as encompassing the 'vital core' of all human lives: a set of 'elementary rights and freedoms people enjoy' and consider to be 'vital' to their well-being. Although this 'vital core', based largely on the capabilities approach pioneered by Amartya Sen, is not specified,[5] its protection 'in ways that enhance human freedoms and human fulfilment' (CHS 2003: 4) is seen as the principal objective of human security. Elements of the 'vital core' include 'fundamental human rights' pertaining to 'survival, to livelihood, and to basic dignity' (Alkire 2003b: 24). As Sabine Alkire, the Report's main architect, notes in a working paper, human security is 'deliberately protective' in that 'it recognizes that people and communities are fatally threatened by events well beyond their control' (Alkire 2003b: 2). Shielding people from danger requires concerted international effort to develop norms, processes and institutions that systematically address insecurities, including those arising from extreme poverty, ill heath and the effects of environmental degradation (CHS 2003: 6). However, protection alone is seen as insufficient to combat human insecurity: human security seeks also 'to *empower* them to act on their own behalf' (CHS 2003: 2-italics mine). Empowerment enables people to develop their potential and become full participants in decision-making (CHS 2003). Protection and empowerment are regarded as mutually reinforcing and needed to achieve greater human security for all.

The antinomy between the 'narrow' and 'broad' approaches masks the *discursive* continuities between the two approaches which are reflected in the practices of international institutions committed to human security. For example, current HSN efforts to achieve greater human security include issues such as the establishment of the International Criminal Court, the protection of children in armed conflict, the control of small arms and light weapons, the fight against transnational organized crime, and the universalization of the Ottawa Convention on Anti-personnel Landmines, as well as other issues associated more closely with the broader perspective on human security such as the promotion of sustainable human development, the alleviation of absolute poverty, providing basic social services for all, and pursuing the goals of people-centred development, is necessary for building human security (HSN 2009). Anchored in the western liberal tradition of rights-based political theory, the individual of human security discourse is unencumbered by the social and cultural mores of his or her community, and invested with equal and inalienable rights. While the narrow approach focuses on 'freedom from fear', the broad approach supplements this 'core' value with 'freedom from want' and 'freedom to take action on one's own behalf' (CHS 2003). Indeed, it could be argued that the fundamental difference between the two approaches is merely that what advocates of the 'narrow' approach assume to be a social fact – the atomized individual – proponents of the narrow approach consider a *project*: the creation of unencumbered individuals out of the culturally differentiated great mass of humanity. Empowerment here acts as a biopolitical technology which constructs the disciplined individuals needed for neo-liberal governmentality. The 'project' of 'Human Security', in other words, entails not only the protection of, but also *the construction of rational, autonomous and self-interested individuals where none exist*.

Critical perspectives on conventional human security discourse

The most persistent criticisms of the concept of human security in general are that it is vague, incoherent, arbitrary and difficult to operationalize. Many critics would agree with Roland Paris that existing definitions of human security 'tend to be extraordinarily expansive and vague, encompassing everything from physical security to psychological well-being, which provides policymakers with little guidance in the prioritization of competing policy goals and academics little sense of what, exactly, is to be studied' (Paris 2001: 88). It is argued here that the very ambiguity of the concept moreover makes it susceptible to incorporation into the hegemonic national security paradigm, thus qualifying its coherence as an alternative perspective or approach. The dangers of co-option are recognized by Ken Booth who argues, somewhat harshly, that 'the concept of human security ... which originally encouraged the idea of a different and more important referent than the sovereign state, has been co-opted and incorporated into statist discourses' (Booth 2005: 266). On the one hand, the human security approach marks a significant departure in security studies in particular and international relations in general since it makes the individual and not the territorially bounded sovereign nation-state as the primary referent object of security. Yet on the other hand, the concept of human security complements or even *reinforces* the doctrine of national security. Indeed, the concept of human security as advocated by the United Nations under ex-Secretary General Kofi Annan in the light of the recommendations of both the ICISS (2001) and CHS (2003) Reports, seeks to (re)*empower* the state by charging it with a 'responsibility to protect' its citizens in a globalizing world (Annan 2005). According to MacFarlane and Khong, human security is 'not about transcending or marginalizing the state' but 'about ensuring that states protect their people' (MacFarlane and Khong 2006: 265). This gives rise to the concern, that 'human' security may be sufficiently malleable to allow itself to be used to legitimize greater state control over society in the *name of protection* (Shani 2007b).

Furthermore, it has been argued that human security is employed by powerful western states and international institutions as a tool of biopolitical control. Biopower refers to:

> the set of mechanisms through which the basic biological features of the human species become the object of a political strategy ... or, in other words, how ... modern Western societies took on board the fundamental biological fact that human beings are a species.
>
> (Foucault 2007: 1)

It is a form of power which has as its target 'population'. However, in contrast to 'sovereign' power, it seeks to 'make live' and ameliorate the living conditions of the population it subjugates and controls. Whereas Berman highlights the ways in which human security participates in the 'securitization' of everyday life in modern western societies (Berman 2007), others, however, have seen human security as complicit in the legitimization of new imperial practices which seek to subjugate, discipline and control the 'surplus populations' (Duffield 2007) of the global postcolonial South through a discourse of 'global governance' (Douzinas 2007) or 'democratic imperialism' (Shani 2007b). In perhaps the most systematic application of a biopolitical framework to North–South relations, Duffield argues that human security attempts to 'secure' the West by containing the 'circulatory' problems of the exclusions and inequalities engendered by capitalism within the postcolonial South. Consequently, it effectively 'securitizes' development and reproduces the colonial racial hierarchy in an age of globalization. Whereas the insured populations of the North are subjected to biopolitical technologies of government which are designed to 'make live', the uninsured 'surplus populations' of the South are condemned to live in a poverty legitimized through recourse to a developmental discourse of sustainability. De Larringa and Doucet (2008) similarly highlight the way in which human security casts the problematique of 'security' in biopolitical terms but see the 'production of human subjectivity that the human security discourse participates in enabling, coupled with the logic of exceptionality in the post-9/11 moment' as 'providing the grounds for an exercise of sovereign power on a planetary scale' (De Larringa and Doucet 2008: 534).

Critically reworked, however, human security has the potential to resist the global exercise of sovereign power under conditions of exceptionality as well as the hegemony of the discourse on national security through a normative commitment to *de-securitization* (Wæver 1995; Buzan *et al*.1998). De-securitization eschews 'emanicipatory ideals' in favour of a manoeuvring of the dynamics of security. Following Buzan, Wæver and de Wilde, 'security' denotes the move which takes politics beyond 'the established rules of the game and frames the issue either as a special kind of politics or as above politics'. If 'securitization' may be understood as an extreme form of politicization, whereby an issue comes to be either politicized or placed above politics, *de-securitization* refers to the process whereby an issue shifts out of the emergency mode and back into the normal bargaining processes of the political sphere (Buzan *et al.* 1998: 23–4). Although it may stop short of 'emancipation',[6] a critical discourse on human security seeks, at the very least, to lessen the power of oppressive structures over human life.

Central to this project is the deconstruction of all other 'natural' political referents which seek to subordinate the individual to its goals. According to Booth, a 'critical theory of security seeks to denaturalize and historicize all human-made, political referents, recognizing only the primordial entity of the socially embedded *individual*' (Booth 2005: 268 – emphasis mine). However, what Booth fails to recognize is that the 'individual' is also a 'political referent' needing to be 'denaturalized and historicized'. A product of an Enlightenment modernity which has sought to erase cultural and gender differences,[7] the liberal conception of the abstract 'individual' has impoverished our understanding of humanity and reduced what it is to be human to 'bare life'(Agamben 1998).

For Agamben, 'bare life' corresponds to the ancient Greek term *zoē*, which expresses the simple fact of living: *bare life is life which can be killed but not yet sacrificed*. This differed from the term *bios* which denoted a qualified life: a life with dignity, endowed with meaning which was consequently considered 'worthy' of sacrifice. In the classical world, *zoē* was excluded from the *polis* and confined to the sphere of the *oikos*: the home. Indeed, the concept of *zoē* made politics possible: 'There is politics because man is the living being who, in language, separates and opposes himself to his own bare life and, at the same time, maintains himself in relation to that bare life in an inclusive exclusion' (Agamben 1998: 8). Agamben contends, following on from insights by Foucault and Arendt, that it is 'the entry of *zoē* into the sphere of the *polis* – the politicization of bare life as such' which 'constitutes the decisive event of modernity' (Agamben 1998: 4). Thus, whereas classical democracy sought to exclude *zoē* from the *polis*, 'modern democracy presents itself from the beginning as a vindication and liberation of *zoē*, and . . . is constantly trying to transform its own bare life into a way of life and to find, so to speak, the *bios of zoē*' (Agamben 1998: 9). It is in this very politicization – or rather 'securitization' – of *zoē* by the sovereign state that modern discourses on democracy and totalitarianism converge.

The 'politicization of bare life' reaches its apogee in the Nazi concentration camps. For Agamben, the camps were not an 'aberration' nor a 'unique event' but the place where politics as the exercise of sovereignty – defined by Carl Schmitt as the ability 'to decide on the state of exception' and exercise power over life and death – is most clearly revealed. As such, it has become 'the fundamental biopolitical paradigm' of the modern west (Agamben 1998: 181). In the camps, some inmates were referred to as *der Musselmann* (the 'Muslims') since 'humiliation, horror and fear had so taken away all consciousness and personality' as to reduce them to apathetic, prostrating subservience. Seeing them from afar, other newer inmates were reminded of Muslims at prayer. 'Mute and absolutely alone', the *Musselmann* were not only excluded from the political and social context to which they belonged like the other camp inhabitants but also from the 'world of men' (Agamben 1998: 185; 2002: 41–87).

Conventional discourses on Human Security (HS) reproduce the modernist conception of the individual, found in its most extreme form in the concentration camps, as 'mute and absolutely alone'. Stripped of membership of the cultural communities through which individuals find meaning, dignity and 'identity' and subject to the totalizing (yet theoretically limited) power of the sovereign state, the abstract individual of conventional HS discourse becomes a 'docile body' at the service of capitalist governmentality (Foucault 2007; 1991) shaped by the disciplinary power of neo-liberalism. 'Disciplinary neo-liberalism' here refers to the extension and intensification of the discipline of capital to social relations. The state, hitherto regarded as the ultimate disciplinary body within society, is itself subject to market discipline: governments seek to prove their credibility, and the consistency of their policies according to the degree to which they inspire the confidence of investors (Gill 2000). This 'disciplinary' neo-liberalism, as Stephen Gill has pointed out, requires a juridical-political dimension in order for it to appear as hegemonic: a 'new constitutionalism' that seeks to 'lock in' the 'rights' of investors and privilege the 'security of capital' over 'human security' (Gill 2003). The new political architecture of the global political economy is provided by new international institutions such as the World Trade Organization (WTO) which 'disciplines' member-states for pursuing policies detrimental to the interests of (multinational) capital and the World Economic Forum at Davos, which provides an arena where government, business and media leaders can meet and coordinate policy goals. Their objectives are 'to create a set of long-term economic and political reforms that gain constitutional status, thus underpinning the extension of the disciplinary power of capital on a world scale' (Gill 2000).

In the case of indebted developing societies, this can be done directly either through the Structural Adjustment Programmes (SAPs) of the IMF/World Bank nexus or, for the recalcitrant few, through 'democratic imperialism':[8] invasion followed by coercive democratization and privatization of state-owned assets

(Shani 2007c). The results have been that states, and citizens, in the global South (as well as North) are increasingly dependent upon the 'impersonal forces of the world market' (Strange 1996) for their 'human' security.

Globalization, migration and human in/security

One consequence of the continued dependence of post-colonial societies on the 'impersonal forces of the world market' has been the increase in international migration from South to North. According to the International Organization for Migration (IOM), migration doubled from 75 to 150 million between 1965 and 2000 (IOM 2003). The UNDP estimates that approximately 200 million people are *international* migrants, that is to say live outside the state of their birth (UNPD 2009:5). However, they account for only 2 per cent of the world's population and this figure has remained remarkably consistent, considering changing demographic patterns and the increase in the global population. Furthermore, the number of international migrants is dwarfed by the approximately 740 million internal migrants displaced in no small measure by the globalization of neo-liberalism. So what has changed? What accounts for *securitization* of migration and the extension of sovereign power over the 'bare life' of the individual migrant (Berman 2007)? A possible answer may have something to do with the *racialization* of migration. Previously, international migration was overwhelmingly from core to periphery or North to South. Castles and Miller estimate that 59 million people left Europe for the New World, Australasia and South Africa (Castles and Miller 2003: 4). However, the socioeconomic inequalities arising from neo-liberal globalization has made migration to the North for many people in the South not only an attractive option, but a necessity, particularly for those from war-torn or conflict-ridden 'failed' states.

Generally speaking, there are three different 'ideal–types' of institutional arrangements by which immigrants can be incorporated into host societies: assimilation, exclusion and multiculturalism (Modood 2005).Whilst assimilation involves the creation of a 'melting pot', as in the US as described in the 1970s by Glazer and Moynihan (1975), where immigrants are expected to take the initiative in adapting to a de-ethnicized, market or secular culture as in France (see later), exclusion involves the participation or incorporation of migrants only into the selected and marked-off sectors of the host society, as in Germany and Japan. Neither involves the state and majority community to change. Multiculturalism is where processes of integration are seen both as two-way and as working differently for different groups. It differs from integration because it recognizes the *social reality* of ethno-cultural groups, not just of individuals and organizations. As Modood points out, this reality can be of different kinds; for example, a sense of solidarity with people of similar origins or faith or mother tongue. It might be an act of imagination but may also be rooted in lived experience and embodied in formal organizations dedicated to fostering group identity and keeping it alive (Modood 2005). Philosophically, it is based on the premise that we are all 'cultural beings, born and raised within a thick culture, which we no doubt can revise and even reject but only by embracing some other culture' (Parekh 2002: 141). Politically, a commitment to multiculturalism tends to involve *active* state policies, in both the public and private spheres, designed to accommodate immigrants in their host market through equal opportunities legislation, granting full access to social service, education and housing, and finally, access to citizenship whilst not requiring immigrants to 'give up' or *privatize* their pre-existing ethno-cultural identities.

In the post-9/11 world, Northern societies have, to varying degrees, watered down or abandoned multicultural approaches to immigration and sought to promote policies which would lead to greater integration of immigrants into the host culture through the *privatization of cultural identities*. It is argued later, that the retreat from – or, in the French case, the rejection of – multiculturalism has resulted in greater *participation exclusion* – the exclusion of ethnic and religious minorities from the public sphere – and *living mode exclusion* – the non-recognition of a way of life which a culturally defined group may choose to have (UNDP 2004) – and thus led to greater human *insecurity* in the 'developed' world.

'Faith' v 'Nation': Laïcité and human insecurity

In March 2004, the French state passed a law which bans conspicuous religious symbols and attire in public schools in order to uphold the principle of *laïcité*, which actively promotes secularism in the public sphere. In France, *laïcité* is an ideological form of western secularism that has developed on two levels and encompasses both legal and philosophical implications. In the first place, it involves a very strict separation of Church and State – a legacy of the political conflict between the State and the Catholic Church that resulted in a 1905 law regulating the presence of religion in the public life. Second, *laïcité* claims to provide all citizens with an ideological and philosophical value system by effectively 'privatizing' religion and excluding it from the public sphere. *Laïcité* therefore defines 'national cohesion by asserting a purely political identity that confines to the private sphere any specific religious or cultural identities' (Roy 2007).

Although the law does not explicitly target any one religious community, Sikh schoolchildren are most affected by the ban since Sikh religio-cultural identity is *embodied* in the five 'signs' or symbols of Sikh identity: Baptized (*amritdhari*) male Sikhs following the edicts of the tenth Guru Gobind Singh (1666–1708), are enjoined to keep their hair, including facial hair, long (*kes*); to carry a comb (*kanga*); wear knee-length breeches (*kachh*); a steel bracelet on the right hand (*kara*); and to carry a sword or dagger (*kirpan*). Those who embody these five symbols of Sikh identity, known as *Kes-dhari* Sikhs, constitute the *Khalsa*, or 'community of the pure'. The *Khalsa* is not merely conceived as a spiritual fraternity of orthodox Sikhs, but as a *sovereign* community which could defend itself and would no longer need the tutelage of a human Guru (Shani 2007a).

Since the wearing of the Five Ks is an integral part of *Khalsa* Sikh identity, the 5,000-strong Sikh community in France have been faced with a stark dilemma: either to cease wearing the religious symbols which are the very embodiment of their faith; or to face exclusion from state schools. Despite the French government's assurance that a 'satisfactory' solution for the Sikh community in France would be sought and the incoming French President Sarkozy's lip service to the principles of cultural diversity and religious freedom, the ban on religious symbols in the classroom has led to the expulsion of six Sikh schoolboys.[9] Furthermore, two adult French-Sikh citizens – Shingara Singh Mann and Ranjit Singh[10] – were unable to renew important documents as they declined to remove their turban for the ID photo.

These cases have been taken up by UNITED SIKHS, a transnational, apolitical organization operating outside the Sikh 'political system' centred on the Golden Temple complex in Amritsar. UNITED SIKHS claimed that the expulsion of the schoolboys was in contravention of Article 9 of the European Convention on Human Rights. Their appeal against the expulsion of three of the schoolboys was, however, recently rejected by the *Conseil D' Etat*, the highest French Court, which argued that it did not constitute an 'excessive infringement upon the freedom of thought, conscience and religion guaranteed by Article 9' (SikhNet 2007). The *Conseil D' Etat*, furthermore, upheld the decision to not allow Shingara Singh Mann to renew his driving licence without having to take off his turban on the same grounds. Although there may appear to be legal grounds for contesting the *Conseil D' Etat*'s verdict, a closer reading of Article 9, however, would suggest that the European Convention on Human Rights is in fact itself complicit in the restriction of individual freedom. On the one hand, Article 9(1) states unequivocally that: 'Everyone has the right to freedom of thought, conscience and religion' yet this right is simultaneously negated by Article 9(2) which makes it subject to:

> *such limitations as are prescribed by law and are necessary in a democratic society in the interests of public safety, for the protection of public order, health or morals, or for the protection of the rights and freedoms of others.*
>
> (Council of Europe 1950 – italics mine)

In short, Article 9 'securitizes' the individual's freedom of thought, conscience and religion by making it possible for the state to deny it in the interests of a 'national' security discourse articulated primarily in terms of 'democratic' governmentality. This discourse, furthermore, shares many similarities with conventional discourses on HS, most notably its stress upon individual freedom and on the necessity of *protection* (thus reproducing the philosophical grounds necessary for the establishment of the *Leviathan* as found in 'social contract' theorizing).

For the French Sikhs, however, the central issue is not individual rights to 'freedom of thought, conscience and religion' but their right to belong to a transnational, sovereign religio-political body: the *Khalsa Panth*. What is at stake is not freedom *per se* but *sovereignty and identity*. By forcing Sikhs to remove turbans and (by implication) cut their hair in order to be citizens, the French state is effectively *secularizing* Sikhism, forcing it to conform to a modern, western definition of 'religion' which has its origins in the Judaeo-Christian tradition (and most particularly in Protestantism). Shorn of their external symbols, Sikhs are deprived of their dignity as Sikhism is *disembodied*. The secularized Sikh's *bios* is consequently reduced to pure *zoē*: a 'bare life' which can no longer be sacrificed in defence of a *Khalsa* which is no longer sovereign (at least in France!). The Sikh thus meekly surrenders to the dictates of the secular state in the same manner as Agamben's *Musselmann* – human but no longer Jewish – submitting to the will of the guards.

Conclusion

Human security, at its most basic, describes 'a condition of existence in which basic material needs are met, and in which human dignity, including meaningful participation in the life of the *community* can be realized' (Thomas 2000: 6-emphasis mine). It follows that a concern with human dignity should include not only a commitment to the protection of the individual from threats of physical violence or the satisfaction of basic material needs but also a commitment to *cultural diversity*. It has been argued that conventional human security discourses reproduce the modernist conception of the individual as a rational, autonomous and self-interested actor, unencumbered by attachment to 'constructed' cultural communities. This not only divests the individual of dignity and identity – rendering her/him 'mute and absolutely alone' – but also serves the interests of the territorialized, sovereign state and global neo-liberalism.

A more critical human security paradigm should therefore seek to 'de-securitize' the 'human' by recognizing the culturally contested and embedded nature of individual identities. Culture here does not refer to a set of all-encompassing, biologically determined and territorially rooted 'primordial attachments' (Shils 1957; Geertz 1963) but 'to the construction, maintenance, and transformation of meaningful and purposeful schemes of existence' (Inayatullah and Blaney 2004: 16). Culture, in other words, is what permits the individual to have a *bios*: to enjoy a life endowed with meaning and dignity; and to lead a life considered worthy of sacrifice. In so doing, it gives the 'mute and absolutely alone' subject of conventional HS discourses a community (or communities) to which to belong and a language in which to voice *difference*, thus blunting the assimilationist drive of the modern nation-state and the homogenizing thrust of neo-liberal globalization. For the 'ultimate sense of belonging to the species' upon which 'thin' universalist conceptions of cosmopolitanism are based cannot, in Agamben's words, 'in any sense be a kind of dignity' (Agamben 2002: 69).

Notes

1 This chapter is a substantially edited and revised version of a paper first presented at a Conference on Globalization, Difference and Human Security, Osaka University, March 12–14, 2008 and subsequently at the annual meeting of the 50th International Studies Association Annual Convention, New York Marriott Marquis, New York City, NY, USA, Feb 18, 2009. The author wishes to thank Mustapha Kamal Pasha and the editors for their constructive comments.
2 This section is an edited and revised version of Shani 2007b: 4–6.
3 Alkire (2003a: 15–39) and Amouyel (2006: 10–23) provide comprehensive surveys of differing conceptions of human security and the 'broad' definition in particular. Hampson distinguishes between a natural rights/rule of law, humanitarian and a more problematic socioeconomic conception of human security (Hampson *et al.* 2002: 4–5).

4 The HSN is a group of mainly western states led by Canada which meet informally at ministerial level to discuss issues pertaining to human security. See Human Security Network (2009).
 5 Alkire (2003b: 2) revealingly refers to it as a 'non-technical' term operating in the 'space' opened up to it by the capabilities approach. Elsewhere, she writes that the 'vital core' comprises 'very rudimentary rights or freedoms, which may be organized within the categories, survival (freedom from premature preventable death), daily life (basic material needs), and dignity' (Alkire 2003b: 28).
 6 Critical Security Studies theorists such as Booth and Jones emphasized that the focus of security studies should be emancipation. Emancipation is defined as the 'freeing of people (as individuals and groups) from the physical and human constraints which stop them carrying out what they would freely choose to do'. Echoing Galtung's conception of peace as liberation from structural violence and Sen's reframing of development as freedom, they see war, poverty, poor education and political oppression as constraints on 'security'. Emancipation, they argue, 'not power or order, produces true security'. Therefore, 'emancipation is theoretically security'(Booth 1991: 319).
 7 See Hudson (2005), Berman (2007), Gibson and Reardon (2007) for a critique of Human Security discourse from feminist perspectives.
 8 The term 'democratic imperialism' here refers to the attempt by the United States to unilaterally and aggressively install pro-western (and pro-market governments) in strategically important areas of the 'developing' world in the post 9/11 period (Shani 2007c: 28).
 9 Jasvir Singh, Bikramjit Singh and Ranjit Singh were expelled in 2004. They were joined in 2005 by Gurinder Singh and Jasmeet Singh in 2006. Maha Singh has, furthermore, not been admitted in any school since 2006 on account of his turban (Mejindarpal Kaur, Personal correspondence, 25 March 2007).
10 Shingara Singh Mann was unable to renew his driver's license and passport as he would not take off his turban for a photo ID and Ranjit Singh, a 69-year-old political refugee, was refused a resident card in 2002 for a similar reason (Mejindarpal Kaur, Personal correspondence, 25 March 2007).

Bibliography

Agamben, G. (1998) *Homo Sacer: Sovereign Power and Bare Life* (trans. Daniel Heller-Roazen), Stanford: Stanford University Press.
—— (2002) *Remnants of Auschwitz: The Witness and the Archive* (trans. Daniel Heller-Roazen), New York: Zone Books.
Alkire, S. (2003a) 'Concepts of human security', in L. Chen, S. Fukuda-Parr and E. Seidensticker (eds) *Human Insecurity in a Global World*, Cambridge, MA: Harvard University Press, 15–40.
—— (2003b) *A Conceptual Framework for Human Security*, Centre for Research on Inequality, Human Security and Ethnicity (CRISE), Queen Elizabeth House, University of Oxford, Working Paper #2, 2002. Online. Available URL: http://www.crise.ox.ac.uk/pubs/workingpaper2.pdf (accessed September 4, 2009).
Amouyel, A. (2006) 'What is human security', *Revue de Sécurité Humaine/Human Security Journal* 1 (1): 10–23.
Annan, K. (2000) *Millennium Report of the Secretary-General of the UN*, New York: United Nations Department of Public Information.
—— (2005) *In Larger Freedom: Towards Development, Security and Human Rights For All*, New York: United Nations Publications.
Berman, J. (2007) 'The "vital core": from bare life to the biopolitics of Human Security', in G. Shani, M. Sato and M. K. Pasha (eds) *Protecting Human Security in a Post 9/11*

World: Critical and Global Insights, Houndmills, Basingstoke, Hants: Palgrave Macmillan, 30–50.

Booth, K. (1991) 'Security and emancipation', *Review of International Studies* 17 (4): 313–26.

—— (2005) 'Beyond critical security studies', in K. Booth (ed.) *Critical Security Studies and World Politics*, Boulder, CO: Lynne Rienner, 259–79.

Buzan, B., Waever, O. and de Wilde, J. (1998) *Security: A New Framework for Analysis*, Boulder, CO: Lynne Rienner.

Castles, S. and Miller, M. J. (2003) *The Age of Migration: International Population Movements in the Modern World*, 3rd edn, Basingstoke: Palgrave Macmillan.

Commission on Human Security (CHS) (2003) *Human Security Now*, New York: Oxford University Press.

Council of Europe (1950) *Convention on the Protection of Human Rights and Fundamental Freedoms*. Online. Available URL: http://conventions.coe.int/treaty/en/Treaties/Html/005.htm (accessed March 1 2007).

De Larringa, M. and Doucet, M. (2008) 'Sovereign power and the biopolitics of human security', *Security Dialogue* 39 (5): 517–37.

Douzinas, C. (2007) *Human Rights and Empire: The Political Philosophy of Cosmopolitanism*, London: Routledge Cavendish.

Duffield, M. (2007) *Development, Security and Unending War: Governing the World of Peoples*, Cambridge: Polity.

Foucault, M. (1991) 'Governmentality', in G. Burchell, C. Gordon and P. Miller (eds) *The Foucault Effect: Studies in Governmentality*, Chicago: University of Chicago Press, 87–104.

—— (2007) *Security, Territory, Population: Lectures at the College de France, 1977–1978* (trans. Graham Burchell), Houndmills, Basingstoke, Hants: Palgrave Macmillan.

Geertz, C. (1963) 'The integrative revolution: primordial sentiments and civil politics in new states', in C. Geertz (ed.) *Old Societies and New States: The Quest for Modernity in Asia and Africa*, New York: Free Press, 105–19.

Gibson, I. R. and Reardon, B. A. (2007) 'Human security: toward gender inclusion', in G. Shani, M. Sato and M. K. Pasha (eds) *Protecting Human Security in a Post 9/11 World: Critical and Global Insights*, Houndmills, Basingstoke, Hants: Palgrave Macmillan

Gill, S. (2000) 'The Constitution of Global Capitalism', paper presented at International Studies Association Annual Convention, Los Angeles, March 15, 2000.

—— (2003) *Power and Resistance in the New World Order*, Basingstoke: Palgrave Macmillan.

Glazer, N. and Moynihan, D.P. (1975) 'Introduction', in N. Glazer and D. P. Moynihan, *Ethnicity: Theory and Experience*, Cambridge, MA: Harvard University Press.

Hampson, F. O. (2002) *Madness in the Multitude: Human Security and World Disorder*, New York: Oxford University Press.

Hampson, F. O., Daudelin, J., Reid, H., Hay, J. B. and Martin, T. (2002) *Madness in the Multitude: Human Security and World Disorder*, New York: Oxford University Press.

Hopgood, S. (2000) 'Reading the small print in global civil society: the inexorable hegemony of the liberal self', *Millennium: Journal of International Studies* 29 (1): 1–25.

Hudson, H. (2005) 'Doing security as though humans matter: a feminist perspective on gender and the politics of human security', *Security Dialogue* 36 (2): 155–74.

Human Security Centre (HSC) (2005) *Human Security Report 2005: War and Peace in the 21st Century*, New York: Oxford University Press.

Human Security Network (2009) *The Human Security Network*. Online. Available URL: http://www.humansecuritynetwork.org/network-e.php (accessed September 4, 2009).

Inayatullah, N. and Blaney, D. L. (2004) *International Relations and the Problem of Difference*, New York and London: Routledge.

International Commission on Intervention and State Sovereignty (2001) *Report of the International Committee on Intervention and State Sovereignty*, Ottawa, ON: International Development Research Centre, December.

International Organization for Migration (IOM) (2003) *World Migration Report: Managing Migration Challenges and Responses for People on the Move*, Geneva: International Organization for Migration. Online. Available URL: http://www.iom.int/documents/publication/en/chap16p291%5F302.pdf (accessed February 2, 2008).

MacFarlane, S. N. and Khong, Y. F. (2006) *Human Security and the UN: A Critical History*, Bloomington and Indianapolis: Indiana University Press.

Modood, T. (2005) *Multicultural Politics: Racism, Ethnicity and Muslims in Britain*, Minneapolis: University of Minnesota Press.

Parekh, B. (2002) 'Barry and the dangers of liberalism', in P. Kelly (ed.) *Multiculturalism Reconsidered*, Cambridge: Polity Press, 133–51.

Paris, R. (2001) 'Human security: paradigm shift or hot air', *International Security* 26 (2): 87–102.

Roy, O. (2007) *Secularism Confronts Islam*, Columbia, NY: Columbia University Press.

Shani, G. (2007a) *Sikh Nationalism and Identity in a Global Age*, London: Routledge.

—— (2007b) 'Introduction: protecting human security in a post 9/11 world', in G. Shani, M. Sato and M. K. Pasha (eds) *Protecting Human Security in a Post 9/11 World: Critical and Global Insights*, Houndmills, Basingstoke, Hants: Palgrave Macmillan, 1–17.

—— (2007c) '"Democratic imperialism", neo-liberal globalization and human in/security in the global South', in G. Shani, M. Sato and M. K. Pasha (eds) *Protecting Human Security in a Post 9/11 World: Critical and Global Insights*, Houndmills, Basingstoke, Hants: Palgrave Macmillan, 17–30.

Shani, G. and. Pasha, M. K (2007) 'Conclusion', in G. Shani, M. Sato and M. K. Pasha (eds) *Protecting Human Security in a Post 9/11 World: Critical and Global Insights*, Houndmills, Basingstoke, Hants: Palgrave Macmillan.

Shils, E. (1957) 'Personal, primordial, sacred and civil ties', *British Journal of Sociology* 8 (June): 130–34.

SikhNet (2007) *French Highest Court Upholds Turban Ban in Schools*. Online. Available URL: http://www.sikhnet.com/sikhnet/news.nsf/NewsArchive/CD6C767746C15575872573B10063CE01 (accessed December 14 2007).

Strange, S. (1996) *The Retreat of the State: The Diffusion of Power in the World Economy*, London: Cambridge University Press.

Thomas, C. (2000) *Global Governance, Development and Human Security: The Challenge of Poverty and Inequality*, London: Pluto Press.

United Nations Development Programme (UNDP) (1994) *Human Development Report 1994: New Dimensions of Human Security*, New York: Oxford University Press.

—— (2004) *Human Development Report 2004: Cultural Liberty in Today's Diverse World*, Oxford: Oxford University Press.

—— (2009) *Human Development Report 2009: Overcoming Barriers: Human Mobility and Development*, Oxford: Oxford University Press.

Wæver, O. (1995) 'Securitization and desecuritization', in R. D. Lipschutz (ed.) *On Security*, New York: Columbia University Press, 46–86.

6 Human security, biopoverty and the possibility for emancipation

David Roberts[1]

It has long been the concern of scholars like Chandler (2008), Duffield (2001), and Sorensen (2002) that Liberal security discourses addressing security in the global South have concealed an agenda directed towards the securing of societies in the global North. Such scholars have identified the so-called 'Security–Development Nexus' as an early casualty of such co-option, whereby 'development' as a concept is rendered less for the social prosperity of people in the South and more for the security of people in the North. Development, then, has been hijacked.

More recently, the Human Security concept has befallen a similar fate. What was intended in an expansive sense as a means of securing a greater number of civilians from a broader range of threats has been manipulated to legitimate violent Liberal interventionism, including 'humanitarian bombing' and 'cosmopolitan policekeeping' (Kaldor 1999), proposed to forcibly subsume non-Liberal behaviour in the peripheries to the dictat of the neo-liberal metropolis. In the process, Liberal scholarship has blamed mayhem and instability in those peripheries on a dysfunctional Other, dislocating their cause from broader phenomena of power and asymmetry in matters of global governance, characterized by neo-liberal hegemony (Kaldor 1999, 2007).

It is no irony that the scholarship co-opting these security discourses is conspicuous in its refusal to consider the role of power in the international system and in global governance. Indeed, the efficacious or indifferent denial of the role of power in global governance – the disconnection of cause from effect – stands out as a key characteristic of the mainstream IR literature, and yet the role of asymmetrical power in the international system is central to understanding relationships between crises in the global margins and causation in the global core. More importantly still, it is central to answering the question of why mainstream security discourses exclude or marginalize a broader rendering of human security, why those discourses persistently refuse to recognize the role of ideational hegemony in the international system and its consequences for broad human security, and how we might make broad human security something more than an empty signifier.

This chapter approaches these matters through the lens of Foucauldian analytics. First, it discusses the biopolitical nature of power in neo-liberal global governmentality and its relationship to broad human security in the global South. Second, it addresses the absence of policy regarding broader human security, which bedevils the concept's coherence and legitimacy, by internationalizing Foucault's analysis of sovereign, territorially-shaped population contingencies. Third, from this approach, the chapter identifies practical, broad human security policy aimed at international, sub-state populations sharing similar lethal threats to their human security.

Power and global governance

The scholarly literature on International Relations has, until recently, mainly considered global governance in technocratic, institutional terms which reflect conventional understandings of power. Numerous articles in leading journals, such as the eponymous *Global Governance*, have focused on the Liberal–Realist instrumentalism of multilateral international institutions and their role in finessing the Kantian and Liberal Peace. In this imagining of the international system, international organizations facilitate cooperation and manage conflict. They perform technocratic functions, which scholars investigate with a view to making existing practices and bodies better at what they already try to do (Rosenau 1995). Power, where it is interrogated, is considered mainly in traditional terms, with respect to matters of military might and organization, or economic prowess. This scholarship is, of course, critical in the sense that it engages with the literature in the positivist traditions of the social sciences and in conformity with mainstream IR intellectual expectations. However, it is not critical in the sense that it does not engage outside of the mainstream; it remains, for the most part, in an intellectual comfort zone buttressed by epistemological and ontological conformity, preferring to direct its resources to theorizing to predict the future in crystal ball fashion, rather than applying its resources to problem-solving for and in the present. It fiddles intellectually while people burn metaphorically.

In this neutral form, global governance is conceived of by Carin *et al.* as 'multilayered regulation' (2006: 3); as a conglomeration of regimes and instructions mobilized primarily by states to achieve the desired outcome of peace and prosperity amidst the destabilizing forces of economic globalization. Rorden Wilkinson comments that this literature tends to emphasize how

> the steady development of international institutions and regimes have, when taken in the aggregate, led to the emergence of a web of international norms, treaties, and conventions that encourage sustained cooperation among states and, in so doing, generate a measure of international governance.
> (Wilkinson 2004: 4)

In a similar vein, James Rosenau defines global governance as something 'conceived to include systems of rule at all levels of human activity – from the family to the international organization – in which the pursuit of goals through the exercise of control has transnational repercussions' (1995: 13). And, within that broad rubric of global governance, which depends on multilayered multilateral institutionalism, Robert Keohane and Joseph Nye represent the main vehicles of global governance as politically passive systems (2000: 37). Rosenau is quite explicit about the role of power in global governance when he writes that 'the organizing perspective is that of governance in the world rather than governance of the world. The latter implies a central authority that is doing the governing, an implication that clearly has no basis in fact' (Wilkinson 2004: 7).

Rosenau's point is a fair one, as long as power is considered in conventional, materialist, Realist-friendly terms. But this is a narrow interpretation of power, and scholars increasingly have turned their attention to more nuanced understandings of power as ideational or ideological; normally this interpretation of power meshes with the conventional to produce an ideas-based logic behind a variety of forms of political authority and force in the international system. According to Barnett and Duvall, persisting in considering power in terms of a Liberal–Institutionalist/state-centric 'central authority' is not just intellectually moribund but also carries with it very real risks in the 'real world' of everyday human lives. They argue that 'failure to develop alternative conceptualizations of power limits the ability of international relations scholars to understand how global outcomes are produced and how actors are differentially enabled and constrained to determine their fates' (Barnett and Duvall 2006: 41). In short, they argue that 'concern with power . . . brings attention to global structures, processes, and institutions that shape the fates and life chances of actors around the world' (Barnett and Duvall 2005: 7–8).

Others have considered power in global governance and identified a variety of forms. Kapstein, for example, suggests that international institutions, at the heart of global governance and neo-liberal praxis, may change or maintain conditions or processes in ways that benefit some more than others (Kapstein 2005). Thus, the architecture of global governance creates and/or perpetuates hierarchies of advantage and disadvantage by dictating and maintaining uneven preferences and practices in a range of economic regimes which aggravate postcolonial asymmetries of relative prosperity and poverty. Facilitating this inertia, Ian Johnstone identifies a second type of power present in global governance as 'productive' (Johnstone 2005). This refers to the ability to maintain adiaphoric denial by means of representing a subjective, incomplete and partisan claim as an objective, absolute and neutral truth that cannot be changed. Economics, for example, is presented in the neo-liberal mainstream as a neutral science when the plethora of contending perspectives and priorities suggest it cannot be so; human nature is presented as universal and a scientific fact when no such scientific evidence has ever existed; common sense is claimed as an absolute when it is a subjective and shifting collection of prejudices and preferences. All claim a universality and reliability which none can prove, but they enjoy productive power since they are accepted and uncritically taken for granted by many, in part because norms are rarely critiqued, in part because many people do not perceive that the world around them is not fixed, and in part because norms are, by their nature, hegemonic.

The third form of power in governance, discussed by Barnett and Duvall (2006) involves structures, or transnational social rules systems which, when combined with the hegemony of productive discourses, are responsible for creating and perpetuating material and capability inequality. And, since these concepts of power permeate the institutions and practices of global governance and are projected by them, governance itself is a form of power. However, even from such an enlightened perspective, structure as power is still considered in relatively conventional terms, such as class and related social and economic divides. In response to this limitation, Felix Berenskoetter argues that power at the global level maintains the institutions, beliefs and practices that underpin it. Perhaps yet more importantly, Berenskoetter maintains that power can also be applied to challenge and change a given scenario, implying clearly that power is 'responsible for both change and continuity' in the international system (Berenskoetter 2007: 13). That is, intentional or unintentional activity is required both to maintain a status quo and to transform it. Berenskoetter further contends that if the exercise of power makes a difference, then 'identifying power is analytically indistinguishable with identifying cause' (Berenskoetter 2007: 13). He adds that 'this is significant because it also means identifying who/what is responsible for the ways things are, or are likely, to be'. According to this perspective, 'power can be made analytically responsible for phenomena of both change and continuity' (Berenskoetter 2007: 13).

Foucault and global governance

Ideational and material power from these perspectives is ever present in global governance. But the means by which it is distributed remains unclear until we turn to Foucault. Foucault is renowned for his contribution to understanding the role of power and government at the national level. He suggests that the rationale of government, or its governmentality, is to discipline and punish in accordance with the achievement of the good life. In this sense, government power is power over the human life within its territorial jurisdiction, and for this reason Foucault refers to such power as biopolitical. Power in this sense emanates from a belief in a particular way of organizing society for a particular outcome, and this power is not solely centralized but is instead disseminated throughout multiple sites which enforce a government's rationale. He referred to such formations as capillary power circulated through multiple institutions, most famously like prisons and schools, where conformity is inaugurated and non-conformity punished. It is the 'calculated management of life' (Foucault 1979: 140). And, as with all management involving human beings, it must inevitably also mismanage.

Recently, aspects of Foucault's governmentality have been applied to considerations of global governance. If national governmentality exercises capillary biopolitical power over territorially-bounded populations, then logically, global governmentality may exercise the same forms of power in similar ways over the global population. Global governance, or global governmentality, is neo-liberal in rationale and authorizes political and economic liberalization. The former is claimed to secure individual human rights and provide and regulate a stable social environment in which the latter can maximize enlightened self-interest directed through commerce for the achievement of prosperity and international security.

In this way, global governmentality comprehensively seeks to exercise power over life, including non-human species, since it regulates the biosphere broadly. Its reach is presently unparalleled historically and its legitimacy, despite compelling contrarian argument and evidence, holds firm. Even in the light of recent 'economic meltdown' and the associated rhetoric demanding the need for change, the neo-liberal idea itself has not received much in the way of criticism from within the elite architectures of power that determine ideological continuity globally. Global governance/governmentality reflects and extends the rationale of neo-liberalism by means of the multilayered regulatory instruments which otherwise form the technical subject-matter of mainstream global governance scholarship, which ignores or refutes the instrumentalism of capillary power that such bodies constitute when scrutinized from a Foucauldian perspective. International Governmental Organizations (IGOs) like the UN, European Commission (EC) and North Atlantic Treaty Organization (NATO), International Non-Governmental Organizations (INGOs) and political charities like Amnesty International, Transparency International, Oxfam and Human Rights Watch, and national advocacy groups in almost every country in the world, all constitute the capillary veins through which neo-liberal ideational power directs planetary life.

Such an application of Foucauldian thought is, according to Michael Merlingen, a fresh means of 'assembling a larger picture of the biopolitical character of the international . . . for the exploration of world order' (Merlingen 2008: 272–73). Ronnie Lipschutz suggests that 'although Foucault wrote only about governmentality within states . . . the extension of his idea to the international arena' points us towards: 'An arrangement of actors and institutions, of rules and rule, through which the architecture of the global articulation of states and capitalism is maintained'(Lipschutz 2005: 235–36).

Fleshing out this approach, Michael Dillon and Julian Reid argue that 'global liberal governance' involves 'a varied and complex regime of power, whose founding principle lies in the administration and production of life' (2001: 41). Global governance, based on the rationale of neo-liberalism through which global governmentality projects itself, engages 'with the detailed knowledgeable strategies and tactics that affect the constitution of life and the regulation of the affairs of populations, no matter how these are specified' (2002: 12–13; Rowland 2008: 801). And, where Foucauldian governmentality necessitates the evolution of domestic state strategies around 'specific problematics, such as those of health, wealth, security, poverty, esteem, culture or migration' (Dillon and Reid 2001: 48), global governmentality also considers and ranks similar matters. Presently, global governmentality prioritizes particular lives, since 'hard' security matters like terrorism, civil war and nuclear proliferation occurring manically and damaging a metaphorical handful of people take precedence over 'soft' security matters like child mortality and poverty occurring chronically that wipe out millions in processes adiaphorically separated from the neo-liberal rationale of global governance. In this sense, global governmentality, as it attempts to govern the global, ensures certain people are secured, and certain people are not. Global governance, or global governmentality, regulates human security.

The biopolitics, and biopoverty, of human security

Human security as a security concept has always been disengaged from causation. In its narrower imaginings, it has been constricted to a meaning associated only with political violence (Mack 2005), or proposed as a framework for dealing with migration and refugees in Europe (Kaldor 1999). At its broadest extremes, it has been proposed as 'freedom from want and fear', or with reference to an ill-defined 'vital core'. In no instance has its causation been traced to power in the international system. Indeed, the converse is true: conditions of human insecurity have quite openly been dislocated from central causation.

The broader variants have also been dismissed from serious debate in International Relations. Whilst advocates have sought to negotiate a space in the public sphere in which the lives of hundreds of millions of lethally vulnerable people might momentarily be prioritized as matters of security, the debate and their security have been dismissed and isolated to matters of 'human rights' or 'development' by the dominant security traditions (for the most part). Upendra Baxi charges that such traditions 'encode power and hierarchy, allocate competencies (who may speak), constructs forms (how one may speak, what forms of discourse are proper), determine boundaries (what may not be named or conversed about), and structure exclusion (denial of voice)' (1998: 129). One of the consequences of the limits set by this discursive pattern of epistemological chauvinism is that the elephant in the room, of power in global governance, is sidelined from security consideration. Mike Pugh, for example, is concerned that 'silence surrounds the role of interventionary core capitalism in perpetuating poverty through neo-liberal policies and the structuring of the global economy' (2005: 9). And for Kyle Grayson, the closing of Realist-dominated mainstream security discourses to matters of broad human security 'functions as a gatekeeper, preventing the intrusion of anything that might unsettle [some] shared norms about what can count as knowledge' and what can count as security (2008: 394). To make human security mean something, it must first expose the role of power in its regulation and then demonstrate policy coherence. Foucault, governmentality and biopolitics help us rethink the regulation and reification of human security.

Neo-liberal global governmentality is directed through multiple international platforms designed to secure conformity with neo-liberal practices. Public and private international finance cooperate in dictating the terms on which large sums of money are disbursed to developing countries. Simultaneously, public international bodies extend neo-liberal beliefs in development programmes that apply costly and fetishized Weberian transparency and auditing systems to monitor local compliance with global dictat, fulfilling the surveillance aspect of biopower. Non-conformity may be punished not with jail but with marginalization in international bodies, exclusion from new borrowing rights or non-forgiveness of older international debts. Similarly, conformity with neo-liberal expectations may be rewarded with debt forgiveness, Most Favoured Nation status, reduced protectionism and so on. Local government policy in developing countries, then, is routinely prescribed to enforce and embed global governmentality.

The power of neo-liberal governmentality is used prohibitively. The Post-Washington Consensus dictates that states subject to their domination, mainly in the developing world but increasingly in the developed world, may not enjoin in particular social practices. The best known and most commonly cited example of this is the application of Structural Adjustment Programmes (SAPs), which direct governments wanting to borrow from the World Bank and IMF (and, indirectly, from private international capital) to reduce the size of the state (since it is claimed to be corrupt and inefficient, as the UK is discovering), to reduce social expenditure in areas like health and education, and to stimulate private business ventures by offering a favourable investment climate. The World Bank decides social policy in many developing countries (Deacon 2004; Yeates 2005). And, since the market increasingly finds it impossible to fund large social support systems, after the state is prohibited and the market withdraws, residual mechanisms like philanthropy and charity bodies are left over (Mishra 2002; Mkandawire 2004). Whereas state social policy may represent a formal part of the social contract, philanthropy and charity are informal and have no obligation to maintain the presence nominally directed by conformity with tax regimes.

Global governance is responsible for the social conditions in which millions of vulnerable people find themselves denied access to elements of human existence that are scientifically, incontestably essential for its pursuance. Beyond socially and academically contested basic needs, there are elemental, fundamental physiological needs that humans have for survival, without which they will die. These form part of the typologies evolved by Abraham Maslow (1943) and Manfred Max-Neef (1989) regarding bare physiological necessities for the continuation of individual biological life. Air is one which presently is not regulated by money. But water and sanitation are others; in the words of Chief John Turey, Head of Crab Town Community Slum in Freetown, Sierra Leone, 'water is life'.[2] We seem to have forgotten this inviolable empirical fact. But it is increasingly regulated by markets, the predominance and preeminence of which are authorized and stipulated by neo-liberal global governance. In this way, global governance is ultimately biopolitical; it holds power over life and death, just as sovereigns did in the period that stimulated Foucault's thinking. It is in this context that I identify the concept of biopoverty.

Biopoverty refers to the calculated mismanagement of physiological necessities – water, nutrition, vaccines – without which civilians die *en masse*. Biopoverty stands at the nexus of the biologically – essentially and the institutionally – prohibited. It is structural and deliberated – calculated from the formula of democracy and capitalism as dual progenitors of peace and prosperity – in character, since it is socially constructed and mobilized by social and institutional rules that determine the in/accessibility of otherwise available life-preserving resources. For brevity, it may be considered the calculated mismanagement of physiological necessity. This is not 'bare-life' as that part of the human excluded from the juridical process to which Agamben refers (1998). Nor is it necropolitics (Mbembe 2003), in which some degree of institutional determinism may be present in the deliberate extermination of life. Biopoverty is not an abstract theory but a way of describing the mortal situation of hundreds of millions of people daily. It is a socially-constructed problem; a consequence, as Thomas Pogge put it so well, 'not [of] bad luck but bad organization' (2008: 531). Biopoverty as a concept reifies human security: it provides definitional coherence around natural science and identifies readily fixable contingencies. If Foucault's thinking has helped elaborate a middle path between narrow and broad human security, the following section suggests how Foucauldian thought might be applied to policy formulation.

A human security, sector -wide approach (SWAp)

In contrast with mainstream neo-liberal adiaphoric denial of power in global governance, a neo-Foucauldian approach offers the means to describe the reach, nature and consequence of power in global governance, and to identify the instruments by which its rationality is disbursed, illuminating cause and effect. However, in addition, Foucauldian analytics also provide the means by which a broad human security policy can be reified; not at the level imagined by the ethos of freedom from fear and want, but neither at the level constrained in the Human Security Report (Mack 2005) by its strict affiliation with political violence, or by intervention agendas concerned with 'any of the moving feast of strategic threats that liberal order is constantly menaced by' (Duffield 2008: 148).

Foucault (1979) determined that governmentality was concerned with the management of a territorially-bound population mainly through focusing on particular contingencies and needs shared by the population, like 'health, wealth, security, poverty, esteem, culture or migration' (Dillon and Reid 2001: 48). Foucault's analysis can be elevated beyond the sovereign to the global level, allowing us to identify transnational populations on the same terms, of shared conditions, contingencies and cures, across nations and below states; and it is on the basis of this that a broader human security approach can be evolved. Indeed, this is not dissimilar to a strategy known in the field of International Development as a Sector Wide Approach (SWAp). In this context, a sector is identified around which national and donor policy may coalesce, avoiding vertical and single issue development projects and approaching a problem more holistically. The *British Medical Journal* has supported the idea of maternal mortality as a sector to be addressed, which, by understanding the causes and risks of maternal mortality, can coordinate a resolution more effectively than a single project-orientated approach can do (Goodburn and Campbell 2001). In this work, however, child mortality is the 'sector' and its transnational shared identity, coupled with the contingencies that cause it and the similarity of cures that resolve it, reflect Foucauldian analytics. The key cause of avoidable child mortality is clean water provision and sanitation venting, so it is these matters that must be treated first.

Presently, the privileged means of providing water and, less frequently, sanitation, takes the form of reluctant, expensive and inevitably exploitative (since this is the essential and ineluctable nature of liberal economics) Transnational Corporations. Water TNCs, which in recent years have asked the World Bank to subsidize the risks they bear in tendering for large projects, mainly serve metropolitan areas and charge very high end-user prices, often proportionately higher than in developed countries. They are also reluctant to engage with populations beyond the metropolis, because there is risk of vandalism and theft, and because very poor people seem unable to pay very high prices for essential services (Hall 2003; Mehrotra and Delamonica 2005). The outcome is that drinking water is expensive and provided only in cities, and sanitation is rarely considered by water TNCs. There is also a substantial risk of failure to deliver in the first instance in either case (Dwivedi and Dharmadhikary 2006). Either way, given that medical science agrees on the absence of clean water as the key cause of child mortality, clean water has not been provided by the private sector in quantities that substantially reduce that mortality rate, least of all in rural areas.

An alternative exists, however. Rather than a top-down, skewed-impact transnational private sector neo-liberal approach to water and sanitation projects that delivers at high end-user prices to a limited audience and which extracts substantial profit to foreign multinationals, instead, a transnational, or transversal, multination, bottom-up indigenous private sector approach to child mortality where rates are highest could be evolved. This approach could mobilize externally-funded local entrepreneurialism aimed at providing low-cost or free water and sanitation focused around the areas worst affected by child mortality. This would be financed by a coordinating body whose rationale lay in those people's needs, rather than the needs of their budget providers and the fantasies of neo-liberal economic analysts in neo-liberal international institutions.

What very poor people in very poor communities often lack is not the capacity to create water flows, but is instead the means to buy, rent or otherwise access, and then maintain, basic re/building equipment, like earthmovers and diggers, trucks and cranes, and, as often as not, low-technology equipment like wheelbarrows, spades and ladders, or commodities like cement.[3] Local initiatives are wide-ranging, when people have the opportunity and support to self-mobilize, and basic projects often have substantial benefit. Building toilets near schools and villages, educating in basic hygiene, sinking bore-holes, repairing existing facilities, connecting cheap plastic pipelines, building paths and roads to accelerate connectivity are all relatively modest exercises that often have quite sudden and disproportionate returns (Stoltenberg 2006; Buchanan and Decamp 2007).[4] In contrast with the minimal outcomes associated with profit-selective TNC involvement, or the absence of any investment at all beyond chance and residue, indigenous provision will likely continue to bring almost immediate reduction in foul water ingestion and intestinal diseases, whilst sanitation cleansing is similarly quickly determinative of health and mortality. It seems reasonable to look for ways this approach could be evolved and accelerated. In order to do this, cash and expertize are necessary where they are absent. To establish and provide for this need, I propose an interface concept, or conduit system I refer to as a Global Water Bank.

This Global Water Bank interface could be located in the parts of the world with the highest child mortality rates and poorest sanitation and water provision (Hall and Lobina 2006), and connect indigenously-determined water and sanitation demand to exogenously subordinate supply of funding and expertize. In this approach, needs are identified, by the people with the needs, in Community-Based

Organizations (CBOs). CBOs would be comprised of representatives of local people and organizations that fully include women where they bear the brunt of water provision. Provision would be focused on those needs, rather than being arrived at on the basis of, for example, the ratio of a developed country's GDP it allocates to aid and development; or on fickle policies that amount to periodic whims that change each time donor governments hold elections at home; or on the degree to which a given humanitarian NGO might be favoured by public funding based on random campaigns in unaffected developed societies.

These needs would then be communicated to donors like the World Bank, with its development role and its range of expertize, by the locally-arrayed Water Banks. Clearly, no multilateral or bilateral donor would likely be willing or able to organize and coordinate thousands of grants and loans to thousands more individuals in hundreds of provinces in dozens of countries. Instead, the Water Bank interface finesses and communicates local demand to the panoply of global public and private donors, reducing duplication of supply and of bureaucratic planning in multifarious approaches that avoidably generate high-cost jobs for people in high-profile institutions and developed countries, which inevitably subtracts from the sum total of available cash (Fernandez 2009; Slaymaker and Newborne 2004). The Water Banks would provide a range of services generated from this demand-led, focused provision including low-key in-country consultancy, relatively modest unconditional grant-making and lending aimed at existing local capacity and capabilities, higher-end funding for distant resources, such as heavy earth movers rentable from neighbouring provinces or countries, and communication facilitation for local private sector needs, like radios and cell phones. Donors would fund, through the Global Water Bank centres, local and regional construction companies, pay for experts to train and retrain community engineers and car mechanics (for example) to maintain bore-holes, and fund educators to demonstrate the efficacy of water treatment. One example might be to employ people to take basic microscopes, routinely found in children's play sets in western countries, to communities unaware of basic hygiene rules and show the microbes in motion in their drinking water, and compare this to their absence in clean water. The same applies to sanitation. In Medinapur, in West Bengal, in the 1990s,

> [p]roduction centres were set up with starter funds where masons (female and male) were employed to manufacture toilet pans and slabs. Prices began at $7.40 and rose to $74. Loans were on offer to those who put down half the price. By the early 2000's bicycle rickshaw carts delivering toilets to customers were a routine sight. By 2006, almost every household in Medinapur had installed a toilet. Hundreds of women and men have been trained in a new occupation and earn a good living.
>
> (Black 2008: 7)

The emphasis is on micro-credits and grants for local people to self-mobilize, deploy their capabilities and connect with resources that lie beyond their immediate purview, to support the expansion of private sector provision of local water needs in areas worst affected by high infant mortality rates by sustaining emerging water-orientated business communities and resource mobilization from distant parties, where necessary.

Some form of evaluation to satisfy donor and global governance audit processes and to evaluate the effectiveness of the projects would be required. The emphasis on bottom-up entrepreneurialism set in CBOs with local accounting can be extended to the evaluation strategy by applying and adapting the idea of Most Significant Change (MSC), which assesses project impact from the perspective of the intended beneficiaries. In this respect, the simple test of whether the proposed interventions are working is if the Under Five Mortality Rate (U5MR) drops, ascertainable epidemiologically and demographically. This departs from the MSC, which does not normally use an indicator as such, and instead rests more on people's stories, reflecting an 'everyday lives' philosophy more attuned to bottom-up improvement than top-down accounting. However, the qualitative, subjective methodology underscored by MSC could readily be applied to the downstream impacts of water and sanitation provision that are measurable by people's stories, the core MSC methodology. For example, the stories of girl children freed from water-bearing and able to take up school could be a measure of the success of such a programme. Using this method provides ample evidence that donor funds are being properly spent.

Built into this system could be a pragmatic acceptance of the constructive role of Common Social Patronage and petty corruption, where monies spent informally securing the cooperation of significant local actors are legitimated by their enshrining in more formal contracts for basic reporting and organizational tasks that would contribute to the implementation of the water and sanitation projects (Fernandez 2009).[5] Furthermore, should the U5MR not decline, such contracts would not be extended. Given the scale of public-elite corruption increasingly common in western democracies and international aid institutions, where nobody benefits other than the thief, pragmatic formalizing of informal procedures, without which the interventions might not be as successful, where the child mortality rate drops, should not present a dilemma for donors.

Conceptually speaking, this strategy can be applied across regions, since substantial proportions of the U5MR are a product of similar resource matters. Tactically speaking, different approaches in specific places would require particular localized responses to be undertaken within the wider strategic imperative of water and sanitation provision. Greater emphasis financially and tactically could be placed on under-exploited and already existing World Bank operations, such as the Local Initiatives Project (LIP), which provides 'financial resources to people wanting to start their own small businesses and to take an active role in rebuilding their livelihoods instead of depending on state social welfare funds', which are often nonexistent (Ohiorhenuan and Stewart 2008: 85). This 'poverties' approach:

> Does not necessarily signal the death of large-scale efforts to alleviate [water] poverty, nor does it require the abandonment of development itself. Instead, [it] forces us to seriously re-think development [and human security] goals and our means of achieving them.
>
> (Ohiorhenuan and Stewart 2008: 727)

This means of accelerating the declination of child mortality is a consequence of understanding power in International Relations in more balanced terms, as being destructive as well as constructive, and of rethinking ideas around populations and contingencies.

Conclusion

Elevating and internationalizing Foucauldian analytics confronts some of the key complaints made about the broader human security concept. First, it overcomes objections based on who to prioritize for human security. If we are unable to agree as adults on the need to protect tens of millions of the most vulnerable children in the world from clearly avoidable lethal illnesses, then any claim to the existence of any universal commonality must surely fall flat, and any reference to the idea of Liberal 'civilization' must only be a nonsense on par with Realist fantasy regarding anarchic inevitability and ontological determinism. Second, it proposes clear policy that has minimal costs relative to conventional approaches, with needs and resources identified and driven by indigenous communities, rather than global governance values or, in the middle of the two, rapidly shifting uni- and multilateral donor priorities and capacities.

Third, it confronts challenges of political naivety by engaging fully with the notion of ideational and material power in the international system by applying a Foucauldian analytic of biopolitics and governmentality to the global level. This demonstrates causation, but also allows for the means by which this situation can be changed, readily, supported empirically by positivist medical epidemiological evidence and analysis. Fourth, the indigenous ownership and direction of needs and responses responds to concerns that the human security concept has been hijacked and manipulated into a 'technology' of Liberal interventionism and global governance.

Foucauldian governmentality and biopolitics provide a reliable and far-reaching descriptive analytic of the international system which unmasks the neo-liberal hubris and sophistry that cloak its cultural ambitions, its failure to achieve them and the ideological narcissism preserving asymmetrical global power and its ideational role in the calculated mismanagement of human security. From this realistic and more honest analysis, we are better able to design alternative means of broadening the pertinence of the human security concept and its reification.

Notes

1 Dr David Roberts, Senior Lecturer, University of Ulster; Chair, Human Security Working Group.
2 Interview with Chief John Turey, Crab Town Community Slum, Freetown, Sierra Leone, 6 June 2009.
3 Interviews with Michael Roy Moses, Community Development Researcher, Children and Women Empowerment Society (CWES), and 7 Village Elders, White Man's Bay Slum Community, Freetown, Sierra Leone, 4 June 2009; interviews with Chief John Turey, Crab Town Community Slum, Freetown, Sierra Leone, 6 June 2009; interviews

with community representatives, Kompong Speu Hospital, Cambodia, 8–12 August 1993; Skype interview, Dr Gustavo Fernandez, MD, (Humanitarian Intervention specialist in Somalia, Darfur and Iraq), Geneva–UK, 11 April 2009.
4 Interviews with Chief John Turey, Crab Town Community Slum, Freetown, Sierra Leone, 6 June 2009; Michael Roy Moses, Community Development Researcher, *Children and Women Empowerment Society* (CWES), Chin-Chin Community Slum, Freetown, Sierra Leone, 10 June 2009.
5 Skype Interview with Dr Gustavo Fernandez, MD, (Humanitarian Intervention specialist in Somalia, Darfur and Iraq), Geneva–UK, 11 April 2009.

References

Agamben, G. (1998) *Homo Sacer: Soverign Power and Bare Life*, Stanford, California: Stanford University Press.
Barnett, M. and Duvall, R. (2005) 'Power in global governance', in M. Barnett and R. Duvall (eds) *Power in Global Governance*, Cambridge: Cambridge University Press.
—— (2006) 'Power in International Politics', *International Organization* 59 (1): 1–32.
Baxi, U. (1998) 'Voices of suffering and the future of human rights', *Transnational Law and Contemporary Problems* 125 (8): 125–70.
Berenskoetter, F. (2007) 'Thinking about power', in F. Berenskoetter (ed.) *Power in World Politics*, London: Routledge, 1–23.
Black, M. (2008) 'We need to talk about . . . toilets', *New Internationalist* 414 (August): 21–27.
Buchanan, A. and Decamp, M. (2007) 'Responsibility for Global Health', in R. Cook and C. G. Ngwena (eds) *Health and Human Rights*, London: Ashgate, 506–23.
Carin, B., Higgott, R., Scholte, J., Smith, J. and Stone, D. (2006) 'Global Governance: Looking Ahead 2006–10', *Global Governance*, 12 (1): 1–6.
Chandler, D. (2008) 'Human Security: the dog that didn't bark', *Security Dialogue* 39 (4): 427–38.
Deacon, R. (2004) *The Politics of Global Social Policy*, Geneva: United Nations Research Institute for Social Development.
Dillon, M. and Reid, J. (2001) 'Global liberal governance: biopolitics, security and war', *Millennium: Journal of International Studies* 30 (1): 41–66.
Duffield, M. (2001) *Global Governance and the New Wars: The Merging of Development and Security*, London: Zed.
Duffield, M. (2008) 'Global civil war: the non-insured, international containment and post-interventionary society', *Journal of Refugee Studies* 21 (2): 145–65.
Dwivedi, G. and Dharmadhikary, S. (2006) *Water: Private, Limited: Issues in Privatization, Corporatisation and Commercialisation of the Water Sector in India*, Badwani: Manthan Adhyayan Kendra.
Foucault, M. (1979) *The History of Sexuality: An Introduction*, London: Allen Lane.
Goodburn, E. and Campbell, O. (2001) 'Reducing maternal mortality in the developing world: sector-wide approaches may be the key', *British Medical Journal* 322: 917–20.
Grayson, K. (2008) 'Human security as power/knowledge: the biopolitics of a defintional debate', *Cambridge Review of International Affairs* 21 (3): 383–401.
Hall, D. (2003) *Financing water for the world: an alternative to guaranteed profits*, London: Public Services International.
Hall, D. and Lobina, E. (2006) *Water as a public service*, London: Public Services International.
Johnstone, I. (2005) 'The power of interpretive communities', in M. Barnett and R. Duvall (eds) *Power in Global Governance*, Cambridge: Cambridge University Press, 185–204.

Kaldor, M. (1999) *New and Old Wars*, Cambridge: Polity.

—— (2007) *Human Security: Reflections on Globalization and Intervention*, Cambridge: Polity.

Kapstein, P. (2005) 'Power, fairness and the global economy', in M. Barnett and R. Duvall (eds) *Power in Global Governance*, Cambridge: Cambridge University Press, 80–101.

Keohane, R. and Nye, J. (2000) 'Introduction', in J. Donahue and J. Nye (eds) *Governance in a Globalizing World*, Washington, DC: Brookings Institute, 1–44.

Lipschutz, R. (2005) 'Global civil society and global governmentality: or, the search for politics and state amidst the capillaries of social power', in M. Barnett and R. Duvall (eds) *Power in Global Governance*, Cambridge: Cambridge University Press, 229–48.

Mack, A. (2005) *The Human Security Report 2005: War and Peace in the 21st Century*, Oxford: Oxford University Press.

Maslow, A (1943) 'A theory of human motivation', *Psychological Review* 50 (4): 370–96.

Max-Neef, M. (1989) 'Human scale development: an option for the future', *Development Dialogue: A Journal of International Development Cooperation*, 1: 7–80.

Mbembe, A. (2003) 'Necropolitics', *Public Culture* 15 (1): 11–40.

Mehrotra, S. and Delamonica, E. (2005) 'The private sector and privatization in social services: is the Washington Consensus dead?', *Global Social Policy* 5 (2): 141–73.

Merlingen, M. (2008) 'Monster studies', *International Political Sociology* 3 (2): 272–74.

Mishra, R. (2002) 'Richard Titmuss and social policy', *Journal of Social Policy* 31 (4): 747–52.

Mkandawire, T. (2004) *Social Policy in a Development Context*, Basingstoke: Palgrave.

Ohiorhenuan, J. and Stewart, F. (2008) *Post-Conflict Economic Recovery: Enabling Local Ingenuity*, New York: UNDP.

Pogge, T. (2008) *World Poverty and Human Rights*, Cambridge: Polity.

Pugh, M. (2005) 'The political economy of peacebuilding: a critical theory perspective', *International Journal of Peace Studies* 10 (2): 23–42.

Rosenau, J. (1995) 'Governance in the twenty-first century', *Global Governance* 1 (1): 13–43.

Rowland, J. (2008) 'Book Reviews: Good Governance and Development; Public Administration and Democratic Governance: Governments Serving Citizens; Learning Civil Societies: Shifting Contexts for Democratic Planning and Governance', *Development in Practice* 18 (6): 801–4.

Slaymaker, T. and Newborne, P. (2004) *Implementation of Water Supply and Sanitation Programmes under PRSPs: Synthesis of Research findings from Sub-Saharan Africa*, London: Overseas Development Institute and WaterAid.

Sorensen, J. (2002) 'Balkanism and the new radical interventionism: a structural critique,' *International Peacekeeping* 9 (1): 1–22.

Stoltenberg, J. (2006) 'Our children: the key to our common future', *The Lancet* 368 (9541): 1042–47.

Wilkinson, R. (2004) 'Introduction', in R. Wilkinson (ed.) *The Global Governance Reader*, London: Routledge.

Yeates, N. (2005) *Globalisation and Social Policy in a Development Context: Regional Responses*, Geneva: UNRISD.

7 Institutionalised and co-opted

Why human security has lost its way

Mandy Turner, Neil Cooper and Michael Pugh

Several chapters in this book argue for a reinvigoration of human security focused on an emancipatory agenda. Our argument is that human security cannot be rescued because it has been institutionalised and co-opted to work in the interests of global capitalism, militarism and neoliberal governance. Some, however, dispute that it has had any impact. Muggah and Krause (2006), for instance, tested its application in Haiti and concluded that it made little difference in policies or outcomes. Indeed, others have argued that there are few examples where human security has actually informed foreign-policy decisions (Owen 2008). Such observations led David Chandler to dismiss human security for being 'the dog that didn't bark' i.e. 'that its integration into the mainstream of policymaking has reinforced, rather than challenged, existing policy frameworks' (2008: 428).

Nevertheless, the rise to dominance of the human security discourse has been quite remarkable. By 2009, only 17 years since its inception, it had made the transition from being a concept created by Mahbub ul Haq, an economist and founder of the *Human Development Report*, to a comprehensive framework for its operationalisation across the UN and development agencies. By expanding the conventional focus on state security to include security in the seven designated realms of the economy, food, health, the environment, the personal, the community, and the political, human security captured the *zeitgeist* of debates in academic and policy communities, particularly the ideas that insecurity causes poverty and that civil wars were *the* major cause of insecurity. Human security was thus regarded as offering a radical alternative to the dominant discourse of international security based on state security and the threat of inter-state conflict.

Since its first elaboration, human security has been further debated and defined through the publications of academics and pronouncements of UN-created bodies (e.g. the UN Trust Fund for Human Security [UNTFHS], the Commission on Human Security, the Advisory Board on Human Security, the Human Security Unit, and the Friends of Human Security, to name but a few), and through the Human Security Network established by the middle-ranking powers, Canada, Norway and Japan. Defined by Chenoy and Tadjbakhsh (2006) as 'the protection of individuals from risks to their physical or psychological safety, dignity and well-being', it also attracted the attention of NGOs, which recognised it had emancipatory potential in its emphasis on human rights and offered a catchy campaigning slogan: eradicating 'freedom from want' and 'freedom from fear'. It can therefore be linked to voices critical of injustices in the global economy – particularly the issues of trade, aid and debt that galvanised the 'Make Poverty History' campaign in 2006. This partly explains why the human security discourse became so popular.

Chandler (2008) argues that this popularity stems from the fact that human security securitises everything, thus creating new enemies for western elites to demonise. Western policymakers have obviously found some aspects of the human security discourse useful, particularly the location of perceived threats to western security (such as terrorism, international criminal networks and migration) in the developing world, which has justified greater military, economic and political intervention (Duffield and Waddell 2006). Others, from a more Realist perspective, argue that human security is just another example of middle powers and international agencies trying to increase their authority and influence (MacLean 2006). Clearly, middle-ranking powers, such as Canada and Japan, as well as UN agencies, have adopted the human security agenda as a way to influence the 'high politics' of international security, as indicated by their insistence that it is *not* a substitute for traditional state security concerns but an important addition.

And yet these explanations cannot satisfactory explain why human security has been adopted by activist and bureaucrat alike, or why radical disagreements continue over whether it fosters emancipation or submission. Our argument is that human security has become a popular discourse largely because of its *perceived* radicalism. It allows bureaucrats working in these institutions to highlight and target some issues traditionally ignored in the state security discourse, while not challenging their positions or that of their governments/organisations, or straying into the dangerous waters of critiquing the global structures of economic and political power.

Human security is a malleable concept, which is where its strength – and the source of its co-option – lies. This chapter explores this co-option and institutionalisation through an analysis of peacebuilding, arms control and economic development. The strength of our argument – that human security has lost its way – lies in the fact that our analysis uncovers identical processes at work in three different policy arenas. We argue that, despite its original radical promise, the human security discourse has been applied in ways that has meant the prioritisation and politicisation of some issues, and the depoliticisation of, and relative silence about, others. This is deeply ironic given that some critics of human security charge that it prioritises everything and thus nothing (Paris 2001). But *what* is prioritised and *what* is left out is critically important.

Human security and the peacebuilding agenda

In common with human security, peacebuilding is a relatively new concept that has rapidly come to dominate academic and policy discourses. Indeed, its entry into the international vocabulary was announced in the same UN document as human security – *An Agenda for Peace* in 1992 – indicating a symbiosis between the two concepts. As outlined in the Commission on Human Security 2003 report, *Human*

Security Now, '[h]elping countries recover from violent conflict, one of the most complex challenges confronting the international community, lays the groundwork for development to take off as well as human security' (Commission on Human Security 2003: 57). The goal of the international peacebuilding agenda is thus to develop human security. In order to achieve this, a peacebuilding industry has emerged: donors, international organisations, international financial institutions (IFIs) and NGOs have developed a dizzying array of definitions, matrixes and 'toolboxes' (e.g. World Bank 1998; OECD–DAC 2001; DFID 2005) as well as a plethora of networks and institutions (including the UN Peacebuilding Commission and the EU Peacebuilding Partnership).

Curiously, however, at the same time, there has been both a broadening and a narrowing of the application of human security in peacebuilding policy. The broadening has taken place in policy documents which, on occasion, read like a wish-list for the 'good society'. The narrowing has taken place in its application, whereby statebuilding, security sector reform (SSR), and rule of law programmes have been prioritised. As pointed out by Vankovska (2007), in the clash between the two versions of human security – broad (freedom from want) and narrow (freedom from fear) – the latter is privileged. This is evident in the recommendation of the UN High Level Panel on Threats, Challenges and Change in 2004 that peacebuilding should focus on statebuilding, which reinforced the Brahimi Report's emphasis on civilian security and rule of law. Given the central role of statebuilding and SSR in peacebuilding practice, these will be explored in this chapter.

There are two key aspects to the discourse surrounding statebuilding and human security. The first is that weak or war-torn states are incapable of governing themselves and cannot (re)build on their own. Their ability to achieve human security, measured as progress towards the Millennium Development Goals (MDGs) (discussed later), is thus dependent on intervention to promote good governance – understood as institution-building to foster neoliberalisation (Paris 2001). This legitimises ambitious and intrusive policies that ultimately deny local sovereignty under the guises of 'capacity-building' and 'shared sovereignty'. While sovereignty has, on occasion, been temporarily annulled through the use of international administrations, governance assistance has been the preferred option of donors supported through coordinated, centralised multi-stakeholder support funds monitored by committees of donors and international NGOs. As a result of these arrangements, donors get control over policymaking, while recipient state elites get external support. Under the rubric of human security and the language of 'partnerships', recipients become 'governance states' with 'contingent sovereignty' that leaves decision-making power with donors (Harrison 2004). These 'partnerships' allow policymakers to engage in 'organised hypocrisy', i.e. they can embrace the principle of sovereignty while in practice contravening it (Krasner 2004: 108). Examples of this include the 2005 Governance and Economic Management Programme in Liberia and the 2005 Poverty Reduction Strategy in Sierra Leone.

The second aspect is that the pursuit of 'good governance' and human security requires local partners, which means finding and supporting local elites that have internalised international policy requirements and are willing to accept aid and guidance. This process has been represented as creating credible 'partners for peace' – and has underpinned donor support for diaspora recruitment to post-conflict governments, as witnessed in Iraq and Afghanistan. It has also legitimised the use of sanctions and violence to overthrow 'bad elites' (elected or otherwise) as witnessed in Palestine. Partnerships with diasporas have been seen as particularly useful as they offer a potential solution to the 'sovereignty gap' by reducing the need for international personnel while, at the same time, helping to 'tick the box' for local engagement and support but from people who are deemed conversant with, and sympathetic to, western interests and sensibilities. While this has been regarded as a way to reduce resentment from local populations, diaspora returnees who have been away from the homeland for many years are often ignorant of the local political economy, often lack a domestic base of support, and can often be more responsive to the needs of donors than their own people. Supporting certain elites as 'partners for peace' also requires isolating and undermining the 'bad' elite – even if that means going against the wishes of the population. Western reaction to Hamas's 2006 election win is a case in point, and offers a stark reminder of the disjuncture between the needs and desires of donors and those of local populations. Sanctions were imposed on an occupied people, military, political and economic support was offered to Hamas's opponents (Fatah), and earlier good governance reforms were undermined by the creation of a Temporary International Mechanism which bypassed the Hamas-led government and channelled aid directly to the people. These processes were a large factor in the subsequent disintegration of the Palestinian Authority into an isolated pariah administration controlled by Hamas in Gaza, and a donor-supported technocratic administration in the West Bank (Turner 2009).

The human security discourse has also played a pivotal role in the development of the concept and practice of SSR, as well as providing justification for greater involvement of the development community in security-related issues. In particular, the UK's Department for International Development (DFID) and the OECD Development Assistance Committee (DAC) have been at the forefront in promoting SSR as central to ending human insecurity (DFID 2002; OECD 2005). This focus fed into and was fed by DFID's strategy in Sierra Leone, where the UK is the largest donor. DFID's Sierra Leone programme had three pillars: SSR, rebuilding the state and delivery of services to citizens (although this last was not supported in the early years). The commitment to statebuilding and SSR was reflected in the funding figures: DFID spent 41 per cent of its budget for Sierra Leone on governance in 2002/3 and 2006/7 compared with 14 per cent for Africa as a whole; and only 6 per cent each for education and health compared with 14 and 21 per cent respectively for Africa as a whole (Poate *et al.* 2008: 10). Given that the lack of educational opportunities for youth has been highlighted as one of the causes of the conflict, this seems short-sighted (Ginifer 2003). Critics also argue that SSR in Sierra Leone helped to create an overdeveloped security force without the concomitant development of civil oversight (Albrecht and Jackson 2009).

This 'democratic deficit' in SSR is also evident in Palestine. Under the realm of capacity-building, the EU sponsored reform of the civil police while a US team led on the development of a Palestinian security force for state security and counterterrorism. Such high levels of external control raises questions about the ownership of national security, but in the Palestinian case this was compounded by Israel's occupation and the 1993 Oslo Accords which, in effect, removed the state security forces from any resistance strategy (Agha and Khalidi 2006). In a 2008 survey of Palestinian civil society views on security, lack of protection against the occupiers and limited oversight mechanisms were identified as key concerns (DCAF and SHAMS 2008). Civil oversight was limited because the Palestinian Legislative Council was paralysed after the 2006 elections due to the detention by Israel of one-third of its members, and the split between the West Bank and Gaza after the Hamas 'coup' in June 2007. This made it difficult to hold the executive and its security forces accountable and has prevented judicial reform. While SSR has as its goal the eradication of 'freedom from fear', creating huge military capacities with limited democratic oversight is a recipe for state repression, human rights abuses and military coups.

The pursuit of human security in the arena of peacebuilding has been portrayed as a radical agenda in its purported support for the creation of legitimate political authority (Kaldor 2007: 187). However, 'capacity-building' and creating 'partners for peace' have simultaneously undermined self-government and democratic accountability, and has legitimised the use of violence in the name of furthering peace and human security. The language of 'peacebuilding from below' – replete in policy documents and proclamations – is, in actual fact, 'peacebuilding from below produced from above'.

Human security and the pariah weapons agenda

If contemporary peacebuilding is best described as a process of 'peacebuilding from below produced from above', then recent human security 'successes' regarding the regulation of pariah weapons might alternatively be described as 'arms control from below within the logic of militarism from above'. This contrasts sharply with the general consensus that views post-Cold War restraints on landmines, cluster munitions and small arms as signal successes of bottom-up civil society action and the human security agenda. This latter notion has become so widespread that it has virtually attained the status of a universal truth – or rather a particularly powerful *regime of truth* that contains common elements. These include the idea that action on pariah weapons represents a profoundly novel post-Cold War shift in the politics of arms control. Thus, the landmines campaign is deemed to have been sustained by an innovative global civil society campaign, aided and abetted by key like-minded states (Mathew and Rutherford 2003). Moreover, it is argued, a key element in the success of such campaigns has been a novel reframing of landmines or cluster munitions as humanitarian problems susceptible to action within the parameters of human security, rather than arms control issues subject to the logics of national security (Williams 2008). In particular, action on both landmines and cluster munitions is represented as a response to a category of weapons that are uniquely odious because of their inability to discriminate between combatants and innocent civilians. This is a narrative of the pariah weapons control agenda as a new, radical, bottom-up endeavour that places the security of the human at the very heart of practice. Yet it is a narrative that is ahistorical in the way it overlooks the long relationship between power, specific models of economy and militarism, and humanitarianism displayed throughout the history of arms trade regulation. In order to illustrate this, it is necessary to make some observations about the history of pariah weapons regulation.

First, there is a *long* history of pariah weapons regulation that includes attempts to impose bans or limits (some more successful than others) on the use of poison, the crossbow, the gun in seventeenth and eighteenth century Japan, dum-dum bullets and the submarine. Such attempts appear with sufficient frequency in history to suggest that the construction of specific types of military technology as particularly odious and therefore deserving of extraordinary measures of control is a normal practice in the history of arms regulation – not a novel phenomenon.

Second, certain themes recur that shed light on the dynamics underpinning the contemporary agenda on landmines, small arms, etc. For example, the framing of restrictions by reference to a humanitarian discourse is quite common. The 1890 Brussels Act (principally an anti-slavery initiative) not only included restrictions on the small arms trade to Africa but was agreed against the backdrop of an intense civil society campaign that included expressions of concern about human welfare: 'the indiscriminate trade in firearms and ammunition has been, and is, a great curse and injury to the native races of Africa' (Fox 1889).

Even US support for restrictions on submarine warfare at the London Naval Conference of 1930 was presented as a response both to public demands for the abolition of the submarine and as a humanitarian initiative, given the level of civilian casualties resulting from submarine attacks on merchant ships in World War I. This was arguably not the prime consideration driving US policy as it was also at a profound disadvantage in the rate of submarine construction compared to the other powers (cited in Manson 1992: 741).

Third, whilst specific examples of pariah regulation may well have been grounded in a humanitarian discourse this tells us little about the broader system of arms trade regulation in which they are located. As Krause and MacDonald have noted, for example, the passage of the Brussels Act occurred in an era that 'saw the fewest restraints and regulations on the arms trade in modern history' (1992: 712). Viewed from a longer historical perspective, shifts towards tighter or looser phases of regulation are more a function of tectonic changes in models of economy that occur in different eras and changes in the security imperatives underpinning regulation rather than specific humanitarian concerns. Thus, the dominance of mercantilism and the emphasis on autarky in the sixteenth century tended to produce a more restrictive approach to the regulation of arms transfers in contrast to the more laissez-faire era of the nineteenth century (Krause 1992).

Whilst the post-Cold War era has not seen a return to the less restrictive approach of the nineteenth century, it has coincided with the dominance of neoliberalism which in turn has underpinned a shift to a more commercial and more permissive attitude to arms transfers in general. The combined effect of this has been to transform the public discourse on *major* weapons transfers into a far more technocratic one focused more around their economic costs and benefits than either the strategic or human security consequences of arms sales. This depoliticisation of major arms transfers (Spear and Cooper 2010) has also been accompanied by the reorientation of arms trade controls away from the governance of East–West relations and towards the management of North–South relations. This provides part of the explanation for contemporary pariah weapons bans, as technologies such as landmines and small arms have become problematised precisely because they are deemed to constitute part of the broader challenge of managing the perceived instabilities of the global South – one element in the broader challenge of creating 'peacebuilding from below produced from above' and in establishing security for (neoliberal) development. One illustration of this is the quite dramatic manner in which small arms have been reframed as post-Cold War instruments of human insecurity rather than as the means to shore up Cold War allies.

Fourth, the construction of specific weapons as beyond the pale (either as a technology per se or when used in particular contexts) has also tended to be a function of two other factors: their socially constructed status as the 'other' of the dominant and legitimised weapons technologies of the day and the interests of powerful actors of the era. For example, the virtual eradication of guns in seventeenth and eighteenth century Japan was facilitated by its construction as the antithesis of the samurai sword and the notions of honour in battle attached to the latter (Perrin 1979). Alternatively, whilst the 1890 Brussels Act was certainly underpinned by a loud humanitarian discourse, the arms trade restrictions enshrined in the Act were animated more by imperial concerns about the impact on colonial order of what had become a massive trade in firearms to Africa (Beachey 1962).

Similar themes also underpin the post-Cold War pariah status of weapons such as landmines, cluster munitions and small arms in those parts of the developing world subjected to the technologies of human security governance (Duffield 2007). For example, the pariah status of such weapons as threats to human security has been made possible, in part at least, because the language of human security has been adopted as a discursive framework within which to legitimise a range of western military interventions from Kosovo to Afghanistan – what Chomsky (1999) has termed 'the new military humanism'. More pertinently, this human-centred language has also been adopted to legitimise the new generation of military technology such as cruise missiles through an emphasis on the way their accuracy permits discrimination between combatants and civilians – between the deserving and the undeserving dead. Conversely, this has also created a discursive space for campaigners to promote the restriction of particular categories of arms that neither fit this representation nor are particularly central to western defence strategies or to the arms industries of the major powers. In other words, campaigners have been able to achieve the macrosecuritisation (Buzan and Waever 2009) of particular kinds of weapons technology such as landmines, but only because this precisely fits in with – and legitimises – the mainstream discourse of security and militarism in the post-Cold War era.

The current global policies on arms transfer control might therefore be summed up as drawing on a discourse of human security to promote the restriction of pariah technologies (and the disciplining of pariah actors) within the context of managing disorder in the global South and within an overall regulatory framework that is *actually* quite permissive. In addition, one consequence of the loud humanitarian discourse around restrictions on landmines and cluster munitions is that it has tended to obscure the rise in global defence expenditure and arms sales after the post-Cold War slump. It has also obscured the fact that the powerful actors in the international system account for the vast majority of global military expenditure and arms sales.

This is not to deny the positive effects of restrictions on landmines or the proliferation of small arms. However, the impact of such programmes is far more ambiguous than proponents of the human security agenda allow. In particular, the overall effect of the contemporary pariah agenda has been to underpin both the western military hegemony necessary for the maintenance of a liberal world order and to legitimise both the instruments and strategies of military intervention designed to extend the 'liberal peace' and promote (neoliberal) development – albeit by war.

Human security and the development agenda

Although human security has been attached to peacebuilding and weapons regulation, the concept initially grew out of an economic development agenda in the United Nations Development Programme. It was thus potentially radical at its very emergence. However, as with the other issues analysed earlier, it lost its way in the process of institutionalising the merger between security and development. Indeed, development was tied to the conditionalities of 'good governance' and neoliberal economic policies. From a perspective that must now include reflections on the 'casino crisis' in capitalism since 2007, human security as a development agenda served two main purposes: alleviating threats to the world's poor and pre-empting post-Cold War threats to the advanced capitalist world in the form, for example, of unrest and war, migration and spread of disease. It would secure protection against instability for societies which claim probity and decorum in their own political, economic and social spheres – albeit themselves sites of gross political and corporate corruption and biopolitical discipline (Hardt and Negri 2000). The packaging of neoliberalism as a 'natural law' of development for achieving human security through growth has constructed a 'virtual telos' – a kind of parody of a Marxist vision of an egalitarian world, reinvented for the marginalised poor. However, strategies to protect the poor from the vulnerabilities of globalisation, as elaborated by Malhotra *et al.* (2003) for example, have been effectively sidelined by the core capitalist states, the IFIs and the World Trade Organisation (WTO). Despite the promise of human security and development via neoliberalism, global inequalities have gathered pace.

The human security development agenda gave rise to the MDGs though the Bush Administration successfully eliminated references to them in the 2005 World Summit Declaration, and they make no appearance in Kaldor's *Human Security* (2007). A series of reports set the framework for pro-poor debates in the mid-2000s.

Perhaps the most prominent arose from a survey of 'progress' towards achieving the MDGs. Released in February 2005, the Millennium Project Report, *Investing in Development*, is striking in its commitment to pro-poor and social protection economics. Its springboard was the measurement of the uneven and halting progress towards the achievement of the MDGs by the target date of 2015. The report acknowledged that market shock therapy would not work for Africa, and recommended a bold revision of international strategy. However, key elements of the 'new' practices were to be 'scaling up success' and 'quick win actions'. These entailed scaling up public investment, capacity building, resource mobilization and development assistance, in order to strengthen governance, human rights, civil society and promote the private sector. A dozen countries should be fast-tracked into 'good governance', and national strategies for development should align with regional initiatives such as the New Partnership for Africa's Development (itself a neoliberal market-oriented enterprise). Developing countries were urged to adopt poverty-reduction strategies, monitored by the World Bank for budgetary prudence, by 2006.

There seems little doubt that such a revisionist programme could have considerable appeal because a massive reduction in the number of deaths from structural violence (though the report never uses that term) could only please supporters of the human security enterprise and supporters of causes from debt relief to the provision of cheap, life-saving drugs for Africa. The report, in effect, captured the debate on the politics of development, for it provided the nucleus of the first half of the UN Secretary-General's subsequent UN reform programme, *In Larger Freedom* (UN 2005). A de-radicalisation process was evident in the High-Level Panel Report, *A More Secure World: Our Shared Responsibility* (2004), which also carried the burden, and sway, of UN sponsorship. As discussed earlier, institutionalisation of the project resulted in the creation of various 'human security' agencies and the UN Peacebuilding Commission. The Commission on Human Security, formed 'to further integrate the human security concept into development', was tasked with mobilising public opinion and operationalising the concept. The debate was now couched as a significant step towards managing capitalism in a way that would apparently benefit the poor and vulnerable populations of the world. It chimed well with grass-roots campaigning to 'Make Poverty History'. Indeed the report called for increases in Overseas Development Aid and more generous debt relief. It required high-income countries to open their markets to developing country exports and raise their export competitiveness through investment.

Nevertheless, embedded in the discourse were assumptions that, taken as a whole, indicate a project of neoliberal economic governance. For example, the High-Level Panel recommended the involvement of economic agencies such as the World Bank at an early stage in peace processes. However, it did not countenance any wholesale change to the policies and programmes of the IFIs or question existing practices. The participation of international economic institutions in peace processes was thus likely to reinforce the neoliberal agenda. The Human Security Commission would work 'to ensure that the widening of choices gained by development would be complemented by the freedom to exercise these choices safely and freely' (UN 2009), but without any indication as to how 'development' of choice could be guaranteed or exercised without, for example, disbanding the WTO.

Marginal policy changes in the realm of social protection have certainly been evident in the IFIs (notably in the World Bank) and aid agencies (notably in DFID) (Ritzen 2005). Nevertheless, the Millennium Project Report was written by (mainly western) economists, led by Jeffrey D. Sachs, a special adviser to Kofi Annan. Sachs had orchestrated structural adjustment, with its devastating consequences for vulnerable sectors of society in Russia and Eastern Europe. Turning his attention to Africa, Sachs claimed that the ratio of capital per person in Africa had declined over generations, trapping people into poverty. The remedy required opening economies up to foreign investment (Sachs 2005: 244; also Collier *et al.* 2004). The application of an anaemic version of human security to development was part of the quest for stability, not just because terrorism was alleged to lurk in underdeveloped places, but also because underdevelopment was an offence to the vision of capitalist development.

Sites of neoliberal evangelism, such as the Davos Forum, could hardly project a vision or structural plan for a material world that would actually re-balance economic power in favour of the poor, since this would damage the competitive logic of capitalism. Revisionists have recognised the chill of failure evident in neoliberal free market economics – as evidenced in the advance of 'responsible capitalism', represented by corporate social responsibility codes. Nevertheless, they do not challenge the fundamentals of an ideology based on the zeal of entrepreneurship, private capital accumulation (including the use of public funds to subsidise it), an otherwise limited role for the state, a self-evident rationality of 'sound economic management' and integration into the world trading system. There is a common prescription: '[w]hatever one's motivation for attacking the crisis of extreme poverty . . . the solutions are the same' (Millennium Project 2005: 1).

The casino crisis has brought about premature manifestations of hubris at the death of the neoliberal agenda (Krugman 2009). However, after a brief bout of 'Keynesian welfare for financial institutions' in the capitalist cores the reinvention of neoliberalism has been evidenced domestically in a myriad of ways, *inter alia* by: fiscal retrenchment in government budgeting, cuts in public sector pay and benefits, and strong (and partly successful) resistance of financial sectors to regulation. After the G-20 summit of 2009, the dominant rhetoric was to close off protectionism but the actual practice was to raise trade barriers in the developed world while using economic 'shocks' as a rationale for conditionality to further promote neoliberalism in the developing world (Molina and Pereira 2008). The IFIs have been the advocates of pro-cyclical policies that increase economic distress (Weisbrot *et al.* 2009). Advanced capitalist countries have continued to exploit the asymmetries and comparative advantages inherent in their power over trade and capital flows. Above all, popular political discourse has shifted from interrogating the *débâcles* of capitalism to how citizens will pay for the crises in the future, thus further pruning any limited gains achieved via the human security agenda.

Conclusion

Human security has lost its way due to its institutionalisation and co-option that has occurred in the service of global capitalism, militarism and neoliberal governance, as illustrated in the spheres of peacebuilding, weapons control and development. The most recent attempt to operationalise human security supports this analysis. In 'Human Security: Theory and Practice', the UNTFHS proposes a 'toolbox' approach for developing, implementing and evaluating the human security concept. Building on the seven security realms originally identified by ul Haq, it adds 'two mutually reinforcing pillars': 'protection' (defined as top-down) and 'empowerment' (defined as bottom-up) as being crucial to the achievement of human security. Both 'pillars' are regarded as being *internal* to states: 'protection' is defined as good governance, the rule of law, social protection and accountability; and 'empowerment' is defined as 'developing the capabilities of individuals and communities to make informed choices and to act on their own behalf'. But there is no discussion of global domination and global inequality or the practices of powerful states and institutions. Insecurities are regarded as emanating from threats beyond anyone's control to prevent (UNTFHS 2009: 6–8). Institutionalisation has emptied out the original radical promise of the human security discourse.

This is not to conclude, however, that the policies and actions that emanate from the adoption of the human security discourse are meaningless – far from it. In peacebuilding, its application has helped to prioritise statebuilding and security sector reform, while sidelining local agency and democratic control; in arms control, the campaign against cluster munitions has crowded out calls for stricter regulation of the conventional arms trade; and in development, aid transparency and the MDGs have become a means to package the restitution of neoliberalism. From a critical perspective, the flawed assumptions of human security in the areas of peacebuilding, arms control and development lie in the silence surrounding structural violence, the misleading packaging of economic convergence and global integration, and the narratives of vulnerability.

The fragilities and limitations of human security indicate that a paradigm shift is necessary. Human security served important purposes, not least in mobilising support for broader concepts of security. But its operationalisation has been subjected to co-option and institutionalisation that emphasises contingent sovereignty, military humanitarianism and neoliberal economic development.

A shift would require welfare practices to have political roots in local societies and political communities that would set their own welfare agendas. Valuable as an ontological enterprise and inherent in the methodology of permanent critique, it would differ from the orthodoxy of human security in several respects. First, it would encompass alternative notions of life that affect the individual, community, the biosphere and planetary environment. Second, it would emphasise the need for dialogue between heterodoxies, incorporating the goal of optimising the life potential of both individuals and diverse forms of community, recognising that the means to reach such a goal would be the object of serial negotiation. Third, it would avoid relativism, since it would include attention to the structures of global capitalism and a reconfiguration of the global economic system to empower communities to have more control over their resources. Fourth, it would invoke the twofold meaning of welfare: well-being and social provision. In policy terms it would reject the current focus on the ameliorative interventions of international agencies and coalitions and the preoccupation with 'exits' arranged around quick fixes.

Such a paradigm shift would need to operate at two levels: continuous and equitable engagement with diverse local cultural and welfare dynamics on the one hand, and restructuring or disempowerment of the existing financial hegemony at a global level. This chapter therefore concludes by proposing the necessity of a new research agenda configured around the development of a 'life welfare' paradigm – one that is value-based, that co-exists with civil society and that de-securitises the human in human security.

Bibliography

Agha, Hussein and Ahmad S. Khalidi (2006), *A Framework for a Palestinian National Security Doctrine*, London: Royal Institute of International Affairs, February.

Albrecht, Peter and Paul Jackson (2009), *Security Transformation in Sierra Leone 1997–2007*, London: GFNSSR and DFID.

Beachey, Raymond W. (1962), 'The Arms Trade in East Africa in the Late Nineteenth Century', *The Journal of African History*, Vol. 3, No. 3, pp. 451–67.

Buzan, Barry and Ole Waever (2009), 'Macrosecuritisation and Security Constellations: Reconsidering Scale in Securitisation Theory', *Review of International Studies*, Vol. 35, No. 2, pp. 253–76.

Chandler, David (2008), 'Human Security: The Dog That Didn't Bark', *Security Dialogue*, Vol. 39, No. 4, pp. 427–38.

Chenoy, Anuradha M. And Shahrbanou Tadjbakhsh (2006), *Human Security: Concepts and Implications*, London: Routledge.

Chomsky, Noam (1999), *The New Military Humanism: Lessons from Kosovo*, London: Pluto Press.

Collier, Paul, V. L. Elliott, Håvard Hegre, Anke Hoeffler, Marta Reynal-Querol and Nicholas Sambanis (2004), *Breaking the Conflict Trap*, Oxford: Oxford University Press.

Commission on Human Security (2003), *Human Security Now: Protecting and Empowering People*, United Nations Publications, August.

DCAF (Geneva Centre for the Democratic Control of Armed Forces) and SHAMS (Center for Human Rights and Democratic Participation) (2008), 'Forum: Delivering Security to the Palestinian People' (Ramllah, Jenin, Tulkarem, Qalqilya, Salfit, Hebron, Nablus, Tubas), Switzerland: DCAF.

DFID (Department for International Development) (2002), *Understanding and Supporting Security Sector Reform*, London: DFID.

—— (2005), *Why We Need to Work More Effectively in Fragile States*, London: DFID, January.

Duffield, Mark (2007), *Development, Security and Unending War: Governing the World of Peoples*, Cambridge: Polity.

Duffield, Mark and Nicholas Waddell (2006), 'Securing Humans in a Dangerous World', *International Politics*, Vol. 43, No. 1, pp. 1–23.

Fox, Francis W. (1889), 'Letter to Lord Salisbury', 17 October 1889, National Archives, Kew.

Ginifer, Jeremy (2003), 'Reintegration of Ex-Combatants', in Mark Malan, Sarah Meek, Thokozani Thusi, Jeremy Ginifer and Patrick Coker, *Sierra Leone: Building the Road to*

Recovery, Institute of Security Studies Monograph 80, Pretoria: Institute of Security Studies.

Hardt, Michael and Antonio Negri (2000), *Empire*, Cambridge, MA: Harvard University Press.

Harrison, Graham (2004), *The World Bank and Africa: the Construction of Governance States*, Oxon: Routledge.

Kaldor, Mary (2007), *Human Security: Reflections on Globalization and Intervention*, Cambridge: Polity.

Krasner, Stephen D. (2004), 'Shared Sovereignty: New Institutions for Collapsing and Failing States', *International Security*, Vol. 29, No. 2, pp. 85–120.

Krause, Keith (1992), *Arms and the State: Patterns of Military Production and Trade*, Cambridge: Cambridge University Press.

Krause, Keith and Mary K. MacDonald (1992), 'Regulating Arms Sales Through World War II', in Richard D. Burns, *Encyclopedia of Arms Control and Disarmament*, New York: Scribner's, pp. 707–24.

Krugman, Paul (2009), 'Beliefs in Collision: How the Bubble was Missed', *International Herald Tribune* (6 September: 1, 17).

MacLean, George A. (2006), 'Human Security in the National Interest? Canada, POGG and the "New" Multilateralism', in Sandra J. MacLean, David R. Black and Timothy R. Shaw (eds) *A Decade of Human Security: Global Governance and Multilateralism*, Aldershot & Burlington, VT: Ashgate, pp. 63–72.

Malhotra, Kamal *et al.* (2003), *Making Global Trade Work for People*, London: Earthscan.

Mathew, Richard A. and Kenneth R. Rutherford (2003), 'The Evolutionary Dynamics of the Movement to Ban Landmines', *Alternatives*, 28, pp. 29–56.

Manson, Janet M. (1992), 'Regulating Submarine Warfare', in Richard D. Burns *Encyclopedia of Arms Control and Disarmament*, New York: Scribner's.

Millennium Project (2005), *Investing in Development: A Practical Plan to Achieve the Millennium Development Goals*, Report to the UN Secretary-General, New York, February.

Molina, Nuria and Javier Pereira (2008), *Critical Conditions: The IMF Maintains Its Grip on Low-Income Governments*, Eurodad. Online. Available URL http://www.eurodad.org/uploadedFiles/Whats_New/Reports/Critical_conditions.pdf (accessed 19 November 2009).

Muggah, Robert and Keith Krause (2006), 'A True Measure of Success? The Discourse and Practice of Human Security in Haiti', in Sandra J. MacLean, David R. Black and Timothy R. Shaw (eds) *A Decade of Human Security: Global Governance and Multilateralism*, Aldershot & Burlington, VT: Ashgate, pp.113–26.

Organisation for Economic Cooperation and Development (OECD–DAC) (2001), *The DAC Guidelines: Helping Prevent Violent Conflict*, Paris: OECD.

—— (2005), *DAC Guidelines and Reference Series: Security System Reform and Governance*, Paris: OECD.

Owen, Taylor (2008), 'The Critique that Doesn't Bite: A Response to David Chandler's "Human Security: The Dog That Didn't Bark"', *Security Dialogue*, Vol. 39, No. 4, pp. 445–53.

Paris, Roland (2001), 'Human Security: Paradigm Shift or Hot Air?' *International Security*, Vol. 26, No. 2, pp. 87–102.

Perrin, Noel (1979), *Giving Up The Gun: Japan's Reversion to the Sword, 1543–1879*, Boston: G. K. Hall.

Poate, Derek, Paul Balgoun and Ines Rothman (2008), 'Evaluation of DFID Country Programmes: Sierra Leone', Evaluation Report EV690, London: DFID, September.

Online. Available URL http://www.dfid.gov.uk/Documents/publications/evaluation/ev690.pdf (accessed 19 November 2009).

Ritzen, Jozef (2005), *A Chance for the World Bank*, London: Anthem.

Sachs, Jeffrey D. (2005), *The End of Poverty: How We Can Make It Happen in Our Lifetime*, London: Penguin.

Spear, Joanna and Neil Cooper (2010), 'The Defence Trade' in Alan Collins (ed.) *Contemporary Security Studies*, (2nd edition), Oxford: Oxford University Press, pp. 394–412.

Turner, Mandy (2009), 'The Power of "Shock and Awe": the Palestinian Authority and the Road to Reform', *International Peacekeeping*, Vol. 16, No. 4, pp. 561–76.

United Nations (1992), *An Agenda for Peace: Preventive Diplomacy, Peacemaking and Peacekeeping*, Report of the Secretary-General, UN doc. A/47/277 – S/24111, 17 June, New York.

—— (2004), *A More Secure World: Our Shared Responsibility*. Report of the Secretary-General's High Level Panel on Threats, Challenges and Change, New York: UN, December.

—— (2005), *In Larger Freedom: Towards Development, Security and Human Rights for All*, Report of the Secretary-General, UN doc. A/59/2005, 21 March, New York.

—— (2009), UN Centre for Regional Development. Online. Available URL http://www.uncrd.or.jp/hs/whatishs.htm (accessed 20 October 2009).

United Nations Trust Fund for Human Security (2009) *Human Security in Theory and Practice: Application of the Human Security Concept and the United Nations Trust Fund for Human Security*, Human Security Unit, Office for the Coordination of Humanitarian Assistance, New York.

Vankovska, Biljana (2007), 'The Human Security Doctrine for Europe: A View from Below', *International Peacekeeping*, Vol. 14, No. 2, pp. 264–81.

Weisbrot, Mark, Rebecca Ray, Jake Johnston, Jose Antonio Cordero and Juan Antonio Montecino (2009), 'IMF-Supported Macroeconomic Policies and the World Recession: A Look at Forty-One Borrowing Countries', Center for Economic Policy Research, Washington DC. Online. Available URL http://www.cepr.net/documents/publications/imf-2009-10.pdf (accessed 5 October, 2009).

Williams, Jody (2008), 'New Approaches in a Changing World: The Human Security Agenda', in Jody Williams, Stephen D. Goose and Mary Wareham, *Banning Landmines: Disarmament, Citizen Diplomacy and Human Security*, Plymouth: Rowman and Littlefield.

World Bank (1998), *Post-Conflict Reconstruction: The Role of the World Bank*, Washington, DC: The World Bank.

Part II

8 The limits to emancipation in the human security framework

Tara McCormack

Introduction

The concept of human security is argued to be one of the most important and serious challenges to the way in which international security has been both theorised and practised for much of the twentieth century.[1] In place of the state-centric security framework, which has both endangered people and ignored the real threats to individuals, the human security framework is argued to have the potential to be an emancipatory and empowering security framework for individuals. In this article I critically engage with these central claims within the human security framework and I will argue that human security cannot live up to its promises.

Most critiques engaging with human security tend to focus on the way in which it may be made workable or criticise it for not being sufficiently distanced from the pluralist security framework. A smaller number of more radical critics have argued that human security represents a new form of control and management of the developing world by the west (for example, Duffield and Waddell 2004, Dillon 2006). My critique aims neither to contribute towards a 'better' version of human security nor to show that human security is part of a new strategy of liberal governmentality. Although I will argue that human security *is* ultimately a conservative security framework this is not, I will argue, because it is a new technique of liberal governance but because it serves to entrench *existing* international power inequalities through pathologising the weak or underdeveloped state and rendering intervention by powerful states and international institutions less clear and accountable. Therefore, in conclusion I argue that the human security framework does not ultimately offer a challenge to contemporary power inequalities or give power to the powerless.

Human security as a challenge to contemporary power inequalities

For advocates of human security, the state-centric pluralist security framework with its formal commitment to non-intervention, sovereign immunity and state equality (Simpson 2004: 231) is argued to be anachronistic in the face of myriad new security challenges (see for example, *An Agenda for Peace* for an early exposition, UN

[1992]1995: 41–42; Debiel and Werthes 2006: 8; Jolly and Ray 2006: 3–4). However, the human security framework promises more than merely an updated security framework. For supporters of human security, the pluralist prioritisation of state security is immoral. The pluralist security framework has a conservative or 'problem-solving' function (Grayson 2004) that prioritises order over justice and human emancipation. The traditional security framework simply ignores the fact that for the vast majority of humanity the real threats are not from military invasion by neighbouring states but, in the words of the 1994 UN Human Development Report (UNHDR), 'from hunger, crime, disease, political repression and environmental hazards' (UN 1994: 22). Advocates of the human security framework furthermore argue that under the cover of sovereign immunity, governments have been able to commit crimes against their own people with impunity. The pluralist security framework simply ignores the fact that, '... states are more often part of the problem than the source of the solution' (Bellamy and McDonald 2002: 373).

Human security is argued to be a paradigm shift in thinking and 'doing' security, from the state-centric to one which takes the individual to be the point of reference,

> human security is perhaps best understood as a shift in perspective or orientation. It is an alternative way of seeing the world, taking people as its point of reference, rather than focusing exclusively on the security of territory or governments.
>
> (Axworthy 1999)

Ethical concerns about the freedom and emancipation of the individual are at the heart of the human security framework. Human security rejects the narrow confines of the pluralist security framework of national or territorial security focused on the state, towards a commitment to human life globally, '(human security) ... puts the individual at the centre of debate, analysis and policy' (Thakur 2004: 347–48; see also Tadjbakhsh and Chenoy 2007: 13). Because of this explicitly normative dimension focused on the individual, the human security framework (in contrast to the pluralist security framework) purports to offer an emancipatory and radical challenge to the status quo and existing power relations (Grayson 2004: 357), a framework which questions the contemporary power structures and economic, social and political frameworks which lead to human insecurity (Newman 2001: 247). Human security is argued to have the potential to give voice and power to the most vulnerable and powerless, particularly women or other 'voiceless' communities (Suhrke 1999: 271–72; MacFarlane 2004: 368).

The framework has been developed and debated in university institutes[2] and by academics and policy practitioners (for example, Glasius and Kaldor 2005; Jolly and Ray 2006; Maclean *et al.* 2007), in inter-state policy networks[3] and developed in major UN reports (for the first full exposition of the human security framework see UN 1994, also 2000b, 2004, 2005) and other reports sponsored by states (CHS 2003; ICISS 2001). Many of the main themes of human security have been central to other security reports (EU 2003; DFID 2005). Human security is not a monolithic concept however, there is some disagreement between both theorists and states that have adopted the framework as part of their foreign policy, about what 'human security' might actually mean and how best to make the concept workable in terms of policy. Japan, for example, has adopted what is often termed the 'broad' definition of human security. This is exemplified in the 2003 report of the Commission on Human Security (CHS) which advocates a definition of human security that encompasses 'freedom from want' and 'freedom from fear', that individuals should be both protected from harm and empowered to live the life that they wish to lead (CHS 2003: 2–4). Canada, on the other hand, has formally adopted a 'narrow' definition of human security in which the focus is on the 'freedom from fear' aspect.[4] This means that ostensibly the focus in Canadian policy is aimed at a more limited 'protection' agenda rather than on empowerment.

Much critical engagement with human security has tended to focus on the lack of conceptual and analytical clarity of the concept, suggesting that the concept adds little in value to understanding human insecurity and leads to difficulty for policy making (see for example the critiques offered by Paris 2001 or Buzan 2004). Acknowledging these problems, theorists and academics have attempted to reach measurable definitions (for example, King and Murray 2002). Sympathetic critics have suggested that the 'freedom from fear' or narrow agenda is the best agenda in terms of coherent policy making (Krause 2004: 367; Thomas and Tow 2002) or have suggested ways in which these apparent problems can be overcome, for example see Taylor Owen's suggestion for a definition that focuses on the level of threats rather than one which focuses on the origin of the threat (Owen 2004).

Other sympathetic critics have argued that rather than a lack of policy potential, the broadness of the concept offers both a holistic approach to the numerous post-Cold War security problems and essential flexibility, because the sources of insecurity vary hugely between and within countries (Jolly and Ray 2006: 14–13; Tadjbakhsh and Chenoy 2007: 10). Grayson, for example, stresses that it is precisely this refusal to play the 'problem-solving' game of definition that gives human security its radical critical potential by enabling it to engage with the broader social and economic structures that give rise to human insecurity (Grayson 2004).

However, whichever definition of human security one adopts within both 'narrow' and 'broad' conceptions there is a belief that the human security framework offers a serious and emancipatory challenge to the traditional security framework. Perhaps not many policy makers or theorists would go as far as Tadjbakhsh and Chenoy, who suggest that individual empowerment is both the means and end of human security (2007: 238) but fundamentally the shift to the individual, whether from a broad or narrow perspective, is argued to represent a transformation in security and a paradigmatic shift towards protecting and empowering the individual, protecting human life and promoting social progress (UN 2005: 9).

For examples of what this means in terms of policies and financial support, the recent report of the UN's Office for the Coordination of Humanitarian Affairs Human Security Unit focuses on nine examples of initiatives in various countries which purportedly protect and empower people (the Human Security Unit takes its definition of human security from the CHS 2003). These include, for example, initiatives focusing on the sexual health of women and girls in three Central American countries, a regional programme in Africa which is giving small engines to local communities (to be run by the local women's groups), a project to raise awareness about 'human trafficking' in Cambodia and Vietnam, giving 'voice to the voiceless' in Africa and Afghanistan through establishing a radio network that broadcasts interviews with impoverished and marginalised members of society such as street vendors (UN 2006).

From a 'narrow' human security perspective, in one of the major post-Cold War security reports (which has been sponsored by the Canadian government), *The Responsibility to Protect*, it is argued that human security must take into account development, social and economic sources of insecurity and is explicitly aimed at modifying the pluralist security framework (ICISS 2001: 14–15). The Canadian government also gives some of the following examples of the means by which a people-centred approach to security may be achieved; the Kimberly process; the Ottawa Convention on the prohibition of the use of land mines; the Kosovo war: the establishment of the International Criminal Court: intervention and peacebuilding in Haiti, and Sierra Leone; and international agreement on terrorism (McRae 2001). Canada's Department of Foreign Affairs and International Trade (DFAIT) Human Security Program funds projects and programmes to do with democratisation, governance and accountability, gender inequality, corporate responsibility, justice and security sector reform.[5] Clearly, even the 'narrow' focus entails an expansive agenda which goes far beyond conflict prevention. All in all, even the narrow perspective offers a 'vast and ambitious' potential agenda (Black 2007: 56).

The radial challenge of human security or entrenching power inequalities?

Inverting existing power relations: Pathologising the non-western state and the merging of security and development

Within the human security framework, there is an explicit merging of security and development (UN 2004, viii; for a critique of the merging of security and development within human security see Duffield, 2001; Duffield and Waddell, 2006) and an erosion of the division between domestic and international security. The 1994 UN Human Development Report (UNHDR), *New Dimensions of Human Security*, highlighted most of the major themes in the merging of development and security which have been developed in major reports from the UN and other international institutions over the past two decades: the links between poverty, underdevelopment, violence and security, and the global interconnectedness of security (UN 1994: 1–3; UN [1992]1995: 41–42; UN 2000a; UN 2005; Carnegie Commission 1997: xviii; ICISS 2001: 4–5). In the words of the ICISS:

> Human security is indeed indivisible. There is no longer such a thing as a humanitarian catastrophe occurring 'in a faraway country of which we know

little' ... In an interdependent world, in which security depends on a framework of stable sovereign entities, the existence of fragile states, failing states, states who through weakness or ill-will harbour those dangerous to others, or states that can only maintain internal order by means of gross human rights violations, can constitute a risk to people everywhere.

(ICISS 2001: 5)

The merging of development and security represents a shift from the formal separation between these two areas that pertained in the pluralist security framework. Underdevelopment within a state was not regarded as a threat to international peace and security. Neither was poverty and associated social, economic and political problems held to affect the rights of a state to international legal equality, non-intervention and the other formal norms associated with the pluralist international system (Simpson 2004: 231; Duffield and Waddell 2004: 18).[6] For examples of international statements on the subject during the Cold War, see the 1965 Declaration on the Inadmissibility of Intervention in the Domestic Affairs of States and Protection of their Independence and Sovereignty (Resolution 2131) and the 1970 Declaration on the Principles of International Law concerning Friendly Relations and Cooperation Between States (Resolution 2625). Within the human security framework however, this indifference to the internal content of a state is one of the major limitations of the pluralist security framework.

Few would wish to dispute the argument that for individuals living in situations of dire poverty and underdevelopment, there is little chance of leading any kind of fulfilled life, even if formal political freedoms exist (UN 2005: 5). However, the merging of development and security has implications that contradict the stated empowering and emancipatory goals of human security. Rather than offering a radical challenge to the contemporary international order and the power inequalities that exist, the merging of development and security enforces them. The biggest threats to global insecurity and instability are located in the very weakest and least developed states whilst the purported interconnectedness of security threats in the post-Cold War world means that this instability and underdevelopment directly affects all states.

In major reports that have been written after the attacks on the World Trade Centre in 2001 (hereafter 9/11), it has been argued that 9/11 'proves' both the way in which poverty and underdevelopment lead to violent extremism against the west[7] and the way in which there is no longer a division between the domestic and international (UN 2004: 12–14). The 2004 *Report of the High Level Panel on Threats, Challenges and Change* uses almost gothic imagery in its portrayal of the threat from underdeveloped states:

International terrorist groups prey on weak States for sanctuary. Their recruitment is aided by grievances nurtured by poverty, foreign occupation and the absence of human rights and democracy; by religious and other intolerance; and by civil violence – a witch's brew common to those areas where civil war and regional conflict intersect. (paragraph 21) . . . Poverty, infectious disease, environmental degradation and war feed one another in a deadly cycle.

(UN 2004: 14–15)

In this framework, not only are the least developed states held to be the most unstable, but social, economic and political instability in the least developed and weakest states is seen to be a serious threat to world stability. The effect of this framework is to pathologise the non-western or developing state. The human security framework presents a strange inversion of the existing power relationships in international relations, whereby the world's most powerful states and military alliances are threatened by the very weakest. Here, the weakest states, whose populations are in daily peril from want of the most basic necessities of life, whose only thoughts must be how to stay alive, and whose states have little control over their own development, are turned into existential threats for the most powerful and developed states. These themes are also central to other major security reports, for example, EU 2003 and DFID 2005.

Some analysts have argued that the 'War on Terror' has twisted the human security agenda, leading to a focus on terrorism and 'hard security' issues (for example, Jolly and Ray 2006: 15; also see the opinions expressed by NGOs in Duffield and Waddell 2006: 10–13). Yet this argument simply ignores that the purported links between poverty and terrorism and the global threats emerging from the poorest and weakest nations have always been an integral part of the human security agenda. One could simply reverse the argument and suggest that perhaps part of the reason for the ease with which the 'War on Terror' has been incorporated into international institutions and the security doctrines of major states is because the 'War on Terror' fits easily into the framework that has already been established by human security. America's 2002 National Security Strategy (NSS) for example, continues many of the themes of the human security framework. The NSS pinpoints major threats in the very weakest states, 'America is now threatened less by conquering states than we are by failing ones' (USA 2002: 1). Reiterating the themes of previous UN reports, it warns of the dangers from terrorists and weapons of mass destruction. Even the declaration of the right to act pre-emptively against such threats was hardly out of keeping with the necessity for pre-emptive intervention articulated in previous reports which focused on human security (for example ICISS 2001: 27). The NSS goes on to promise assistance in rebuilding Afghanistan so that it does not again provide a haven for terrorists and stresses the need to engage in development and overcome poverty (USA 2002).

Moreover, the argument that the 'War on Terror' has had a malign influence on the human security framework ignores the fact that human security has always been an initiative emerging from the major international institutions and powerful western states. There is no 'golden age' of human security policy in which the 'voiceless' and most vulnerable set international and national security policy priorities. Even before the 'War on Terror' the human security agenda was set according to western priorities (albeit in the name of the poor and disempowered. See for examples Schittecatte 2007 and O'Manique's critical engagement with the securitisation of AIDS (O'Manique 2007).

If, as claimed, the human security framework offers a critical perspective on the very sources of global inequality and poverty and underdevelopment (Grayson 2004; Newman 2001: 247) then it does not seem logical that the focus is entirely upon the weakest and least powerful of states. Edward Newman points out the one of the problems with the idea of the 'empowered' individual is that much human insecurity results from structural factors and the distribution of power that is beyond the control of individuals (2004: 358). This critique can equally well be applied to the focus on the weakest and least developed states, states that will in the contemporary international context have the least control over their own internal development and security and are most at the mercy of, for example, fluctuating terms of trade. Here, international inequality, unfair trading regimes and the lack of autonomy allowed to the poorer states under World Bank and IMF programmes such as 'Poverty Reduction Strategies' (see Pender 2007 for a critical discussion of these strategies) are all excluded from the human security framework.

Thus broader international factors, such as international power inequalities and the contemporary international economic system, are excluded from any analysis of why a state remains underdeveloped and the focus is squarely upon internal factors within these poor and underdeveloped states. Yet the internal focus of human security also excludes the context that gives rise to societal instability. Rather than understanding social, economic and political problems and the resulting insecurity of daily life as a *consequence* of poverty and underdevelopment, poverty and underdevelopment are understood to be *caused* by these social, economic and political problems and the resulting lack of security. Thus human security programmes do not understand development in terms of, for example, expanding the industrial resources of the state, but focus on how to overcome underdevelopment through 'empowering' women, see DFAIT's Human Security Program and UN 2006 for examples of the way in which these assumptions direct funding (see Pupavac 2005 for a critique of the human security approach to development).

Some advocates of human security seem not dissimilar to the Victorian landowners and industrialists who blamed the poverty of the working classes upon the fecklessness and idleness of the workers rather than the systemic exploitation of the economic order. Unsurprisingly, today's powerful states and international institutions close their eyes to international inequality and terms of trade (for example) and argue that the lack of development within a country is due to instability or lack of women's rights. Yet ironically it is surely the case that the weaker a state is, the more it must be hostage to international trading regimes and regulations and control from multinational bodies and ultimately far less in control of its own development. Rather than challenging contemporary international power inequalities, the human security framework seems simply to ignore them as irrelevant. A stance which can hardly been seen to pose a challenge to those international power inequalities.

From state sovereignty to no sovereignty?

As part of the radical challenge of human security, the framework promises a shift from a state-centric security framework to one which places the individual at the centre, as the Commission on Global Governance argues (CGG), 'Too often in the past, however, preserving the security of the state has been used as an excuse for policies that undermined the security of people' (CGG 1995: 81). Whilst no one could dispute the argument that states have often been the source of great insecurity and danger (to say the very least) to their own citizens, the claims of human security must be investigated on their own terms. To what extent does this shift in state sovereignty in favour of the individual live up to its claims? In this following section I will argue that the shift away from state sovereignty has implications that contradict the claims to empower people and to give the citizens of weak or impoverished states 'real' sovereignty. Rather than empowerment, if that is understood as giving political power and control to the citizens and establishing clear lines of accountability and responsibility, the transformed sovereignty of the human security framework has the potential to disempower citizens in weak states as it allows for the rehabilitation of intervention and regulation by either the international community or powerful states.

The human security framework is posed as a challenge to state security. However, it is not the state in its entirety that is problematic, but state sovereignty, as it was understood as part of the old security framework that is the problem. It is the pluralist norms of formal sovereign equality and non-intervention that are understood to be barriers to human security and it is these aspects of state sovereignty that are to be challenged. In the human security framework therefore state sovereignty is not abandoned, 'sovereignty does still matter' (ICISS 2001: 7), but modified. Within the human security framework state sovereignty is redefined in a way which places human security at its centre (ICISS 2001: 15). It is argued that real content is given to state sovereignty through prioritising human security. This modification of sovereignty transforms sovereignty into what it really should be, showing that the 'irreducible locus of sovereignty is in the individual human being' (MacFarlane 2004: 368). The security of states is no longer an end in itself, 'States are now widely understood to be instruments at the service of their people, and not vice versa' (Annan 1999: 81).

The state therefore still has a role to play in the protection of human security, as the 2004 UN High Level Panel on Threats, Challenges and Change argued, 'the front-line actors in dealing with all the threats we face, new and old, continue to be individual sovereign States' (UN 2004: 1). However, through the modification of state sovereignty, sovereignty becomes less of an inherent political right or juridical fact of a state but becomes instead something which depends upon to what extent the state upholds its responsibilities' to its citizens and its role in the international realm (UN [1992]1995: 44). This argument in which the formal norms of the pluralist framework of sovereign equality and non-intervention are modified is developed in most major UN reports and reports from other organisations and is also found in academic writing from both the 'narrow' perspective (for example, Thomas and Tow 2002: 189–90) and perspectives that critique the narrower perspective in favour of a broader approach (for example, Bellamy and McDonald 2002: 376). This aspect of the human security framework has been comprehensively explored in the ICISS, in which the Commission has argued sovereignty must be re-characterised in terms of 'sovereignty as responsibility' (ICISS 2001: 13; UN 2004: 17). Sovereignty is no longer something that is an assumed property of a state, rather it is something that must derive from the states' treatment of its own citizens. States are responsible and accountable to their citizens, when the state fails in terms of this responsibility towards its citizens the international community may hold that state to account (ICISS 2001: 8, 13–14).

The re-characterisation of sovereignty and the overturning of the pluralist formal norms of non-intervention and sovereignty equality entails rehabilitating a wide range of potential interventionary strategies. For example, pre-emptive intervention to prevent conflict is recommended. The ICISS argues that the international community needs to move from a, '. . . "culture of reaction" to that of a "culture of prevention"' (ICISS 2001: 27). There is also much greater scope for post-conflict intervention. Whilst the pluralist security framework aimed at reaching a settlement between parties to a conflict, the human security framework aims at transforming the societies from within through extensive intervention in its internal structures (UN[1992]1995: 62; see DFAIT's aforementioned human security program). *The Brahimi Report* (UN 2000a) argues for an extensive strategy of post-conflict intervention in order to ensure human security, which entails:

> [r]eintegrating former combatants into civilian society, strengthening the rule of law (for example, through training and restructuring of local police, and judicial and penal reform); improving respect for human rights through the monitoring, education and investigation of past and existing abuses; providing technical assistance for democratic development (including electoral assistance and support for free media; and promoting conflict resolution and reconciliation techniques).
>
> (UN 2000a: 3)

The re-characterisation of sovereignty challenges the formal pluralist norms of sovereignty equality and non-intervention, and potentially allows for a wide range of intervention and/or regulation of states that are failing to live up to their responsibilities. In this context, the question of which states or institutions are to have the role of upholding the states responsibilities and intervening to ensure that the state does live up to its responsibilities is posed. The ICISS argues that, whilst ideally this would be the job of the Security Council, in the absence of the political will to take action, other bodies, such as regional organisations or coalitions of willing states or even individual states should step in (ICISS 2001: 53–55). Human security, '. . . brings together states, international organisations, . . . NGOs, and individuals in radically new combinations' (McRae 2001: 20).

This, of course, for the supporters of human security is precisely the point. Many states, it is argued, are not fit to rule themselves. However, the re-characterisation of sovereignty contradicts the claims of human security to be an emancipatory and empowering framework that gives sovereignty to people and challenges existing power frameworks. As has been shown, human security does not challenge the sovereign state framework in its entirety, rather the human security framework holds certain states to account, particularly the poor and underdeveloped state which are seen to be failing in their 'responsibility to protect'. Human security therefore introduces a division between those states, which can provide human security for their citizens, and those, which cannot (Duffield and Waddell 2004: 18). This implies a shift towards a more hierarchical order in which international institutions or major states have greater freedom to act on behalf of the citizens of other states. Formal inhibitions on intervention are weakened and major states or institutions have potentially more freedom to intervene, regulate and decide if a state is being a 'good international citizen'.

This distinction and division between states is problematic in terms of the purportedly emancipatory and empowering goals of human security for several reasons. In the first place, we must ask who is it that is empowered with agency in the re-characterisation of sovereignty, and it is difficult to see how this is the citizen of the weak or impoverished state. As we have seen, weak and developing states have the potential to be subjected to greater international scrutiny, regulation and possibly intervention but any number of international agencies, or states, or coalitions of the willing. Whilst the relationship between a state and its citizen is de-privileged, a weak or unstable state may become more subject to international scrutiny and international institutions and other states have potentially greater freedom to intervene (in a number of ways) in the name of the states own citizens, yet those citizens will have little control or influence over the supposed agents of their own emancipation and empowerment. The institutions or states are not accountable to, or representative of, those on whose behalf they are intervening. In fact, however bad a state is, there is at least a possibility that the citizens of that state can gain power or change the political system, this is an impossibility in terms of international institutions or powerful states. Clearly, the citizens of Afghanistan, for example, have no possibility of gaining political control of the US or Britain or deciding on NATO policy

The relationship between the intervening states or institutions or NGOs and those on whose behalf action is being taken, is not therefore a political relationship in which (at least formally) there is a relationship of representation and control. Here there is a divorce between the exercise of power and control or accountability of that power. Any agency that intervenes to empower and emancipate the individual must be one that is external to the individual, with no reciprocal relationship of obligation and control. Rather than empowering individuals, the shift away from the pluralist security framework endows external institutions with agency, for example NGOs, other states and international organisations. Here, a political relationship (or potential political relationship, however problematic) between the state and its citizen is replaced with a direct relationship with an unaccountable international institution or foreign state.

In an international realm marked by vast power inequalities, the problematisation of the poor or underdeveloped state and the re-characterisation of sovereignty as responsibility does not challenge the international status quo and international power inequalities. It can be safely argued that in the contemporary context only certain states and international institutions will be making any decisions about who is a good international citizen. In the foreseeable future Moldova or Botswana will not be measuring human insecurity in, say, deprived areas of the US, Britain, Japan or Canada and deciding upon action. Rather, this shift can be seen to actually reinforce international power inequalities, whereby the weakest and poorest states lose even the formal protection of the pluralist norms of sovereign equality and non-intervention. International institutions and powerful states are potentially allowed a far freer role in terms of intervention and regulation of weaker states, whilst the ad hoc nature of the potential intervening parties (whether single states, coalitions of the willing or international or regional institutions and organisations) can only lessen the potential for control by the citizens of weak and impoverished states.

From political interference to moral imperative: depoliticising western intervention and regulation

The final point to be made in conclusion to this section is that the human security framework has the effect of depoliticising and idealising western intervention and regulation. Intervention is no longer understood politically, or challenged on such grounds, but is understood in terms of a moral and ethical framework in which powerful states and international institutions have a moral obligation to intervene on behalf of citizens of other states. For example, the ICISS argues that there is a responsibility for states and international institutions to react to problems within states (ICISS 2001). International intervention is no longer a matter for political contestation, but is seen as a moral duty of the powerful to help the weak (for example, Blair 1999).

Indeed, depoliticising the way in which intervention is understood is explicitly part of the rationale of the ICISS (2001: 16–17). Intervention therefore becomes more difficult to contest and understand. However, whatever position one might take politically regarding intervention, whether military or otherwise, this framing simply evades the substantive issues at stake in any intervention. It is of little surprise that the organisation of developing states, the G77, has expressed its reservations about the concept and potential policy based upon human security (Tadjbakhsh and Chenoy 2007: 35–37). Moreover, because of the way in which the human security framework focuses on internal factors within an underdeveloped state and excludes broader questions of the existing international economy, unequal power relations and the weak position that poor and underdeveloped states occupy in terms of their ability to control or influence their own economic development, intervention and regulation are idealised. The material consequences of intervention, however benign the intent, are excluded from analysis and debate, and problems emerging from any interventionary policies are simply understood as a consequence of existing social or economic problems. Because of this, powerful states or international institutions become less accountable for their actions. Rather than challenging existing power inequalities and empowering the citizens of weak and impoverished states, this shift can only serve to further disempower.

Conclusion

The aim of this article is not to call for a return to some 'golden age' of state security. One should be under no illusions about the pluralist security framework which was a highly ideological framework in which formal equality masked substantive inequality with often brutal consequences. However, the inequities of the pluralist security framework do not mean that we ought not to take a critical approach to human security and interrogate some of its central claims. The aim of this article has been to draw out some of the inherent problems with the human security framework in its own terms.

The central claims of the human security framework are that it represents an emancipatory and empowering security framework for individuals in poor and developing countries, a progressive step away from the narrow conceptions of military and territorial security that have traditionally dominated international relations. I have argued that the human security framework cannot live up to its promises to empower the citizens of poor and developing countries. In the contemporary international context (which is marked by great power inequalities between states), the rejection of the pluralist security framework by major international institutions and the adoption of ostensibly emancipatory and empowering policies and policy rhetoric has the consequence of problematising weak or unstable states and allowing international institutions or powerful states a far more interventionary role.

Through pathologising the weak or underdeveloped state and re-casting sovereignty in terms of 'responsibility', the formal links between the state and its citizens are problematised and international institutions and states have potentially greater freedom to intervene in or regulate weak or failing states. However, there are no mechanisms by which the citizens of states being intervened in might have any control over the purported agents or agencies of their emancipation. The human security framework does not ultimately offer a challenge to contemporary power inequalities or give power to the powerless. Rather, the human security framework serves to entrench international power inequalities and allows for a shift towards a hierarchical international order in which the citizens in weak or unstable states may arguably have even less freedom or power than under the old pluralist security framework.

Notes

1 This is a shortened reprint of 'Power and Agency in the Human Security Framework' published in the *Cambridge Review of International Affairs*, 21 (1) (2008).
2 For example, the Human Security Institute at the Simon Fraser University, Vancouver, Canada.
3 See the Human Security Network established by Canada and Norway, now with 13 members, http://www.humansecuritynetwork.org
4 See the website of the Department of Foreign Affairs and International Trade, http://geo.international.gc.ca/cip-pic/library/humansecurity-en.aspx
5 See the DFAIT website for more details, address as aforementioned.
6 In this specific historical context of the division of the world into ideological blocs, and the

need to ensure that the newly independent nations were not tempted into the Soviet bloc, the West adopted policies that stressed the promotion of independent development (understood as material development and to be achieved through state-led industrialisation) for the newly independent states. For the West then, its security was to be achieved through the independent development, and ultimately modernisation, of the newly independent states, see Pupavac 2005.
7 This remains entirely unsubstantiated. It is of note that one of the few empirical investigations into the background of recent terrorists groups has found the opposite. Marc Sageman (2004) has shown in his study of 400 Al-Qaeda terrorists that three- quarters come from the upper or middle-classes and had gone to study abroad.

Bibliography

Annan, K. (1999) 'Two Concepts of Sovereignty', *The Economist*, (September 18–24): 81–82.

Axworthy, L. (1999) *Human Security: Safety for People in a Changing World*, Canada: Department of Foreign Affairs and International Trade.

Bellamy, A. J. and McDonald, M. (2002) '"The Utility of Human Security": Which Humans? What Security? A Reply to Thomas & Tow', *Security Dialogue*, 33 (3): 373–77.

Black, D. R. (2007) 'Mapping the Interplay of Human Security Practice and Debates: The Canadian Experience', in MacLean, Sandra J., Black, David R. and Shaw, Timothy M., *A Decade of Human Security, Global Governance and New Multilateralisms*, Hampshire, UK: Ashgate, 55–62.

Blair, T. (1999) '*Chicago Speech*', Doctrine of the International Community, Speech Given to the Economic Club of Chicago, Thursday 22 April 1999, Available URL: http://www.globalpolicy.org/globaliz/politics/blair.htm

Buzan, B. (2004) *Security Dialogue*, 35 (3): 369–70.

Carnegie Commission (1997) *Preventing Deadly Conflict, Final Report of the Carnegie Commission on Preventing Deadly Conflict*, New York: Carnegie Corporation of New York.

CGG (1995) *Our Global Neighbourhood*, the Report of the Commission on Global Governance, Oxford: Oxford University Press.

CHS (2003) *Human Security Now*, the Report of the Commission on Human Security, New York: Commission on Human Security.

Debiel, T. and Werthes, S. (eds) (2006) *Human Security on Foreign Policy Agendas, Changes, Concepts and Cases*, Germany: Institute for Development and Peace, INEF at the University of Duisburg-Essen.

DFID (2005) *Fighting Poverty to Build a Safer World, a Strategy for Security and Development*, London: DFID.

Dillon, M. (2006) *The Biopolitics of Human Security*, Paper presented at the annual meeting of the International Studies Association, Town & Country Resort and Convention Center, San Diego, California, US.

Duffield, M. (2001) *Global Governance and the New Wars, the Merging of Development and Security*, London: Zed Books.

Duffield, M. and Waddell, N. (2004) *Human Security and Global Danger, Exploring a Governmental Assemblage*, University of Lancaster: Department of Politics and International Relations.

—— (2006) 'Security Humans in a Dangerous World', *International Politics*, 43 (1): 23.

EU (2003) *A Secure Europe in a Better World. European Security Strategy*, Brussels. Online. Available URL: http://www.consilium.europa.eu/uedocs/cmsUpload/78367.pdf

Glasius, Marlies and Kaldor, M. (eds) (2005) *A Human Security Doctrine for Europe*, London: Routledge.

Grayson, K. (2004) 'A Challenge to the Power over Knowledge of Traditional Security Studies', *Security Dialogue*, 35 (3): 357.

HSC (2005) *Human Security Report 2005, War and Peace in the 21st Century*, New York: Oxford University Press, published for the Human Security Centre, University of British Colombia.

ICISS (2001) *The Responsibility to Protect*, the Report of The International Commission on Intervention and State Sovereignty, Ottawa, Canada: International Development Research Centre.

Jolly, R. and Ray, D. (2006) *National Human Development Reports and the Human Security Framework: A Review of Analysis and Experience*, Institute of Development Studies, Sussex: The Human Development Report Office [UNDP], New York, NY, US.

King, G. and Murray, C. J. L. (2002) 'Rethinking Human Security', *Political Science Quarterly* 116 (4): 585–610.

Krause, K. (2004) 'The Key to a Powerful Agenda if Properly Delimited', *Security Dialogue*, 35(3): 367–68.

MacFarlane, S. N. (2004) 'A Useful Concept That Risks Losing its Political Salience', *Security Dialogue*, 35 (3): 368–69.

MacLean, S. J., Black, D. R. and Shaw, T. M. (2007) *A Decade of Human Security, Global Governance and New Multilateralisms*, Hampshire, UK: Ashgate.

McCormack, T. (2008) 'Power and Agency in the Human Security Framework', *Cambridge Review of International Affairs* 21(1): 113–28.

McRae, R. (2001) 'Human Security in a Globalised World', in Rob McRae and Don Hubert, *Human Security and the New Diplomacy*, Canada: McGill-Queen's University Press, 45–58.

Newman, E. (2001) 'Human Security and Constructivism', *International Studies Perspectives*, 2 (3): 239–51.

—— (2004) 'A Normatively Attractive but Analytically Weak Concept', *Security Dialogue*, 35(3): 358–59.

O'Manique, C. (2007) 'The "Securitisation" of HIV/AIDS in Sub-Saharan Africa: A Critical Feminist Lens', in MacLean, Sandra J., Black, David R. and Shaw, Timothy M., *A Decade of Human Security, Global Governance and New Multilateralisms*, Hampshire, UK: Ashgate, 161–76.

Owen, T. (2004) 'Human Security – Conflict, Critique and Consensus: Colloquium Remarks and a Proposal for a Threshold-Based Definition', *Security Dialogue*, 35 (3): 373–87.

Paris, R. (2001) 'Human Security, Paradigm Shift or Hot Air', *International Security*, 26 (2): 87–102.

Pender, J. (2007) 'Country Ownership, the Evasion of Donor Accountability', in Bickerton, C., Cunliffe, P. and Gourevitch, A., *Politics Without Sovereignty, A Critique of Contemporary International Relations*, London: Routledge, 112–30.

Pupavac, V. (2005) 'Human Security and the Rise of Global Therapeutic Governance', *Conflict, Security and Development*, 5 (2): 161–81.

Sageman, M. (2004) *Understanding Terror Networks*, Pennsylvania: University of Pennsylvania Press.

Schittecatte, C. (2007) 'Towards a More Inclusive Global Governance and Enhanced Human Security', in MacLean, Sandra J., Black, David R. and Shaw, Timothy M., *A Decade of Human Security, Global Governance and New Multilateralisms*, Hampshire, UK: Ashgate, 129–43.

Simpson, G. (2004) *Great Powers and Unequal States, Unequal Sovereigns in the International Legal Order*, Cambridge: Cambridge University Press.

Suhrke, A. (1999) 'Human Security and The Interests of States', *Security Dialogue*, 30 (3): 265–76.

Tadjbakhsh, S. and Chenoy, A. M. (2007) *Human Security, Concepts and Implications*, London: Routledge.

Thakur, R. (2004) 'A Political Worldview', *Security Dialogue*, 35 (3): 347–48.

Thomas, N. and Tow, W. T. (2002) 'The Utility of Human Security: Sovereignty and Humanitarian Intervention', *Security Dialogue*, 33 (2): 177–92.

UN (1994) United Nations Human Development Report, *New Dimensions of Human Security*, New York: United Nations.

—— ([1992] 1995) *An Agenda for Peace*, Second Edition, New York: United Nations.

—— (2000a) *Report of the Panel on United Nations Peace Operations, known as The Brahimi Report*, New York: United Nations.

—— (2000b) *We the Peoples, the Role of the United Nations in the 21st Century*, New York: United Nations.

—— (2004) *A More Secure World: Our Shared Responsibility, Report of Secretary-General's High Level Panel on Threats, Challenges and Change*, New York: United Nations.

—— (2005) *In Larger Freedom; Towards Development, Security and Human Rights for All*, New York: United Nations.

—— (2006) *Human Security for All – Integrated Responses to Protect and Empower People and Communities, A Look at Nine Promising Efforts*, New York: Human Security Unit, Office for the Coordination of Humanitarian Affairs.

USA (2002) *The National Security Strategy of the United States of America*, Available URL: http://www.whitehouse.gov/nsc/nss.html

9 Rethinking global discourses of security

David Chandler

Introduction

The history of the radical challenge of 'human security' is often written by its advocates – from its first usage, in the United Nations Development Programme's 1994 *Human Development Report*, until today – in terms, which pose the centrality of the struggle between realist, traditional, state-based, interest-based approaches and new, liberal, cosmopolitan, deterritorialised, values-based approaches, which focus on individual human needs. For some authors, this struggle is still at the heart of how they conceive of international relations and questions of security; and one which, after 9/11 and with the ongoing disaster of Iraq, is more important than ever (see, for example, Kaldor 2007). This struggle for the heart and soul of global policy-making is often posed, by its advocates, as one between two different 'paradigms', two entirely different outlooks on the world: one paradigm reproducing current power relations and inequalities and insecurities, the other paradigm challenging this view, recognising the interconnectedness, interdependence and mutual vulnerabilities of security threats and the need for collective, collaborative, human-centred responses.

More recently, the frameworks of human security advocates have been challenged by radical critics, asserting that rather than universal claims of 'human security' empowering individuals, they, in fact, represent the expansion of new relations and technologies of governance, through which global regulatory norms operate on behalf of neoliberal capitalism, framed through the 'biopolitical' imperative of securing populations rather than the security of states. The universal framing of human security has therefore been understood as constitutive of a new globalised international order, both by the radical advocates and radical critics of 'human security'. This chapter will first highlight the success of constructivism in challenging traditional rationalist framings of security and then draw out how the move to idealist constructions has been reinforced through approaches which have sought to criticise human security on the basis of its universalising claims.

Global ideas versus state interests

Writing in the aftermath of the end of the Cold War, constructivist theorising, which challenged the structural fixity of neoliberal and neo-realist thought, found a ready audience. It appeared that the study of states and state interests could no longer adequately explain international politics. Instead, the research focus shifted away from fixed identities and narrow material interests to one which emphasised the power of norms and ideas. Alexander Wendt argued that it was not just the distribution of power that was important but also the 'distribution of knowledge': the intersubjective understandings which constitute the state's conception of its self and its interests. As examples, he stated that having a powerful neighbour in the US meant something different to Canada than it did for Cuba and that British missiles would have seemed more of a threat to the Soviet Union than to the US (1992: 397). It was the interaction between states that shaped their identities and interests. Rather than power, it was subjective conceptions that were important; therefore: 'if the United States and Soviet Union decide that they are no longer enemies, "the cold war is over"' (1992: 397).

The collapse of the Soviet Union, through implosion rather than military defeat, fundamentally challenged realist perspectives of state interests and the importance of military power, and thereby facilitated the revival of more idealist perspectives of change – based on social interaction rather than material interests. As Wendt famously stated, inversing the rationalist framework: 'Identities are the basis of interests' (1992: 398). The focus on ideas, rather than interests, led to a more expansive understanding of social interaction, giving a central role to idea-promoting and idea-generating non-state actors, particularly activist NGOs. It is at this point that the concept of transnational or global relations comes in, in distinction to international relations, i.e. relations between states. The international sphere is no longer seen as one in which states project their national interests, instead the process is reversed; through participation in international and transnational relations, the national interests of states are constituted.

In this way, the end of the Cold War could be held not just to discredit realist approaches but also to provide compelling evidence of the role of non-state actors in the development of state 'identities' and interests. Over this period, the growth of international human security approaches and frameworks is one of the leading examples, held to demonstrate the strength of constructivist approaches: 'because international human-centred norms challenge state rule over society and national sovereignty, any impact on domestic change would be counter-intuitive' (Risse and Sikkink 1999: 4). The assumption that human security norms challenge nation-state interests therefore asserts that norm changes cannot come solely from state agency but must also stem from the influence of transnational non-state actors. Even where states may use the normative rhetoric, such as human rights concerns, it is the influence of non-state actors which serves to prevent these from being used in a purely instrumental way.

For constructivist theorists, the shift in the articulation of foreign-policy goals, from a narrow framing of national interests to global framings of human security, demonstrated the growing capacity of moral values to constrain the interests of power. A leading article in *Foreign Affairs*, for example, argued: 'Humanitarian intervention . . . is perhaps the most dramatic example of the new power of morality in international affairs' (Gelb and Rosenthal 2003: 6). As Mary Kaldor asserts:

> The changing international norms concerning humanitarian intervention can be considered an expression of an emerging global civil society. The changing norms do reflect a growing global consensus about the equality of human beings and the responsibility to prevent suffering ... Moreover, this consensus, in turn, is the outcome of a global public debate on these issues.
>
> (2001: 110)

Crucial for the constructivist perspective was the belief that this 'global public debate' took place not on the terms of power but those of morality. Sikkink argues that activities of non-state actors have been able to 'transform', 'modify' and 'reshape' the meaning of sovereignty because sovereignty is a product of a set of 'shared' or 'intersubjective understandings about the legitimate scope of state authority' (Sikkink 1993: 413, 441). The human security orientated debates on international humanitarian intervention and human rights form the core of the idealist constructivist thesis. Jack Donnelly, for example, views this dialogue as a 'promising sign for the future' because it is a debate which takes 'place largely within a space delimited by a basic moral commitment' to the human rights cause (1999: 99–100).

The constructivist 'turn' in international relations fundamentally challenged the previous rationalist assumptions of the pursuit of pre-formed state interests in the international sphere. It was alleged that in today's globalised world, with the emergence of transnational linkages, committed transnational ethical campaigners were capable of changing the identity, and thereby the interests, of leading states. What is crucial to this thesis is the socially-constructed identity of the state actor rather than the alleged structural constraints, where ideas are understood to be merely a reflection of pre-given material interests. The non-instrumentalist assumptions made for discourses of human security rest heavily on the constructivist framework, which assumes a connection between moral or ethical discourse and a power to shape identities and interests.

Very few commentators have attempted to understand the rise of 'human security' frameworks outside the constructivist framework and, as will be drawn out, this framework forms the basis of the critical shift against human security after the end of the 1990s. The fundamental break involved in the constructivist approach was that of inversing the relationship between states and the international or global sphere. Where, previously, states were the key objects of study – as the core actors and instrumentally-orientated rational subjects constituting the international sphere – within the constructivist framework, state policy frameworks were the products of international or global discourse. The subject of study switched from privileging the formation of state interests at the domestic level to privileging their communicative interaction, the declarations of norms and values, which were held to shape state identities and policy-making. Taking on board the starting logic of realism – that states pursue their narrow strategic self-interests – constructivists assumed that it was the external pressures of global interaction and campaigning NGOs which explained the shifting nature of the discourses of foreign policy.

While the constructivist focus on discourse remains very much central to dominant perceptions of human security, the constructivist framework, outlined earlier, tends to reflect the sensibilities of the 1990s rather than the 2000s. There can be little doubt that nearly 20 years after human security was first taken up by the United Nations, its integration into the policy-making and policy practices of leading western states and international institutions, has revealed that talk of two different 'paradigms' – the radical counterposition of 'individual' and 'state-based' approaches, or between 'critical theory' and 'problem-solving' frameworks – has been much exaggerated. The framework of human security, as an approach which challenges power, has now been comprehensively questioned and opposed by numerous counter-approaches which argue that human security cosmopolitan frameworks have now become the dominant discourses in which power is strengthened and reproduced (for example, Rogers 2002; Duffield 2007; Douzinas 2007; Jabri 2007). However, as intimated earlier, the constructivist assumptions: that the discourses or ideas should be the ontological focus of study, and seen to be explanatory of the practices and interactions of the subjects themselves – have not been challenged.

In the 1990s debate, the advocates of human security posed a radical challenge to the state-based frameworks of traditional security approaches. In the following decade, the radicals appeared to be on the other side, critiquing human security as the ideological tool of biopolitical, neoliberal global governance. Both approaches counterpose human security to state-based frameworks and both posit the discourse as the project of new global agency: for liberal advocates, this was global civil society; and for radical poststructuralist and critical realists, this was US hegemony or neoliberal empire. This chapter argues that the paradox of human security is that there is an assumption of a new transformative globalising actor which has led the transformation of state-based approaches to security, yet this is established on the basis of the universal nature of the discourse rather than a study of the actors engaged in the practices of policy-making. There is little analysis of the dynamics leading western states and state-based international institutions to call for human security approaches to be mainstreamed. These two competing paradigms through which 'human security' is increasingly understood, appear to be shaped less by academic commentators' understanding of the practices of human security on the ground than by their normative perspective towards the abstract framework of liberal cosmopolitan policy approaches.

Human security as a challenge to power

Many human security advocates present their views as a radical challenge to the traditional discipline and practices of international relations. This view is particularly strongly articulated by critical security theorists who argue that their theoretical approach 'places suffering humanity at the centre of its theoretical project' and that they place 'the powerless and disposed at the heart of theory and emancipatory practice' (Wheeler 1996: 126, 128). Ken Booth, for example, abstractly counterposes the needs of the powerless to those of the inherently oppressive inter-state system, viewing the privileging of universal human rights as a progressive blow against:

> Westphalia, [which] in its time, had represented a sort of anchorage, after the ravaging wars of religion. But the grammar of the system of state sovereignty and statism constructed from the seventeenth to the twentieth century led to the Holocaust and atomic warfare . . . In the killing fields at the apogee of Westphalia – Dachau and Hiroshima – 'Hell was here'.
>
> (1999: 65)

The view of two radically separate paradigms – state-based and human-based – allows human security advocates to idealistically engage with both the theory and the practice of human security. On the one hand, there is often a tendency to conflate the aspirations of human security theorising with policy practices in reality, for example, Shahrbanou Tadjbakhsh and Anuradha Chenoy state:

> With human security [the individual 'qua person', rather than 'qua citizen'] becomes the ultimate actor taken into account. His/her security is the ultimate goal, to which all instruments and political actors are subordinated. Elevating the person as the ultimate end is made possible by defining this new actor in terms of his/her vulnerabilities on the one hand, and his/her capacity to affect change on the other.
>
> (2007: 13)

Here, it is clear there is no mediation between abstract theoretical or policy claims and policy practice. 'Individuals qua persons' clearly have different and differing security concerns making it impossible for them to be the 'ultimate actor' to which international institutions are subordinated. Even Amartya Sen recognises that the 'human-centred' approach, highlighted in his seminal book, *Development as Freedom*, still involves political processes of collective decision-making, choices and policy trade-offs (1999: 33–34). The assertion that 'individuals qua persons', i.e. outside a political process, can suborn power, makes little sense in theory, let alone practice (see Chandler 2003); nevertheless, this view highlights how human security advocates have a highly abstract understanding of the transformative potential of human security approaches.

This abstract perspective is clearly expressed when the reality of policy does not match the promise of the aspirations. This does little to undermine the advocacy of human security as the problems are always put down to the vestiges of realist thinking, 'statist' outlooks, material interests or often the disruptive role of the US, described by Mary Kaldor as the 'last nation state' (2003). For the more naïve advocates, it appears that all that holds back their brave new moral world is the self-interest of 'powerful states, aspiring regional hegemons, and entrenched elites that are interested in retaining their power within the nation states structures' (Tadjbakhsh and Chenoy 2007: 93). In this framework, human security is merely a way of framing a pure, unsullied, ethical or normative perspective. Analyses of practices on the ground which fall short of this merely indicate that policy actors have not quite managed to fully adopt such a purist approach.

On the one hand, a constructivist framing can easily counterpose ethics to interests, enabling academic theorists to present the limits of human security declarations as due to the interference of interests, which undermine the development and implementation of ambitious transformative policies. On the other hand, the constructivist approach enables advocates to articulate human security as in the self-interest of powerful elites, on the basis that their interests are fluid reflections of changing identities. In this way, the relationship between ethics and interests is never a stable one as interests inevitably collapse into ethical claims. Therefore 'securing people is not just an ethical imperative, it is the best strategy to secure the state and the international system' (Tadjbakhsh and Chenoy 2007: 21). The radical counterposition between state and human interests is rarely sustained: 'thus human security transforms, rather than replaces the national security discourse and is not an alternative to state security' (2007: 167; see also MSG 2007).

The constructivist framing helps to explain the ambiguity of the 'human security' paradigm, in which the discourse is, on the one hand, a radical, emancipatory paradigm shift and, on the other, it is less an ethical, normative challenge to realist calculations of self-interest than an adaptation of realist understandings to a more globalised and interdependent world. It is often not clear in human security advocacy – where the interdependence of threats and responses is crucial to the argument – whether the merging of ethical imperatives with security and self-interest is an empirical assertion or a normative one. The openly admitted lack of clear causal understandings of these interconnections often serves to keep the question off the agenda (Tadjbakhsh and Chenoy 2007: 243).

The critical advocates of human security discourses do not counterpose the interests of postcolonial peoples to those of western elites. Rather, the argument is couched in terms of the compatibility of interests once there is a shift from backward and unenlightened views of self-interest to a view of self-interest which fits today's interdependent, globalised, complex world. The nature of the advocacy discourse itself highlights the possibility that a debate about human security and the renegotiation of the meaning of self-interest has been generated from within western elites rather than imposed by radical activism from outside. However, the question, which constructivist theorists do not pose, is why political elites would seek to present themselves as acting in the interests of global humanity rather than the collective self-interest of their own constituents? This is because the globalised nature of the discourse comes methodologically prior. This is why there is no starting point of separate political subjects with distinct or differing interests, as in classical rationalist frameworks. The starting point is the intersubjective discourse, which asserts a shared global ethical concern.

One challenge to critical and constructivist theorists, who have posited the emancipatory potential of human security approaches, has come from critical and empirically-grounded analysts, concerned less with the discourse than with the practices. Some authors have suggested that, on the ground, there appears to be little difference between traditional agendas of state-based security and radical human security approaches. In an interesting study, Robert Muggah and Keith Krause develop an approach they state is informed by what they see as the weakness of 'constructivist/critical International Relations' – the tendency to 'treat discourses as significant themselves, without examining the link to actual practices' (2006: 115, n.10). In an attempt to consider the relationship between discourse and practice, they seek to examine the differences between pre- and post-human security interventions, comparing and critically examining similar UN missions in Haiti – UNMIH (1993–95) where there is no human security discursive framework and MINUSTAH (United Nations Stabilisation Mission in Haiti) shaped by the human security agenda – and conclude that this shift in 'paradigms' 'has not necessarily translated into radically new practical strategies, much less positive outcomes *in situ*' (2003–5: 122).

One of the strongest criticisms of human security frameworks is that they merely serve the interests of power in offering palliative treatment, merely token support, for the poor and marginalised. In the words of Paul Rogers, the concerns of human security, eager to extend the security agenda to poverty reduction and social security, are merely 'liddism' – attempts to keep the lid on the resistance of the postcolonial world (2002). Catherine Schittecatte, in an interesting study, highlights how, regardless of the normative debate on 'narrow' and 'broad' understandings of the concept of human security, the areas which have gained more attention and resources and increasingly included leading roles for non-state actors, have been those which 'reflect ongoing priorities of the most powerful members and organisations of the international community' (2006: 130). Most progress has been made in the 'freedom from fear' area, with the revival of ideas of 'Just War' intervention, while there has been little interest in mainstreaming 'freedom from want' approaches that go beyond palliative measures to 'challenge the philosophy of market liberalism' (2006: 132).

The critical empirically-grounded studies tend to emphasise that the human security agenda has done relatively little to influence policy-making in practice, despite the ambitious rhetoric. In fact, this is often the most surprising aspect for empirical researchers, who regularly note that the human security framework has 'been promoted less assertively at the local level than the strategic policy guidelines had led us to expect' and that policy changed much less in practice than government rhetoric might have led researchers to believe (for example, Schümer 2008: 149). Zoë Marriage's empirical study of international post-conflict assistance in Africa argues that abstract framings of human-centred policy-making in terms of aid provision are less guides to action than all-purpose justifications for inconsistent and ad hoc practices on the ground (2006). Tanja Schümer's study, of DFID policy in Sierra Leone, similarly highlights the lack of relationship between discursive claims of human security programmes orientated to humanitarian and individual needs and ad hoc practices on the ground, emphasising that this disconnection was never acknowledged or addressed at senior policy-making level or in the field (2008).

Human security as a mechanism of power

While empirical studies have challenged the claims of the transformative challenge to traditional policy-making posed by human security advocates, they have rarely theorised why it is that foreign policy discourse should have undergone such a radical reframing despite the lack of a clear change in practices. These critical empirical perspectives have tended to be marginalised by more theoretically-orientated critical approaches to human security, which have developed particularly since 9/11. These approaches have been provided by writers who tend to be associated with poststructuralist frameworks, often drawing on theorists such as Carl Schmitt, Michel Foucault and Giorgio Agamben. International legal theorist Carl Schmitt's work on the concept of the sovereign exception and the dangers of universalist ethical appeals to the 'human' (see Schmitt 1996; 2003) has been used to argue that human security approaches pose a fundamental challenge to the UN international legal order (for example, Zolo 2002). In the recent work of Vivienne Jabri (2007) and Costas Douzinas (2007) this framework is melded with post-Foucaultian readings of human security as an exercise of biopower. In this framework, new global governmental practices are highlighted which are legitimised through the privileging of human development and human security over and above the formal rights framework of sovereignty and non-intervention.

This framework is posed particularly sharply in the 'biopolitical' emphasis of Mark Duffield's book *Development, Security and Unending War* (2007) which develops the themes of his earlier work, focusing on the shift from inter-state war to the perception of underdevelopment as a source of international insecurity. For Duffield, the discourse of human security is one of permanent emergency and unending war. He argues that human security is a key reflection of the dominance of biopolitical framings of international relations – interconnecting security and development concerns – through having 'life' or the population as a reference point rather than the state (2007: 118). Human security discourse seeks to universalise or globalise security problems of instability by positing the responsibilities of the west to intervene and manage insecurity at the same time as seeking to contain the risks of instability through a focus on non-material development, in terms of the technologies of community-based self-reliance.

Duffield argues that the threat of terrorism is not a direct replacement for the threat of communism. The management of Cold War threats of inter-state conflict relegated the importance of the postcolonial world; where there was intervention this was at arm's length, mediated politically through inter-state relations, where selected states would be supported and provided with aid, often against the will and needs of their populations. Duffield states that, today, the west seeks to intervene biopolitically to reconstruct 'ineffective' or 'failing' states on the basis of satisfying the unmet needs of their populations (2007: 129). For Duffield, there is nothing progressive in the biopolitical framing of security in terms of permanent instability. The human security approach is seen to blur the divisions and power relations shaping security discourse at the same time as instituting a racial discourse of biopolitical division between the secure and the insecure – those living under effective and ineffective governance; those developed and those deserving of development. This bifurcation is captured in the descriptive and contingent division between the 'insured' – those living in mass-consumer society with social welfare protections – and the 'uninsured' – those living in underdeveloped societies where instability is an ever-present threat and where the development solution is self-reliance and containment through the social engineering of community-support mechanisms.

Human security, under the aegis of the 'human' offers a divisive vision of the world, where the west has both a security 'interest' and a 'values-based' desire to 'secure', to 'develop', to 'protect' and to 'better' the 'other', whose insecurity threatens the security of western consumer society as the instabilities associated with conflict, poverty and alienation threaten to spill over into and to destabilise the west. The desire to contain instability is understood as the need to address the threatening unmet needs of the unsecured, uninsured and insecure non-western 'other'. Because the development solution of self-reliance and sustainable development does not offer to bridge the development gap with the west but instead to contain it, the limitations of self-reliance are continually coming to the fore, promising an unending war where interventionist development techniques are continually being reinvented and perfected.

However, there is a danger that this reading of Foucault's biopolitics can easily result in the discourse of human security being considered abstractly, detached from today's political context. There is a danger of slipping into a traditional realist framework – which merely reads the rhetoric of ethical universals as the ideological expression of acts of power and interest – or of reinterpreting all interventions, legitimised through the rhetoric of the interests or needs of those being intervened in, as biopolitical attempts to divide, regulate and shape the world (see also Buur *et al.* 2007). In which case, rather than reading the discourse of human security as progressive because of its universal claims, it is critiqued, equally idealistically, merely on the hegemonic implications of these claims.

Duffield reads the human security discourse as a biopolitical discourse, privileging the importance of the governance and regulation of life and human needs over sovereign power based on force and coercion. This approach appears to be just as abstract as the frameworks of theorists advocating the radical and transformative nature of human security. The conclusion Duffield draws from the discourse is that Foucault's framework of governmentality is being applied at the global level and, therefore, that the human security discourse expresses the rise of a new globalising hegemonic power. Where the advocates of human security posit the existence of an immanent progressive force, existing external to states – such as global civil society – Duffield, and a growing number of other theorists, such as Hardt and Negri (2001), use post-Foucaultian frameworks of analysis to posit the external existence of hegemonic power: 'empire' or some similar deterritorialised manifestation of sovereign power on a global level (see, for example, Jabri 2007; Douzinas 2007).

Ironically, whilst Foucault understood his work on biopower and governmentality as a correction to the reading of his work on disciplinarity, which created the impression of merely asserting 'the monotonous assertion of power' (Foucault 2007: 56; see also Baudrillard 1987: 33), Duffield, in effect, essentialises or naturalises the concept of biopower to argue that 'liberal' discourses of progress are essentially new forms of governing and controlling populations. In emphasising the hegemonic frameworks and interests underpinning idealistic approaches of advocates of human security, Duffield appears to throw the baby of human agency out with the bathwater of development, rejecting modernising aspirations towards democracy and development for recreating oppressive neoliberal biopolitical frameworks of control and regulation.

Despite the differences in their views of whether the shift from state security to human security is to be welcomed or criticised, both the advocates of human security and their radical critics seek to ground their position of critique on the basis of their 'global solidarity' with the non-western poor and marginal. Both sets of theorists see growing global insecurity as a product of the instrumental pursuit of western self-interest within the framework of globalisation – for advocates of human security, the object of critique is attempts to address the globalised world through state-based security frameworks; for post-Foucaultian critics, it is neoliberal attempts to contain and impose biopolitical order on the postcolonial world.

Where the advocates of human security assert a challenge to vested interests, their critics express a concern that power interests are being pursued and reproduced precisely through the discourse of human security. The realist or poststructuralist assertion of the relevance of interests and power relations, revealed behind the universalist claims of human security, appears to follow the same approach as that of the critical and liberal claims of advocates – merely reading off from the self-assertions of western or international actors. This may well allow critical theorists, on both sides of the human security divide, to oppose 'power' and vicariously take the side of the oppressed and marginalised but it does not begin to address the question of why security concerns should have become globalised through discourses of human security nor how these discourses of power could have become mainstreamed so rapidly.

The human security paradox

In order to ground an understanding of the rapid rise of human security approaches, it is necessary to unpack the globalising of security discourse – which poses the existence of globalised struggles over the direction of security – and to go beyond the globalised discourses to study the policy actors themselves. The rapid mainstreaming of human security reflects and codifies major changes in the articulation of foreign policy since the end of the Cold War. The mainstreaming of human security reflects a major transformation in the discourse and practices of the international sphere, one in which the policy-makers and practitioners have been ahead of and facilitated the radical academic advocates of these approaches.

To suggest that these changes can be understood as due to the impact of new immanent forces for progress and emancipation seems untenable in the wake of disillusionment with 1990s visions of change. On the other hand, the radical critics of human security appear to merely stand the idealism of human security advocates 'on its head' to argue that it is the universalising interests of power rather than the cosmopolitan ethics of empowerment which drives the discourse. Neither framing satisfactorily grounds the existence of a new universal subject as the agent of human security as a universalising discourse. Both approaches suggest that human security has been transformative of international relations, yet neglect to investigate why the discourse has been mainstreamed by leading western states and state-based international institutions or to explain why there should be so little contestation over such an allegedly radical reshaping of power relations.

Rather than assessing the changing discourses of international relations on their own terms, a much more mediated and contingent approach to understanding the appeal of human security frameworks is suggested here, highlighting that it is precisely the lack of political contestation over the international security agenda which drives the human security framework. There is no structuring clash of collective political subjects, either in terms of Left and Right or in terms of Great Power or inter-imperialist rivalries. In fact, the international sphere, so long the realm of realpolitik and strategic interaction, has been transformed and hollowed out with the attenuation of traditional frameworks of political contestation.

The security agenda is expanding, but this cannot be explained in terms of a radical challenge, either from above or from below. Rather than an opportunity to put the most vulnerable at the top of the security agenda or, alternatively, a blank cheque for imperial domination, the rise of the discourse of security appears to reflect the disorientation of western elites. This analysis would indicate that, in today's world, discourses of power are pale imitations of the universals of the past. In which case, the relationship between discourse or ideological reflection and underlying power relations and interests may be much more mediated and contingent than when there was a world of clearly articulated subjects. It is vital, therefore, that our understanding of the changing dynamics and practices of the international sphere starts from the real relations through which power and policy operate and then works through to an understanding of the discourses and ideological reflections. In conclusion, three dynamics, behind the ease with which human security has been integrated into mainstream security agendas, are suggested; dynamics which attempt to go beyond the abstract framing of the discussion.

First, there is the desire to exaggerate new post-Cold War security threats. It is clear that political elites and radical advocates of human security approaches both share a normative desire to exaggerate the existence of threats. It is here that human security advocates come into their own, outdoing any 'dodgy dossiers' about Saddam Hussein's Weapons of Mass Destruction with their assertions that in our globalised world, everything is interconnected and interdependent, and that therefore 'dysfunctionality in one sphere is structurally and sequentially expressed in other sub-systems and leads to a vicious circle of causes and effects' (Shaw *et al.* 2006: 16–17). Allegedly, we are approaching a 'tipping-point' for Armageddon, where 'drugs, disease, terrorism, pollution, poverty and environmental problems' are 'mutually reinforcing' (2006: 17). In the absence of traditional enemies, human security approaches fill the gap with the securitisation of every issue from health, to the economy, to the environment.

It might appear that the 'human security' lobbyists, seeking to 'securitise' their campaign interests, from climate change to global poverty, are promoting the needs of power to direct itself, and articulate its needs 'biopolitically', in response to these multiple threats to human life. But rather than a blank cheque for imperial domination, the rise of the discourse of human security can be read, instead, as a reflection of the disorientation of western elites. First, this exaggeration of threats can indicate a search for a policy agenda rather than a strategic manipulation of one. Second, the exaggeration of fears appears to reflect a real existential crisis within western elites, which have lost their sense of purpose and social connection (see Furedi 2007). Radical critics may be mistaken in understanding the human security agenda as a confident assertion of a new post-imperial 'empire', rather it can be better grasped as reflecting a sense of weakness and lack of capacity.

Second, the task is a responsive one, locating agency in the threats rather than with western elites. The problematisation of the non-western states and societies, facilitated by the human security framework is as central to security discourses shaped by the unilateral 'realist' war on terror as it is by the multilateral 'critical' discourses of poverty-reduction, sustainable development and climate change adaptation. It seems that many 'realists' have no disagreement with the 'human security' argument that the world's poorest countries now pose the biggest security threat to the west. The critical poststructuralist approach challenges the discourse of failed states but agrees with the underlying identification of the problem of the postcolonial world and the 'circulatory' problems for global capital which it represents.

While this appears to offer the agenda of western intervention and the return of imperial rule, this would be to read discourses of the past into the present. Human security framings pose little optimism about the west resolving the problems emanating from the postcolonial 'other', or of the restoration of a new secure order. This is a discourse where agency is, in fact, relocated, by common consensus across the liberal/realist spectrum, in the 'other'. The west is seen as vulnerable and weak – high technology, consumerism, welfare, even liberal democracy – are seen negatively, as exposing us to threat. Rather than a security agenda of control, management and strategic intervention, this is one of ad hoc reactions and damage limitation.

Third, there is the facilitation of short-term policy-making in the absence of clear strategic foreign policy visions. In the absence of the geostrategic Cold War order and the domestic framework of the politics of Left and Right, leading western states and international institutions have found it difficult to draw up long-term strategic visions of the future (see, for example Chandler and Heins 2007). Human security approaches have assisted in the process of rationalising these difficulties and legitimating the lack of clear strategy. Human security advocates suggest that, first, the interdependence of threats means that 'threats should not be prioritised', second, that 'policy-making is not a vertical process but a networked, flexible and horizontal coalition that needs a complex paradigm', and third, that the prioritisation of human security goals and outcomes 'may be a futile exercise', as the interdependence of threats means that work in one area may achieve little success if the intervention is not comprehensive and holistic enough to tackle all the relevant factors (Tadjbakhsh and Chenoy 2007: 17).

Human security approaches therefore enable governments and policy-makers to opt out of taking responsibility for foreign policy, encouraging a shift from strategic thinking to sound bites and ad hoc policy-making. What may appear to some critics of human security as a useless 'shopping list of threats' (Krause 2004) is, in fact, the mainstay of both national and international security agendas, where governments lack strategic priorities. Multilateralism and the integration of non-state actors in policy-making is also a reflection of governments' increasing unwillingness to take accountability for policy-making and implementation. Furthermore, human security approaches argue that causal relationships are impossible in an interconnected world (Paris 2004), making it much easier for governments to evade responsibility by seeking praise for their 'good intentions' rather than being held to account for the policy-consequences of their actions.

Conclusion

Rather than understanding the growth in human security agendas through the prism of two fundamentally different transformative paradigms – one based on an immanent global emancipatory challenge from below, the other upon an immanent global source of domination and regulation operating above the level of nation states – it may be better to see security policy, and foreign policy-making in general, as beset by a process of fragmentation, hollowing out the subjects of international relations and producing an absence of paradigms or clear frameworks of operation. The attraction of human security approaches would appear to be that they, on the one hand, reflect this confusion, portraying the external world as a complex and ever-more threatening environment, and, on the other hand, legitimise and institutionalise the lack of policy-making capacity, encouraging the shedding of policy responsibility and viewing the world as less open to strategic intervention.

References

Baudrillard, J. (1987) *Forget Foucault*, New York: Semiotext(e).
Booth, K. (1999) 'Three Tyrannies', in T. Dunne and N. J. Wheeler (eds) *Human Rights in Global Politics*, Cambridge: Cambridge University Press.
Buur, L., Jensen, S. and Stepputat, F. (2007) 'Introduction: The Security-Development Nexus', in L. Burr, S. Jensen and F. Stepputat (eds) *The Security-Development Nexus: Expressions of Sovereignty and Securitisation in Southern Africa*, Cape Town: Nordiska Afrikainstitutet, Uppsala/HSRC Press.
Chandler, D. (2003) 'New Rights for Old? Cosmopolitan Citizenship and the Critique of State Sovereignty', *Political Studies*, 51 (2): 339–56.
Chandler, D. and Heins, V. (2007) 'Ethics and Foreign Policy: New Perspectives on an Old Problem', in D. Chandler and V. Heins (eds) *Rethinking Ethical Foreign Policy: Pitfalls, Possibilities and Paradoxes*, London: Routledge.
Donnelly, J. (1999) 'The Social Construction of International Human Rights', in T. Dunne and N. Wheeler (eds) *Human Rights in Global Politics*, Cambridge: Cambridge University Press.

Douzinas, C. (2007) *Human Rights and Empire: The Political Philosophy of Cosmopolitanism*, London: Routledge Cavendish.
Duffield, M. (2007) *Development, Security and Unending War: Governing the World of Peoples*, London: Polity.
Foucault, M. (2007) *Security, Territory, Population: Lectures at the Collège de France 1977–1978*, Basingstoke: Palgrave.
Furedi, F. (2007) *Invitation to Terror: The Expanding Empire of the Unknown*, London: Continuum.
Gelb, L. H. and Rosenthal, J. A. (2003) 'The Rise of Ethics in Foreign Policy', *Foreign Affairs*, 82 (3): 2–7.
Hardt, M. and Negri, A. (2001) *Empire*, New York: Harvard University Press.
Jabri, V. (2007) *War and the Transformation of Global Politics*, Basingstoke: Palgrave.
Kaldor, M. (2001) 'A Decade of Humanitarian Intervention: The Role of Global Civil Society', in H. Anheier, M. Glasius and M. Kaldor (eds) *Global Civil Society 2001*, Oxford: Oxford University Press.
—— (2003) *Global Civil Society: An Answer to War*, Cambridge: Polity.
—— (2007) *Human Security: Reflections on Globalisation and Intervention*, London: Polity.
Krause, K. (2004) 'The Key to a Powerful Agenda, if Properly Defined', in J. P. Burgess and T. Owen (eds) 'Special Section: What is "Human Security"', *Security Dialogue*, 35 (3): 367–68.
Madrid Study Group (MSG) (2007) '*A European Way of Security: The Madrid Report of the Human Security Study Group comprising a Proposal and Background Report*', Madrid, 8 November.
Marriage, Z. (2006) *Not Breaking the Rules, Not Playing the Game: International Assistance to Countries at War*, London: Hurst & Co.
Muggah, R. and Krause, K. (2006) 'A True Measure of Success? The Discourse and Practice of Human Security in Haiti', in S. J. Maclean, D. R. Black and T. M. Shaw (eds) *A Decade of Human Security: Global Governance and New Multilateralisms*, Aldershot: Ashgate.
Paris, R. (2004) 'Still an Inscrutable Concept', in J. P. Burgess and T. Owen (eds) 'Special Section: What is "Human Security"', *Security Dialogue*, 35 (3): 370–72.
Risse, T. and Sikkink, K. (1999) 'The Socialisation of International Human Rights Norms into Domestic Practices: Introduction', in T. Risse, S. C. Ropp and K. Sikkink (eds) *The Power of Human Rights: International Norms and Domestic Change*, Cambridge: Cambridge University Press.
Risse, T., Ropp, S. C. and Sikkink, K. (eds) (1999) *The Power of Human Rights: International Norms and Domestic Change*, Cambridge: Cambridge University Press.
Rogers, P. (2002) *Losing Control: Global Security in the Twenty-First Century*, London: Pluto.
Schittecatte, C. (2006) 'Toward a More Inclusive Global Governance and Enhanced Human Security', in S. J. Maclean, D. R. Black and T. M. Shaw (eds) *A Decade of Human Security: Global Governance and New Multilateralisms*, Aldershot: Ashgate.
Schmitt, C. (1996) *The Concept of the Political*, Chicago: University of Chicago Press.
—— (2003) *The Nomos of the Earth: in the International Law of the Jus Publicum Europaeum*, New York: Telos Press.
Schümer, T. (2008) *New Humanitarianism: Britain and Sierra Leone, 1997–2003*, Basingstoke: Palgrave.
Sen, A. (1999) *Development as Freedom*, Oxford: Oxford University Press.
Shaw, T. M., Maclean, S. J. and Black, D. R. (2006) 'Introduction: A Decade of Human Security: What Prospects for Global Governance and New Multilateralisms?', in S. J. Maclean, D. R. Black and T. M. Shaw (eds) *A Decade of Human Security: Global Governance and New Multilateralisms*, Aldershot: Ashgate.

Sikkink, K. (1993) 'Human Rights, Principled Issue-Networks, and Sovereignty in Latin America', *International Organisation*, 47 (3): 411–41.

Tadjbakhsh, S. and Chenoy, A. M. (2007) *Human Security: Concepts and Implications*, London and New York: Routledge.

UNDP (1994) United Nations Development Programme, *Human Development Report 1994*, Oxford: Oxford University Press.

Wendt, A. (1992) 'Anarchy is What States Make of it', *International Organisation*, 46 (2): 391–425.

Wheeler, N. J. (1996) 'Guardian Angel or Global Gangster: A Review of the Ethical Claims of International Society', *Political Studies*, 44 (1): 123–35.

Zolo, D. (2002) *Invoking Humanity: War, Law, and Global Order*, London: Continuum.

10 Human security and the securing of human life

Tracing global sovereign and biopolitical rule[1]

Marc G. Doucet and Miguel de Larrinaga

Introduction

The central argument advanced in this chapter is that rather than opening the avenue for an expansion of a humanist and cosmopolitan ethics as many conventional readings advocate, the more fundamental labour of the concept of human security is to bring about a unique dual exercise of sovereign power and biopower which furthers the rule of the liberal order via a global regime of governmentality. This regime of governmentality, of which human security is, among others, a component,[2] assembles forms of power that seek to govern populations in the borderlands of the global liberal order. Following Michel Foucault, such a regime of governmentality brings to bear on populations forms of knowledge and rationalities of power which, in line with its origins in the individualizing and totalizing effects of pastoral power seeks to secure the well-being of 'all and each' (2007: 128). The argument here is that human security as a governmental rationality with the globe as its plane of operation is bound up with forms of power that are meant to target the health and welfare of populations, and in doing so must specify along particular lines rather than others what '(un)healthy' and '(un)secure' populations look like. At the same time, we argue that the concept of human security also brings to light a form of sovereign power which much of Foucault's work on modern forms of power 'under the rubric of a multiplicity of force relations' sought to sever (Neal 2004: 375). Drawing from the work of Giorgio Agamben, the latter part of this chapter explores how human security brings to the forefront the connection between biopower and the juridico-political order by further entrenching and defining the grounds for the conditions of 'exceptionality' and 'emergency' which assist in legitimizing and authorizing sovereign power's international interventions in zones where, as the UN Human Security Unit dramatizes, 'the threshold below which human life is intolerably threatened' is deemed to have been met (Human Security Unit 2009: 7). Using Agamben, human security is read as qualifying human life in a biopolitical form (what Agamben calls 'bare life'), and thus rendering humans amenable to the potential exercise of sovereign power. This potential exercise of sovereign power appears in the work that human security performs on behalf of laying the groundwork for the suspension of foundational elements of conventional inter-state law (e.g. the suspension of the rights of sovereignty and territorial inviolability as advanced in the responsibility to protect doctrine) by assisting in defining 'cases of violence which so genuinely "shock the conscience of mankind", or which present such a clear and present danger to international security, that they require coercive military intervention' (ICISS 2001: 31). Thus, in the concept of human security we find not only elements of governmentality which operate on the field of the health and welfare of populations, but we also find the groundwork for the potential articulation of sovereign power, which draws from life constituted as bare in order to justify or authorize international interventions.

Biopower and sovereign power

In *The History of Sexuality*, Foucault describes biopower as a form of power which has as its goal the 'subjugation of bodies and . . . control of populations' (1979: 93). In contrast to disciplinary power which centred on the body of the individual, biopower 'massifies' power by having as its object the general mass of the population (Foucault 2003: 243). However, as with disciplinary power, biopower continues to function at the capillary or micro-political level of the individual, while at the same time drawing from technologies of power which target the individual from the vantage point of the mass of the population. With the particular and the collective as their plane of operation, the strategies and tactics of biopower which emerged out of the eighteenth century are also marked by having the health and welfare of the population as their main target. In other words, biopower is understood by Foucault as a form of power which seeks to improve life or make life live by developing rationalities and technologies used by the state and other authorities which are meant to, for instance, combat disease or foster the mental and physical wellbeing of the population. As such, the health and welfare of the population becomes for the first time a properly political problem and is central to the emerging 'art of government'. As Stuart Elden notes quoting Foucault, such a form of power meant a fundamental shift in the contract between the state and the people. With biopower, the contract 'has moved from a territorial pact where [the state] is the guarantor of frontiers – "you will be able to live in peace in your frontiers" – to a pact of population: "you will be guaranteed"' (2007: 563).

With life and population as its main targets, Foucault then lays out the main distinction between forms of biopower and the main economy of power that preceded it, namely the power of sovereignty. In *Society must be Defended*, Foucault writes:

> Beneath that great absolute power, beneath the dramatic and somber absolute power that was the power of sovereignty, and which consisted in the power to take life, we now have the emergence, with this technology of biopower, of this technology of power over 'the' population as such, over men insofar as they are living beings. It is continuous, scientific, and it is the power to make live. Sovereignty took life and let live. And now we have the emergence of a power that I would call the power of regularization, and it, in contrast, consists in making live and letting die.
>
> (Foucault 2003: 247)

Thus, biopower is 'the power to make live' whereas the power of sovereignty ultimately rested on 'the right to kill' (Foucault 2003: 240–47). As such, Foucault's understanding of the power of sovereignty approximates an understanding of the old sovereign right invested in the king's body and later in the state. Sovereignty is seen as the principle and practice enshrined in the juridical order which reserves in the last instance the right to use deadly force in the enforcement of its order, both within and beyond its borders. Thus, with biopower we have a form of power that massifies and reaches into a widening array of social fields by working at the capillary level in order to manage the health and welfare of the population; whereas with the power of sovereignty we have a form of centralized power which, in reserving the right to kill, claims to be absolute.

In contrasting a form of power that seeks to make life live with another that reserves the right to kill, the temptation is to see the two forms of power as incompatible, and, at least potentially, working against each other. However, Foucault also described how the power of sovereignty could circulate *within* biopower. In order for this to take place, he argued that 'caesuras within the biological continuum' had to be introduced (Foucault 2003: 255). These breaks were provided by bringing racism into the analysis of the technologies and rationalities of biopower. As Thomas Lemke highlights, modern racism for Foucault is 'a vital technology since it guarantees the function of death in an economy of bio-power. Racism allows for a fragmentation of the social that facilitates a hierarchical differentiation between good and bad races' (2005: 8). In doing so, racism can be seen as introducing into biopower the principle of sovereignty insofar as it allows for a distinction to be made between a within and a without; or between an inclusion and an exclusion. In a sense, racism allows biopower to appropriate and deploy within the population the boundary drawing labour of sovereignty.

In bringing the power of sovereignty into the realm of biopower, racism also tends to unmoor sovereignty from its old friend/enemy distinction as embodied in the juridico-institutional model of territorial sovereign state. As the power of sovereignty enters the terrain of biopower, Foucault argued that the war-like relationship of the friend/enemy distinction as the ordering principle of state sovereignty that we find in Schmitt's work would be replaced by a biological relationship. In this scenario, the figure of the enemy no longer appears as an opponent or rival but has a tendency to become framed as a threat to the biological life of the population. Foucault argues:

> [. . .] racism makes it possible to establish a relationship between my life and the death of the other that is not a military or warlike relationship of confrontation, but a biological-type relationship. [. . .] And the reason this mechanism can come into play is that the enemies who have to be done away with are not adversaries in the political sense of the term; they are threats, either external or internal, to the population and for the population. [. . .] Once the State functions in the biopower mode, racism alone can justify the murderous function of the State.
>
> (2003: 255–56)

From Foucault's perspective, the caesuras introduced by racism allow sovereignty's right to kill to operate in relation to the health and welfare functions of biopower. Biopower incorporates sovereignty as a technology of power which is capable of drawing the necessary lines between populations that will be made to live, and those that form a generalized threat and will be allowed to die or, in more extreme cases, be killed. Once the power of sovereignty enters into a biological relationship, the category of the enemy tends to lose its political standing. Rather, the category is assimilated to a generalized threat which is seen as threatening the health and well-being of the population not unlike other threats such as disease, overpopulation or economic crises. Thus, both forms of power can coexist despite what may appear as contradictory logics between making life live and taking life.

In *Homo Sacer*, Giorgio Agamben sets out explicitly to rearrange the relationship between biopower and sovereign power suggested in Foucault's work. Rather than seeing biopower as merely a modern form of power and intimating that it has displaced or somehow subsumed the power of sovereignty and the juridical order, Agamben argues that '*the production of a biopolitical body is the original activity of sovereign power*' (1998: 6 (emphasis in the original)). In other words, for Agamben, sovereign power is not secondary but rather is intimately bound up with the production of biopower as a form of power which has life as its primary terrain. In speaking in terms of origins, Agamben makes it clear that we need to consider the connection between biopower and sovereign power far before Foucault had envisioned it; and we also need to reconsider the relationship between the two that Foucault had proposed. Indeed, Agamben claims that the seeds for a form of power which has life as its field of operation were laid in Aristotelian thought. He argues that as soon as the originary division between *zoē* which 'expressed the simple fact of living common to all living beings (animals, men or gods)' and *bios* which 'indicated the form or way of living proper to an individual or a group' (Agamben 1998: 1) was made, a life amenable to sovereign power was potentially at hand even though sovereignty itself had yet to emerge. However, whereas the ancients saw such a division as necessary for the separation of politics from the mundane task of sustaining life, western modernity and the juridico-institutional model of the sovereign nation-state with its attendant forms of governance has tended to make *zoē* the central frame for all politics. For Agamben, once the sustenance of life becomes the primary terrain of politics, it opens itself to political calculations and thus decisions (i.e. acts of sovereignty) which will operate along life's only continuum: life/death; making live/letting die; sustaining life/killing life. Such calculations become the political drive for the emergence of the extreme experiences in the west during the twentieth century, which for Agamben culminate in the Nazi death camps.[3] He then illustrates the end logic of the calculations that lead to these death camps through the concept of the state exception and the figure of *homo sacer* (or bare life).

As Agamben writes, 'the state of exception is an anomic space in which what is at stake is a force of law without law' (2005: 39). In their more dramatic and concrete forms, states of exception have historically taken the form of emergencies, insurrections, martial law or war. In these situations, law is declared to have been suspended by state authorities in one form or another, but the force that law assumes remains. Contrary to liberal theory, sovereign power for Agamben is thus structured by the exception rather than the law or a social contract between the people and the sovereign. In the state of exception, *homo sacer* embodies a form of life that is revealed as bare, Agamben argues, because the life of *homo sacer* can be suspended by sovereign power. Life lived in death camps was life subject to being killed at the whim of authorities and without the act of killing constituting a homicide or a sacrifice.[4] While camps appeared as exceptional spaces outside of normal society and its laws, they were spaces which were constituted as such through sovereign power's ability to create them legally via a declaration of a state of exception. It is in this sense that the humans that found themselves in such camps were included within the juridical order through an exclusion; or rather they were included by the very fact of being excluded. Agamben thus identifies *homo sacer* as the human that is proper to the exercise of sovereign power because the life of *homo sacer* is rendered possible by sovereign power's ability to declare a state of exception. Importantly, such a life then must be understood as not being reserved or limited to 'non-citizens', i.e. those outside the juridical order. Rather, each and all are potentially *homo sacer* to sovereign power because each and all face the possibility that sovereign power can, by declaring a state of exception, suspend life in ways that would render it bare. Thus, sovereign power marks the moment when the mere fact of living (*zoē*) of each and all is held open to being politicized at the hands of sovereign power.

In tying sovereign power to the logic of the exception Agamben then clearly retains as central to the modern condition the connection between biopower and the juridical order, the latter of which Foucault saw as secondary to the emerging economy of power of governmentality. In doing so, he also retains the old paradox of sovereignty as a form of power which is at once inside and outside the law. As such, Agamben continues to see sovereignty in Schmittean terms as 'he who decides on the exception' (Schmitt 1985: 5). Sovereign power is the power of acting both without and within the legal order: without the law in having the power to decide to suspend the existing legal order in self-defined and self-authorized exceptional circumstances, yet remaining within the law as he to whom the juridical order grants the power to suspend its own validity. However, contrary to Schmitt, the state of exception for Agamben is not merely a juridical act, but is above all an ability to determine forms of life or to qualify life. He writes:

> If the exception is the structure of sovereignty, then sovereignty is not an exclusively political concept, an exclusively juridical category, a power external to law (Schmitt), or the supreme rule of the juridical order (Hans Kelsen): it is the originary structure in which law refers to life and includes it in itself by suspending it.
>
> (1998: 28)

This means that in order for sovereign power to exist in juridical terms, life qualified as bare must be made available. Without bare life sovereign power would be unable to constitute itself as it would not find a form of life amenable to its exercise.

While many authors have recently used Agamben's work to read the 'exceptional times' of the contemporary period (see for instance Huysmans (2008); Aradau (2007); Willis (2006); and Edkins *et al.* (2004)), the implications of his reading of sovereign power, biopower and the juridical order extends far deeper than what appear as extraordinary or unique historical moments. Indeed, within the context of late modernity, what appears to be the exception, i.e. sovereign's power ability to suspend life and render it bare, comes to determine the rule.[5] This is the case not only because the contemporary moment appears to be marked by governance as permanent crisis (Diken and Laustsen (2002)), but also because the point of reference which drives all 'normal political life' becomes the form of life lived in the exception. Nowhere does this appear more evident than in the expansion of the language of human rights in the post-WWII era. Following Hannah Arendt, Agamben's reading brings to light the profound irony of the expansion of human rights (1998: 126–35).[6] At the same time that human rights are declared at the end of the eighteenth century to be the 'rights of man' implying the universality of rights, they are immediately framed by the nationality and nativity of citizenship, which has the effect of tying them almost inextricably to the sovereign state and the inter-state system. Moreover, as rights progress, they are increasingly framed in terms of rights to the sustenance of life (Caldwell 2004: para. 50). This appears to be even more acute in the language of international human rights than is the case in the national sphere. Thus, drawing from an Agambenian perspective, what is often perceived to be the central turning point in the struggle to codify universal human rights and thereby begin the process of curtailing from above the impunity of sovereignty (which culminates in such institutions as the International Criminal Court (ICC)) can be seen as actually furthering the labour of defining and entrenching political life in its biopolitical form which, as we saw earlier, are precisely the conditions that render sovereign power possible. Much of the language of universal human rights is built on the figure of a human for whom the provision of the basic necessities of life (food, shelter, health and security) is understood as the basic and ultimate defining goal. In this light, extending the language of human rights to the international realm expands the terrain of sovereign power to 'humanity' by setting the terms of humanity's political life in a biopolitical form (Caldwell 2004). The troubling conclusion then is that rather than somehow working against sovereignty, or domesticating the international as many liberal scholars propose, international human rights law actually opens the conditions of possibility for an exercise of global sovereign power by defining at the global level life biopolitically. In other words, the life defined in the language of human rights is precisely the form of life that feeds sovereign power. Once the language of international human rights qualifies and codifies humanity's life as bare, the legal and biopolitical ground is set for potential acts of sovereign power with the globe as their plane of operation. Such acts of sovereign power can come in the form of international interventions that take place through the suspension of certain foundational elements of international law often in the name of securing insecure (bare) life. As we will explore later, we can read the concept of human security as furthering this process in its extreme by centring the language of human rights almost exclusively in biopolitical terms. As noted at the onset of this chapter, in the name of human rights and human development, human security labours to identify 'the threshold below which human life is intolerably threatened'. Not only does human security define life biopolitically, it also works towards legitimating the possibility that killing life (without homicide or sacrifice) to protect life may be unavoidable if military intervention is deemed necessary once all other options have failed.

Biopower, sovereign power and human security

In (re)defining security threats as above all threats to human life, what we argue in this section is that the central labour of the concept of human security begins by defining the human and human life in biopolitical terms. This is the case for both the broad 'freedom from want' (as it emerged with the 1994 UNDP Human Development Report and institutionalized through the UN Commission on Human Security and the UN Human Security Unit) and narrow 'freedom from fear' (as formulated by the *Responsibility to Protect* doctrine and the 2005 World Summit Outcome Document) understandings of the concept of human security. However, whereas the broad conceptions of human security tend to operate on the terrain of the biopolitics of governmentality, the more narrow formulations bring to light the relationship between sovereign power and biopower examined previously.

Human security, biopolitics, and governmentality

The formal origins of the concept of human security stem from the changing humanitarian concerns of the UN as it was confronted with the end of the Cold War. The most well-recognized early move came in the UNDP's 1994 report which furthered the process of shifting the referent of security from the state to the individual and tying security to the issue of development and human rights.[7] As advanced by the report, security was to be understood as emerging from the 'legitimate concerns of ordinary people who s[eek] security in their daily lives' (UNDP 1994: 22). Shifting the referent of security to the individual also obviously entailed shifting the perception of the origins of threats. Ranging from the chronic and quotidian – 'hunger, disease and repression' – to the sudden and disastrous – 'hurtful disruptions in the patterns of daily life' (UNDP 1994: 23) – security threats were to the be understood as no longer tied to the particular interests of the state, but rather tied to the 'universal concern[s]' (UNDP 1994: 22) of all people. The often quoted seven dimensions of security threats identified by the report (economic, food, health, environmental, personal, community and political security) were in part a tactical move in trying to raise the level of concern for human development among state representatives by explicitly drawing from the high value content of security (MacFarlane and Foong Khong 2006: 148). At the same time; however, this initial move sought to transcend the state insofar as it brought into question its role as a provider of security relative to other actors – e.g. IOs, NGOs and non-military government agencies – while simultaneously suggesting that state military actions and priorities (e.g. spending on defence) were potential sources of insecurity.

In shifting its referent from the state to the individual and in making the quotidian conditions of life rather than extraordinary history-making moments the primary field from which security threats emerge, human security as initially formulated combines two key elements that are central to the potential establishment of a regime of global governmentality which has the health and welfare of populations as its frame of intervention. The first and most obvious element is that human security clearly defines the human and security threats in biopolitical terms. Indeed, the threats to human life rather than traditional military threats to the state are the nodal point which ties the spectrum of human security definitions from broad to narrow. The second key element is that human security operates on the terrain of contingency by defining these threats as emerging from everyday lived life. As with Foucault's understanding of the forms of governmental rationalities which sought to manage through statistical knowledge of the population the problems that emerged from the contingent (disease, economic crisis, birth rates and so on), the shift towards human security can be read as an effort to develop forms of governmental rationalities at the international and global level which also seek to respond to and manage threats perceived as emerging from the contingency of life.

Initially, the attempt to develop governmental rationalities based on a human security perspective was largely limited to properly assessing and measuring threats to human life. Without the proper 'data set', a true account of human insecurity would be lacking. One of the examples of this effort can be found in the 2005 Human Security Report which claimed that 'no annual publication maps the trends in the incidence, severity, causes and consequences of global violence as comprehensively' (Human Security Centre 2005: viii) as the report. This effort to map the 'real' threats to human life within a post-Cold War environment was modeled on the UNDP's Human Development Reports. The governmental rationalities that have since privileged the connection between human security and development have been particularly present in the Japanese-sponsored Commission on Human Security and the subsequent work of the UN's Human Security Unit created in 2004. As the UN system has sought to mainstream the concept of human security, funding has started to target specific development programmes with a stated focus on human security. The UN Trust Fund for Human Security (UNTFHS) reports that over 180 projects in some 60 countries have employed and sought to operationalize the concept of human security from 1999 to 2008. According to their funding parameters, these projects are meant to provide 'concrete and sustainable benefits to people and communities threatened in their survival, livelihood and dignity' (UNTFHS 2008: 2). The parameters further stipulate that projects should utilize a 'top-down protection' and 'bottom-up empowerment' framework which is intended to promote partnerships with a variety of entities (civil society groups, NGOs, and other local entities) through an integrated (i.e. multi-UN agency including such bodies as UNDP, FAO, UNICEF, UNHCR, ILO, WFP, UNFPA, OHCHR, IOM, UNODC and WHO[8]) and multi-sectoral (i.e. conflict and poverty, displacement and health, education and conflict prevention) approach. A recent sampling provided by the UN Human Security Unit detailed how projects: collaborated with UN agencies and the provincial government of Ituri to enhance the delivery of education and healthcare services; helped government ministries train police officers and members of administrative and judicial offices in the western Department of Sonsonate, El Savador; aided in ensuring access to basic health and social services for rural communities in the Semipalatinsk nuclear testing area; assisted local governments in training entrepreneurs in the municipalities of North and South Mitrovice/a and Zvecan, Kosovo; facilitated improving farming techniques in rural communities in post-conflict Liberia; partnered with government and civil society in Moldova to provide assistance to victims of human trafficking; provided training in partnership with international NGOs and other UN bodies for alternative livelihoods to ex-poppy farming households in Shan state, Myanmar; and helped enhance disaster prevention tools in collaboration with NGOs and the local and national authorities to assist the vulnerable communities of Quispicanchis and Carabaya in Peru (Human Security Unit 2009: 15–32).[9]

With such a broad range of human security projects, one would be hard pressed not to conclude that almost any 'sustainable human development' project has a human security component. Indeed, a more thorough assessment of the projects goes further in revealing the slipperiness of the concept in that it can be grafted to almost any initiative from funding sports and art workshops to training police, educators and healthcare providers. It was reported that the broadness of the concept was even formally debated during the 2008 thematic debates on human security in the UN's General Assembly which was held as a follow-up to the 2005 World Summit. Some participating member states highlighted how human security was at risk of 'conceptual overstretch'. They warned that if everything became subsumed under human security, the concept would no longer have any added value and would limit its 'operational applicability' (UN General Assembly 2008: 2). In analytical terms this may indeed be an accurate evaluation of human security; however, from the reading we are developing here, the breadth of the concept is explained by having tied its understanding of security threats to the life of the human. Once security is attached to quotidian life, and by extension the contingency of life itself, then potentially everything is open to the logic of (in)security. This sheds new light on what Foucault (2007: 45) meant when he said that apparatuses of security 'have the constant tendency to expand; they are centrifugal' once population and contingency become the terrain of security. Thus, if as Duffield (2007: 114) argues, the real valued added of human security is as a 'mobilizing, integrating and colonizing concept of post-Cold War international governance' it is precisely because human security defines the human and threats to human life in biopolitical terms. Such grounds render the concept of human security amenable to the 'complex forms of global coordination involving multi-levelled state–non-state agreement and extensive divisions of labour between governments, UN agencies, NGOs, private companies, civil society groups and militaries' (Duffield 2007: 114) because security is biopoliticized. From this standpoint, the question of its analytical purchase and operationalization for state representatives becomes secondary in that it is precisely the performative dimension of the concept as a quilting point for mobilization and coordination among complex assemblage of governmental authorities that becomes central once life of the human species becomes security's referent. This helps to explain why, despite the diplomatic controversy surrounding the concept (see notably Bellamy (2009a) and (2009b)), particularly in the post-9/11 context, it has continued to inform and be advanced by the foreign policy of countries like Japan and organizations such as the EU and the UN (on the EU and human security see Kaldor *et al.* (2007) and the Study Group on Europe's Security Capabilities (2004)). If the purchase of human security has remained, it is, we argue, precisely because it has tied concerns for security to the provision of the sustenance of life, thereby allowing it to frame almost any development initiative as a human security concern.

The connection between human security and development, as explored earlier, assists in laying the groundwork for micro-level interventions associated with the development of a regime of global governmentality which has the health and welfare of populations as its plane of operation. However, this is only one dimension of the labour human security performs on behalf of preparing a ground open to forms of intervention. The more controversial end of the debate surrounding human security has often entailed opposition to the concept's potential use in helping to authorize military interventions to protect civilian populations based on humanitarian goals. What we will argue hereafter is that this potential points to the relationship between biopolitics and sovereign power elaborated via Agamben's work earlier.

Human security, biopolitics and sovereign power

The more narrow conception of human security which has been associated with the notion of 'freedom from fear' is generally understood to have emerged from the *Responsibility to Protect* report authored by the International Commission on Intervention and State Sovereignty in 2001. Focused on developing a set of international norms that would direct the conduct of states and the international community in 'extreme and exceptional cases' (ICISS 2001: 31), the report signaled a shift away from the broad development concerns of the Human Development Reports. In contrast to the broad panoply of threats which informed the UNDP's understanding of human security, the threats are narrowed down to 'violent threats to individuals' (Human Security Centre 2005: viii) such as 'mass murder and rape, ethnic cleansing by forcible expulsion and terror, and deliberate starvation and exposure to disease' (Report of the Secretary General's High-level Panel on Threats, Challenges and Change 2004: 65). Emphasis shifted from an understanding of threats which stem from a broad set of political, social, economic and environmental contingencies which emerge from the contingency of daily life, to what was deemed to be the 'avoidable catastrophe[s]' of gross violations of human rights (High Level Panel on Threats, Challenges and Change 2004: 65). While the life of human beings continues to be security's referent, the role of the state in the provision of security and insecurity is brought back into prominent focus. With this return of the state, we also see a return to the central question of the legitimate use of violence and the monopoly of its means in the form of potential military interventions as a response of last resort to gross violations of human rights held as inviolable. As such, this re-coupling of state and security is not framed in terms of territorial inviolability but in relation to the inviolability of the most fundamental universal human rights: the right to life and security of person (Art. 3, UDHR). Within this framework, security is tied to the ability or inability of the state to fulfill its responsibility to protect the human beings within its care.

At play in defining internationally the parameters of a responsibility to protect is not only the development of new norms of intervention, but also, and perhaps most importantly, we find a significant discussion regarding the minimal threshold of life that would authorize the legitimate suspension of a foundational component of conventional inter-state law. In other words, we can isolate an effort to establish and bring into law a set of norms that concurrently call for the suspension of certain foundational elements of international law in 'cases of violence which so genuinely "shock the conscience of mankind," or which present such a clear and present danger to international security, that they require coercive military intervention' on the part of the international community (ICISS 2001: 31). In this, the concept of human security plays a central role by identifying and defining those extreme and exceptional circumstances that not only set the conditions for the suspension of the law but also for its refounding in the language of new international norms on intervention. However, this suspension of conventional inter-state law in the name of human security entails more than the temporary hiatus of the international juridical order. Returning to Agamben, the relationship between the exercise of sovereign power and the state of exception is tied to the form of human life that is rendered bare. For Agamben, this structural feature of sovereign power's relationship to life is made most evident in exceptional circumstances. In the reading provided here, human security performs an important task as it assists in the delineation of these circumstances by sovereign power. It does so, as we have seen, by initially constructing the data set that informs the exceptional circumstances that define the range of threats to human life. This begs the question: how does human security contribute to the legitimation of the law's suspension when the norms of its discourse have not yet been codified in international law? In operating inside and outside the law in its efforts to codify the authorization of international intervention on humanitarian grounds, human security can be understood here in Agambenian terms as functioning in a zone of indistinction in relation to the law. This zone of indistinction is made evident by the fact that this authorization has yet to receive the status of international law and yet it must invoke the force that law normally assumes. The human security discourse thus finds itself complicit in the paradox of sovereign power in relation to the law: it must suspend international law while simultaneously invoking its force.

Where the broad range of the discourse of human security assists most clearly in the exercise of sovereign power is in its definition of human life as measured by the basic threshold required to sustain life. As illustrated earlier, this narrow conception of human security originated most clearly with the ICISS report and was formalized and institutionalized through the General Assembly's 2005 World Summit Outcome Document and Security Council Resolution 1674 adopted in April 2006. The potential exercise of sovereign power in the form of humanitarian interventions is tied to instances in which the gross violation of the most basic rights is deemed to be taking place in moments of 'hurtful disruptions in the patterns of daily life'. The troubling relationship between sovereign power and human rights identified by Agamben and explored earlier in this chapter emerges clearly in the narrow conception of human security. Indeed, human security defines humanity's political life biopolitically in the extreme; not only because it limits what is understood as human rights to the most basic threshold of life, but also because it defines human rights within the explicit context of moments marked by 'crisis' and 'emergency'. It thus further helps set the ground for the potential exercise of sovereign power via the ability of authorities to declare a state of exception in response to crises and emergencies. As Caldwell (2004: para 31) notes in her reading of Agamben, 'human rights and sovereignty share the same referent: an indeterminate and precarious bare life.' However, for Agamben, this relationship between human rights and sovereignty tends to remain 'secret' (1998: 133) in that the expansion of the language of human rights often appears in the form of efforts to curtail sovereign power. What can be brought to light with regards to the present reading, is that through the human security discourse this secret solidarity between human rights and sovereign power is not only laid open but it is also trumpeted.[10] It is laid open and trumpeted because the intent of human security is to compel sovereign power to intervene on behalf of protecting those most basic rights that it defines, and defines human life in biopolitical terms in order to do so.

Conclusion

This chapter has argued that the concept of human security enables a unique exercise of sovereign power and biopower which runs counter to the aims of those who read this concept as a further development of a humanist or cosmopolitan ethics. The work of Foucault and Agamben, we argued, offers us a vantage point from which to develop a reading of human security that unveils this exercise of sovereign power and biopower. Human security assembles these two forms of power by making human life the primary referent for security and by defining the human and security threats in biopolitical terms. Such a concept has shown itself as instrumental in setting the ground for the further development of a global regime of governmentality in which micro and macro levels of intervention have become increasingly necessary not only to manage the provision of the sustenance of life but also to respond to the needs of governing a world increasingly framed in terms of crisis and emergency.

Notes

1 This chapter draws from an analysis initially developed in de Larrinaga and Doucet (2008). The first draft was presented at the ISA-Canada/Canadian Political Science Association (CPSA) meeting, Carleton University, Ottawa, May 26–29, 2009. We would like to thank Colleen Bell as well as the other panelists and participants for their useful comments. As always, any errors or omissions remain the sole responsibility of the authors.

2 On the concept of sustainable human development, see for instance Duffield (2005)and (2004) and Duffield and Waddell (2006) and (2004).
3 Using Arendt, Patricia Owens (2009) notes that Agamben's reading of the Nazi death camps tends to gloss over their uniqueness in terms of the form of total domination they put into practice.
4 On the unavailability of sacrifice within the context of the current war in Iraq as drawn from an Agambenian reading, see the excellent piece by Pin-Fat and Stern (2005).
5 It is for this reason that Agamben makes the bold claim that sovereign power's ability to declare the state of exception is in fact 'the hidden foundation' of the entire western political system (1998: 8–9). As soon as a form of non political life is defined, i.e. bare life, the terrain is set for sovereign power to hold all life as potentially bare.
6 On Owens' reading (2009), there are, however, very important differences between Agamben and Arendt which must not be neglected. Most significantly, for Arendt human rights open possibilities which extend beyond sovereignty's grasp.
7 An account of the history of the concept of human security as it unfolded in the UN system is provided by MacFarlane and Foong Khong (2006) and Bellamy (2009b).
8 United Nations Development Programme (UNDP), Food and Agriculture Organization (FAO), United Nations Children's Fund (UNICEF), United Nations High Commissioner for Refugees (UNHCR), International Labour Organization (ILO), United Nations World Food Programme (WFP), United Nations Population Fund (UNFPA), Office of the High Commissioner for Human Rights (OHCHR), International Organization for Migration (IOM), United Nations Office on Drugs and Crime (UNODC), World Health Organization (WHO).
9 More detailed scholarly analyses of the application of the concept of human security are found in MacLean *et al.* (2006) as well as Thomas and Tow (2002).
10 What should, however, be made clear here is that we are not advocating a wholesale rejection of humanitarianism, but shedding light on the potential dangers of further defining humanitarianism in terms of the provision of life defined biopolitically. On the possibility of responding to or moving beyond bare life, see Owens (forthcoming) and Edkins and Pin-Fat (2005).

Bibliography

Agamben, G. (1998) *Homo Sacer: Sovereign Power and Bare Life*, Stanford CA: Stanford University Press.
—— (2005) *State of Exception*, trans. by Kevin Attell, Chicago: University of Chicago Press.
Aradau, C. (2007) 'Law Transformed: Guantánamo and the "Other" Exception', *Third World Quarterly* 28 (3): 489–501.
Bellamy, A. J. (2009a) 'Realizing the Responsibility to Protect', *International Studies Perspectives* 10 (2): 11–128.
—— (2009b) *Responsibility to Protect: The Global Effort to End Mass Atrocities*, Cambridge: Polity Press.
Caldwell, A. (2004) 'Bio-Sovereignty and the Emergence of Humanity', *Theory & Event* 7 (2) pages n.a.
de Larrinaga, M. and Doucet, M. G. (2008) 'Sovereign Power and the Biopolitics of Human Security', *Security Dialogue* 39 (5): 497–517.
Diken, B. and Laustsen, C. B. (2002) 'Security, Terror, and Bare Life', *Space & Culture* 5 (3): 290–307.
Duffield, M. (2004) 'Carry on Killing: Global Governance, Humanitarianism and Terror', *Working Paper 23*, Copenhagen: Danish Institute for International Studies.
—— (2005) *'Human Security: Linking Development and Security in an Age of Terror'*, paper prepared

for the German Development Institute (GDI) panel 'New Interfaces Between Security and Development', 11th General Conference of the European Association of Development Research and Training Institutes (EADI), Bonn, 21–24 September.

—— (2007) *Development, Security and Unending War: Governing the World of Peoples*, Cambridge: Polity Press.

Duffield, M. and Waddell, N. (2004) *'Human Security and Global Danger: Exploring a Governmental Assemblage'*, Department of Politics and International Relations, University of Lancaster. Online. Available URL: http://www.bond.org.uk/pubs/gsd/duffield.pdf (accessed 21 December 2006).

—— (2006) 'Securing Humans in a Dangerous World', *International Politics* 43 (1): 1–23.

Edkins, J. and Pin-Fat, V. (2005) 'Through the Wire: Relations of Power and Relations of Violence', *Millennium: Journal of International Studies* 34 (1): 1–24.

Edkins, J., Pin-Fat, V. and Shapiro, M.J. (eds) (2004) *Sovereign Lives: Power in Global Politics*, New York: Routledge.

Elden, S. (2007) 'Governmentality, Calculation, Territory', *Environment and Planning D: Society and Space* 25 (3): 562–80.

Foucault, M. (1979) *The History of Sexuality, Vol. 1: Introduction*, Harmondsworth: Penguin.

—— (2003) *Society must be Defended: Lectures at the Collège de France 1975–1976*, trans. by David Macey, New York: Picador.

—— (2007) *Security, Territory, Population: Lectures at the Collège de France 1977–1978*, trans. Graham Burchell. Houndmills: Palgrave Macmillan.

Human Security Centre (2005) *The Human Security Report 2005*, Oxford: Oxford University Press.

Human Security Unit, Office for the Co-ordination of Humanitarian Affairs (2009) *Human Security in Theory and Practice: An Overview of the Human Security Concept and the United Nations Trust Fund for Human Security*. Available URL: http://www.ochaonline.un.org/Reports/tabid/2186/language/en-US/Default.aspx (accessed 20 May 2009).

Huysmans, J. (2008) 'The Jargon of Exception – On Schmitt, Agamben and the Absence of Political Society', *International Political Sociology* 2 (2): 165–83.

International Commission on Intervention and State Sovereignty (ICISS) (2001) *The Responsibility to Protect*, International Development Research Center (IDRC), Ottawa.

Kaldor, M., Martin, M. and Selchow, S. (2007) 'Human Security: A New Strategic Narrative for Europe', *International Affairs* 83 (2): 273–88.

Lemke, T. (2005) 'A Zone of Indistinction – A Critique of Giorgio Agamben's Concept of the Biopolitics', *Outlines* (1): 3–13.

MacFarlane, S. N. and Foong Khong, Y. (eds) (2006) *Human Security and the UN: A Critical History*, Bloomington, IN: Indiana University Press.

MacLean, S. J., Black, D. R. and Shaw, T. M. (eds) (2006) *A Decade of Human Security: Global Governance and New Multilateralisms*, Hampshire: Ashgate.

Neal, A. (2004) 'Cutting Off the King's Head: Foucault's Society Must Be Defended and the Problem of Sovereignty', *Alternatives: Global, Local, Political* 29 (5): 373–98.

Owens, P. (forthcoming) 'Beyond Bare Life: Refugees and the "Right to Have Rights"', in Alexander Betts and Gil Loescher (eds) *Refugees in International Relations*, Oxford: Oxford University Press.

Pin-Fat, V. and Stern, M. (2005) 'The Scripting of Private Jessica Lynch: Biopolitics, Gender, and the "Feminization" of the U.S. Military', *Alternatives: Global, Local, Political* 30 (1): 25–53.

Report of the Secretary General's High-Level Panel on Threats, Challenges and Change

(2004) *A More Secure World: Our Shared Responsibility*, New York: United Nations Department of Public Information.

Schmitt, C. (1985) *Political Theology: Four Chapters on the Concept of Sovereignty*, Massachusetts: MIT Press.

Study Group on Europe's Security Capabilities (2004) *A Human Security Doctrine for Europe: The Barcelona Report of the Study Group on Europe's Security Capabilities*, 15 September 2004. Available URL: http://www.centrodirittiumani.unipd.it/a_laurea/esami/ppsuenu/HSDoctrineEurope.pdf (accessed 20 May 2009).

Thomas, N. and Tow, W. T. (2002) 'The Utility of Human Security: Sovereignty and Humanitarian Intervention', *Security Dialogue* 33 (2): 177–92.

United Nations (2005) *'2005 World Summit Outcome'*, A/RES/60/1. Available URL: http://www.un.org/summit2005/documents.html (accessed 17 April 2007).

United Nations Development Program (UNDP) (1994) *New Dimensions of Human Security*, Human Development Report 1994, Oxford: Oxford University Press.

United Nations General Assembly (2008) *Summary of the General Assembly Thematic Debate on Human Security*, 62nd session, Available URL: http://www.un.org/ga/president/62/ThematicDebates/humansecurity.shtml (accessed 20 May 2009).

United Nations Trust Fund for Human Security (UNTFHS) (2008) *Guidelines for the United Nations Trust Fund for Human Security*, New York, Fourth Revision, 17 March.

Willis, S. (2006) 'Guantanamo's Symbolic Economy', *New Left Review* 39: 123–31.

11 Problematizing life under biopower

A Foucauldian versus an Agambenite critique of human security

Suvi Alt[1]

Although the contemporary world is often described as being plagued by insecurity, uncertainty, breakdown, alienation and despair, there is also a parallel discourse that celebrates the possibilities of human rights, human development and, more recently, human security. Humanity and security are often interlinked in both contemporary international relations theory and practice, the discourse of human security being one of the most interesting examples of the nexus between 'humanity' and 'security'. The concept of human security was first coined in the 1994 *Human Development Report* of the United Nations Development Programme (UNDP), but the idea of developing more 'human' understandings of security is part of a larger process of redefining security that began in the 1970s and 1980s. The end of the Cold War, the spread of globalization and democratization, the strengthened role of NGOs and the transformation of the role of the state are some of the most significant changes in the international system that have contributed to an alteration of conceptions of security (Tadjbakhsh and Chenoy 2009:1).

Despite human security often being described as 'a radical, rather optimistic package' (Gasper 2005: 234) and 'exactly the paradigm needed for the South today' (Tadjbakhsh and Chenoy 2009: 37), the concept has also received a lot of criticism. However, much of this critique has not been directed at problematizing the assumptions about both 'security' and 'the human,' which the discourse of human security underwrites.[2] 'Security' is often left unproblematized in the human security discourse and problematizing the 'human' of human security is a road even less travelled. Only lately has there been a growing body of works that engage critically with these concepts. These works originate from Foucauldian points of departure and many also draw on the work of Giorgio Agamben.[3]

In political science and international relations, the works of Agamben and Foucault have often been used together, and even conflated. For instance, in Chapter 10 of this volume, Doucet and de Larrinaga, drawing on the works of Foucault and Agamben, approach human security as an instrument of the contemporary assemblage of biopower and sovereign power. They focus on human security as the 'responsibility to protect,' thereby emphasizing the role of sovereign power. This chapter, in contrast, examines material which offers a broader conception of human security. This broader conception of human security is most clearly spelt out in the *Human Security Now* (2003) report by the Commission on

Human Security, Survival, Livelihood and Dignity (CHS). The broad conception of human security is based on the view that health as well as social and economic welfare (freedom from want) are as important to people's security as physical and political security (freedom from fear). Understanding human security in these terms allows for taking the workings of biopower more fully into account. While this chapter also recognizes the intimate relationship between biopower and sovereign power, its main aim is to problematize the widely assumed conflation of Foucault and Agamben. Indeed, this chapter suggests that Foucauldian and Agambenite perspectives offer very different kinds of critiques of human security. Against this background, the aim of this chapter is thus to answer two interrelated questions. First, what are the differences between a Foucauldian and an Agambenite critique of human security? Second, how do these differences play out with regard to conceptions of the human and the agency of the human of biopower?

In essence, the differences between a Foucauldian and an Agambenite critique of human security result from their rather different understandings of life, power and politics. While for Agamben biopower is an ancient phenomenon, for Foucault it is distinctively modern. Whereas Agamben's account of power is essentially metaphysical, for Foucault power is historical and idiomatic. Agamben deals with power on the level of ontology, which leads him to believe in the power of philosophy to bring about social change. In contrast, Foucault understands resistance as internal to power and calls for both practical and theoretical engagement with the discourses that shape our being as subjects. Furthermore, while Agamben sees rights and normative discourse as being irreparably tainted by the power that captures life, Foucault allows for the possibility of using rights as a tactic of resistance. Agamben exhibits great lack of faith in political contestation, while Foucault believes that problematization and competition between discourses can reshape politics.

Most obviously, however, Agamben and Foucault differ in their accounts of the human of biopower. The Foucauldian perspective suggests that the human in the human security discourse is the subject of a power exercised through both technologies of the self and technologies of domination. Human security can thus be read as a technique of biopower that works through administering, regulating and correcting life. An Agambenite reading, in contrast, relates the discussion on human security to the concept of bare life; a form of human (de)subjectivity that forms the core of Agamben's political philosophy. In this volume, de Larrinaga and Doucet frequently refer to the 'form of life' that human security proposes, but their account leaves unexamined the actual content of this form of life, which is said to be amenable to both sovereign power and to biopolitical technologies and rationalities. But can we say that it is the same kind of life that is amenable to both Foucauldian and Agambenite biopolitics? Exploring these differences is important with regard to both the theoretical discussion surrounding biopower and biopolitics in International Relations[4] as well as to the practice of human security and the lives lived by its subjects.

In other words, readings that conflate Agamben with Foucault fail to recognize the very different accounts of life offered by Foucauldian and Agambenite treatments of biopolitics. Furthermore, discussions of Agamben's concept of bare life often leave the implications of ascribing bare life to human security unexamined. This chapter therefore makes explicit how Agamben's philosophical radicalism may be in danger of turning into political passivism when applied as a political analytical tool. In contrast, a Foucauldian account, especially when drawing on his later works, leaves more room for the political agency of the subjects of human security. While the works of both Foucault and Agamben can be used to argue that the discourse of human security limits the potentiality of being human, it is nevertheless necessary to recognize the very different implications for politics these readings entail.

Foucauldian biopoliticized life – Helping others to help themselves

Foucault's work offers ground for various critiques of human security. Although discipline and biopower – as distinct modalities of power – can be considered to raise different problematizations, their close relationship may also make it useful to examine them together. Hence, discipline and biopower can be considered to be working together for the 'subjugation of bodies and control of populations' (Foucault 1990: 140). Biopower is aimed at improving the lives lived by its subjects and works at the level of the population. Unlike discipline, which is addressed to individual bodies, biopower is applied to the mass population and the processes, such as birth, death, production and illness that characterize it (Foucault 2004: 242–43).

In the human security discourse, protection and empowerment are the means through which humans are to be made secure. A key aspect of this is the health of populations. In the *Human Security Now* report, the CHS (2003: 73) argues that 'People further their own security by setting aside savings and investing in physical, financial and human assets (a savings account, health insurance or education),' which is considered to ultimately enable them to be in charge of their own lives. Importantly, it is no longer the state that has the responsibility to resolve peoples' needs for health (Rose 2001: 6). Rather, the CHS (2003: 95) suggests that 'Many of the unnecessary deaths can be prevented by better health behaviour – stopping smoking, eating more healthful foods, getting more exercise, practising safe sex'. 'Health and human security are knowledge-based and socially driven' and, therefore, the population needs to be educated to 'adopt healthful behaviour, seek health services and participate in democratic decision-making to protect their own health' (CHS 2003: 103). The state of health, illness and patterns of diet of populations have thus become of interest to governments and are the variables that techniques of power are interested in (Foucault 1990: 25). However, the use of biopolitical techniques of health promotion do not necessarily only result in better health and greater well-being but also – as a result of normalization – in a limitation of the possible range of action of its subjects.

Furthermore, while good health is considered an end in itself, the CHS (2003: 96) also contends that 'Good health is a precondition for social stability'. Global infectious diseases, for example, pose a problem to states because their 'economic costs are staggering. And government credibility is questioned' (CHS 2003: 98). 'Disease and poverty go hand in hand. So, too, do disease and conflict', the CHS (2003: 95) states. Direct links are thus made between both disease and poverty, and disease and violence. As with health, throughout the *Human Security Now* report, questions of insecurity, violence, illness, ageing and education are discussed with regard to their impact on the economy. This represents the dissemination of biopower through 'distributing the living in the domain of value and utility' (Foucault 1990: 144). HIV/AIDS, for example, is seen as 'having a devastating impact on the most productive segments of the population' and, therefore, with populations ageing, 'keeping the most productive segments of the population healthy will be among the biggest challenges' (CHS 2003: 16).

Practically anything that poses a threat to the construction of active and able humans can be considered a human security threat. Human security aims to construct a mode of being that is economically useful. This aim is entangled with concerns 'to ensure population, to reproduce labor capacity, to perpetuate social relations' (Foucault 1990: 37). Failure to take care of oneself results in harm to others. Therefore, the CHS (2003: 98, 101) also considers self-directed violence as a public health problem. The harm one directs towards one's own body is not a private issue but rather of public concern. Individuals must thus be free to master their lives but only as long as they do not cause harm to the kind of person they are supposed to be (healthy, active and able). In the *Human Security Now* report, insecurity and the threat of violence are thus associated with the poor, the uneducated, the ill as well as those deprived of the rights and responsibilities that a democratic form of government entails. Conversely, 'security' is related to educated, healthy, active, self-caring humans who live in strong democratic states with market economies. Indeed, these factors determine how insecure – and, ultimately, dangerous – a person or group of people is deemed to be.

In addition to strategies that protect people from 'menaces,' human security also includes 'empowerment strategies that enable people to develop their resilience to difficult conditions' (CHS 2003: 10). According to the UNDP (1994: 24), human security aims at making people better able to master their lives themselves so that they would not 'become a burden on society'. The UNDP thus appeals to a neoliberal logic whereby people are encouraged to take more responsibility for their own lives in order to reduce the need for governmental care. Neoliberal policies leave it to the individual to prepare against risks (Foucault 2008: 145). Social risks, such as unemployment, poverty and illness, are thus transformed into problems of 'self-care' (Lemke 2002: 59). As a technology of the self, human security aims to modify people's conduct so as to better contribute to the well-being of all people. Foucault (1997: 97) traces 'the care of the self' back to ancient Greek culture where it was a generally accepted principle that 'one could not attend to oneself without the help of another'. Today, people in all parts of the world also need help to help themselves. In this environment, human security promotes the construction of enterprising, active, rational subjects who can manage and discipline themselves. However, an effective use of the technologies of the self requires governance. The CHS (2003: 68) makes it clear that 'Without effective governance, people are not empowered'.

Agambenite bare life – Inclusive exclusion of the human of human security

In contrast to Doucet and de Larrinaga's chapter in this volume, which starts out with a discussion of Agamben's concept of the 'state of exception', the focus in this chapter is placed on the form of human (de)subjectivity that arises from Agamben's work, namely 'bare life'. Agamben (1998: 1) bases his conceptualization of 'bare life' on the distinction the ancient Greeks made between *zoē* (the living common to all living beings) and *bios* (the form of living characteristic of an individual or a group). In the modern state, the realm of bare life converges with the political realm, producing a zone of indistinction between exclusion and inclusion, bios and zoē (Agamben 1998: 6–9). Agamben sometimes uses the terms 'zoē' and 'bare life' interchangeably, which should not, however, conceal the significant difference between the two. Bare life is the zoē that has been captured by sovereign power (Schaap 2008: 10). Basically, bare life is the politicized form of pure biological life (Mills 2004: 46).

How then is bare life to be understood with regard to human security? Agamben (1998: 179) claims that the discourse of development is so appealing these days, because it coincides with the biopolitical pursuit to produce a people without fracture; a people in which everyone is included (or the people of the excluded is eliminated). In the human security discourse, the quest for a people without fracture is about bringing security to the insecure, health to the unhealthy and possession to the dispossessed: 'human security requires including the excluded' (CHS 2003: 5). Agamben (1998: 133) argues that the problem of humanitarian organizations, despite all good intentions, is that they are only able to conceive of the human as bare life. Only bare life can be the object of aid and protection. Therefore, humanitarianism shares a 'secret solidarity' with the power it is supposed to be critiquing (1998: 133).

Humanitarian emergency strips people of their history, culture and identity (Duffield 2007: 34). Humanitarianism is thus often unable to recognize the distinct forms of life, the bios, of people. And even if it is able to recognize them, it is unable to work with them. Furthermore, the objects of aid are characterized by a profound sense of lack. The lack may be actual (e.g. lack of clean drinking water) but it may also be imagined or relative (e.g. lack of knowledge). Especially in the latter case, the lack is to be addressed by constructing the objects of aid as certain kinds of subjects of human security. It is then the people who refuse to be integrated and assimilated into the national political body that become bare life (Agamben 1998: 179). The project of human security may therefore mean inclusion for those who accept its specific conception of being human but (inclusive) exclusion for those who refuse it. Chandler (2008: 466) pointedly notes that the human security discourse is assumed to have a radical impact because the idea of the 'human' is in itself considered radical and progressive. But how do we conceive of the human? Historically, there is no such thing as a universal or definite definition of the human. The threshold between the human and the inhuman is 'an essentially mobile threshold that, like the borders of geopolitics, moves according to the progress of scientific and political technologies' (Agamben 2002: 156).

According to Agamben (1998: 9–11), modern democracy is aimed at transforming bare life into a way of life, into a particular kind of bios. Western politics has, however, failed to achieve this aim with the result that bare life is included in the *polis* merely through its exclusion (1998: 9–11). The paradox of modernity is that it inevitably produces bare life, but is then unable to tolerate it (Agamben 2000: 34). Human security can thus be regarded as an attempt to alleviate the suffering that is necessarily produced by the international system, which the discourse of human security also supports. According to Youssef (2008: 154), in the Agambenite state of exception that the international order is now in, humans are produced as 'non-rights-bearing, apolitical, nonagentive victims' that are managed through humanitarianism. Can we then say that the subjects of the human security discourse are apolitical and nonagentive victims? Is it not the case, as Neal (2006: 42) argues, that the use of the term 'exception' only serves to reinforce sovereign exceptionalism rather than to critique it? According to Schaap (2008: 16–17), Agamben is positing the existence of a secret transhistorical essence of biopolitics that only his philosophy is able to reveal. Every application of the term exception should therefore be wary of describing political problems as a confirmation of the formal sameness of sovereignty and security over time (Neal 2006: 36). Are we thus ourselves part of the process of de-subjectivizing the people which human security claims to be helping by invoking concepts such as bare life? This is indeed a valid criticism. However, it does not seem to be Agamben's intention to deprive the dispossessed and the naked of the possibility of agency; or of what he frames as *potentiality*.

Mills (2008: 69, 79) also raises the question of the value of the concept of bare life as a diagnostic tool. Those using the concept often fail to recognize the vast philosophical apparatus that comes with it, and the inconsistency of their political aims with those of Agamben. Using the concept of bare life to describe an absence of rights with the aim of arguing for the appropriation of those rights is quite inconsistent with Agamben's aims. What role then does the agency of subjects play in Agamben's thought? When read only through the concepts of bare life, state of exception and camp, Agamben's work appears to give a rather bleak picture of the possibility of political agency. According to Connolly (2004: 26), Agamben's thought leads us to a historical impasse because he is not able to offer a way out of the logic he describes. The (im)possibility of political agency is a relatively underexamined aspect of his work and would certainly deserve further exploration.[5] Agamben's understanding of the possibility of (political) agency is something that goes beyond ordinary conceptualizations of political subjectivity or resistance. One does, therefore, need to look beyond bare life and the camp to Agamben's concepts of potentiality and whatever-being to get an understanding of the 'coming community' or 'coming politics' he is advocating.

Politics or potentiality?

Agamben's formulation of political liberation is based on his conceptualization of potentiality. For Agamben,

> to be potential means: to be one's own lack, *to be in relation to one's own incapacity*. Beings that exist in the mode of potentiality *are capable of their own impotentiality*; and only in this way do they become potential.
>
> (Agamben 1999: 182)

Furthermore, 'potentiality maintains itself in relation to actuality in the form of its suspension; it is *capable* of the act in not realizing it' (Agamben 1998: 45).

There is a significant parallel here to Agamben's discussion of the exception and law, where the exception is in relation to the law in the form of its suspension. This means that the exception is not completely outside the law – or the sovereign. The exception is only abandoned by the sovereign. Or, we could say that the sovereign is potential with respect to the exception. The sovereign is in relation to its own incapacity, which is the exception. It achieves pure potentiality because it is able to keep its power suspended between the law and the exception. This would imply that to resist the power that captures life, (bio)sovereign power would need to be deprived of its exclusive access to potentiality. Potentiality would need to be constituted so as to escape the principle of sovereignty (Agamben 1998: 47). For Zevnik (2009: 96), the location for an Agambenite resistance is the point where bare life changes into 'whatever-being,' which is a form of being that escapes such Enlightenment categories as 'human' and 'rational.' In the light of Agamben's work, this point can be found through a rethinking of the concept of potentiality.

This discussion of potentiality is closely related to Agamben's understanding of modal categories. For Agamben,

> Possibility (to be able to be) and contingency (to be able not to be) are the operators of subjectification, the point in which something possible passes into existence. [. . .] Impossibility, as negation of possibility (not [to be able]), and necessity, as the negation of contingency (not [to be able not to be]) are the operators of desubjectification, of the destruction and destitution of the subject.
>
> (Agamben 2002: 147)

Hence, the way in which all different conceptualizations of human security understand 'being secure' as a necessity without which something fundamental is lacking works to desubjectify and destruct the subject. It is not enough, however, to simply reshape human security so as to accept the non-necessary, the 'not being' something that is currently deemed necessary. Thus, throwing oneself on the side of 'not being secure' – as radical as it may appear – is not enough. To be truly contingent, one has to be able to 'not not-be' (Agamben 1993: 105); to be able to experience the limit between being secure and insecure. This kind of contingent 'whatever-being' (Agamben 1993: 86) would thus be able to entirely escape the terms of debate that underlie the human security discourse.

Agamben's (1993: 86) whatever-being finds its home in the 'coming community' where humans have given up their search for a proper identity and where 'singularities form a community without affirming an identity'. Human security on the other hand presupposes the identity of the 'human' as the most fundamental identity that is then followed by the identity of the citizen, for example. From the Agambenite perspective, to adopt these identities is only to play along in sovereignty's game. 'The hypocritical dogma of the sacredness of human life and the vacuous declarations of human rights' only serve to hide sovereign violence and the possibility of escaping it through whatever-being (Agamben 1993: 86). Agamben (1998: 181) thus rejects law, rights and normative discourse, and claims that 'every attempt to found political liberties in the rights of the citizen [. . .] is in vain'. Surrendering oneself to the illusory discourses of rights, law and security only reinscribes the relation between sovereignty and life. Although the new 'form-of-life' Agamben envisions is located completely outside of the triad of bios, zoē and bare life (Mills 2008: 76), its threshold can be found in bare life (Agamben 2002: 69). The seemingly high point of lack or deprivation simultaneously becomes the source of the 'coming'.

In *Remnants of Auschwitz*, Agamben (2002) rejects all attempts to found ethics on the dignity of human life. In doing so, Agamben stands in sharp contrast to the discourse on human security that attempts to found life in a 'freedom to live in dignity'. Instead of founding ethics on the basis of the dignity of life, Agamben (2002: 69) looks for 'a new ethics, an ethics of a form of life that begins where dignity ends'. Whereas human security is 'the ethics of ultimate ends' (Tadjbakhsh and Chenoy 2009: 20), Agamben (2002) is gesturing towards means *without* end. But is it possible to have a politics that would escape the biopolitical task contemporary politics is pursuing? According to Agamben (2007: 10), 'this must for now remain in suspense'. Although this enigmatic answer may please those with a passion for intrigue, it may be less satisfying for those looking for practical political guidance.

As opposed to Agamben's rather philosophical understanding of the possibility of political liberation, Foucault's perception of resistance does not look to reify philosophy as a source of social and political transformation. Although Foucault allows for the possibility of resistance, he does not explicitly advocate resistance to power in general. Agamben, in contrast, argues for the necessity and the urgency of resistance to (or rather a move beyond) a power that captures life. In fact, the Agambenite perspective does not even allow for the tactical application of concepts such as human rights (or human security, for that matter) because biopolitical subjection is always already inscribed in them (Schaap 2008: 18). While Agamben would reject all conceptions of rights, Foucault (2002: 474–75) sees value in using rights as a strategy of resistance. In fact, for Foucault (2004: 265), subjects are manufactured through relations of subjugation and power and, therefore, one cannot escape power. Power is omnipresent but, significantly, 'not because it embraces everything but because it comes from everywhere' (Foucault 1990: 93). From a Foucauldian point of view, it would be questionable to talk about the construction of subjects without a view to their own role in the process. Rather than simply disciplined and regulated from above, people govern themselves through various techniques of the self that need to be taken into account in any analysis of the human subject (Foucault 1997: 177).

Hence, there is no 'free' subject that exists prior to a power that works through the discourse of human security. For Foucault (2004: 24–29), all social bodies are characterized, traversed and constituted by multiple circulatory relations of power. Power in a Foucauldian sense can therefore also mean an 'empowerment' of subjects (Lemke 2002: 53) and not simply their subordination or construction from above. One should not even desire an escape from power because power entails the possibility of resistance. Hence, from a Foucauldian viewpoint, the discourse of human security has to be seen as both a form of resistance in itself (to traditional understandings of security, or to material and social inequality, for example), and as something to be resisted. The need for resistance to the workings of human security would be decided on by concrete subjects in concrete situations. Biopower does not appear as something that necessarily *has to be* resisted (Prozorov 2007: 59). In any case, if there is to be resistance, it is to be a 'plurality of resistances', each of them a special case (Foucault 1990: 96). Indeed, for Foucault (1990: 143), life is not inescapably integrated into techniques of governance; it escapes them constantly.

The uneasy conflation of Foucauldian and Agambenite biopolitics

While Agamben (1998: 6) argues that 'the production of a biopolitical body is the originary activity of sovereign power', Foucault's (1977: 144) genealogy instead rejects the search for origins and focuses on particular configurations of relations of power and their historically contingent 'conditions of emergence'. If biopower is aimed at improving the lives lived by its subjects and works at the level of life-as-species, as Foucault (2004: 242) defines it, and if it is 'a power bent on generating forces, making them grow, and ordering them' (Foucault 1990: 136), then there appears to be a significant contradiction between Foucauldian and Agambenite biopolitics also with regard to both the subject of biopower and the objectives of biopower. In fact, Foucault's biopower is certainly not a power that is based upon 'bare life' (Ojakangas 2005: 11). The view of Diken and Laustsen (2002: 293), for example, that 'modern biopolitics as a whole reduces the citizen to bare life (to Foucault's "docile bodies")' only works to disguise the differences between Foucauldian and Agambenite biopolitics and further attests to the uneasy conflation of Agamben and Foucault in social sciences.

At its most conceptually specific, 'bare life' means the inclusion of natural life in politics through its exclusion, thereby abandoning life to sovereign violence (Mills 2008: 107). This kind of life is very different from the lives of Foucauldian biopolitics and docile bodies that essentially are bodies 'that may be subjected, used, transformed and improved' (Foucault 1991: 136). Indeed, within International Relations, there are crucial differences as to what is deemed most characteristic of biopower. According to Hardt and Negri (2004: 19), 'when individualized in its extreme form, biopower becomes torture'. At the opposite end of the line, Ojakangas (2005: 27) regards the caring middle-class Swedish social democrat as the ultimate figure of biopower. The reason why these differing accounts, while all illuminating in their own right, seem so confusing when looked at simultaneously, is because of the confusion as to what form of biopower one is concentrating on, the Agambenite, the Foucauldian or some other one. Indeed, the differences between what is meant by the 'biopolitical' are often elided in the works of those who deploy the concept (Coleman and Grove 2009: 490).

Foucault seems to imply that there could or should be a way of being a subject different from the life lived by the biopoliticized subjects of, say, human security. Dillon (2004: 54) states that 'There is an excess of (human) being over its (powerful) appearance'. What would this being be like? Foucault himself fails to provide an idea of what life might actually become beyond the omnipresent power of liberal regimes (Reid 2006: 70). Agamben certainly attempts to imagine life beyond the capture of power, but his suggestions require a radical rethinking of both ontology and politics. Agamben is gesturing towards an entirely different ontology, one in which the question of human security would be posed in an entirely different fashion, if it were posed at all. Whereas a Foucauldian perspective would see human security as a discourse that is constantly being reshaped, an Agambenite perspective would claim that it cannot be reshaped. From the Agambenite perspective, it appears that it will not be possible to express any truly meaningful critique of the contemporary social order through a concept such as human security, no matter how it is formulated.

Conclusion

The existence of a great deal of suffering, hardship and fear in the world can hardly be denied. The difficult conditions that the discourse of human security describes are indeed part of everyday life for many people around the world. However, in claiming to provide an all-embracing solution to the problems people face in their lives, the discourse of human security in fact limits the range of possible solutions. The striving for a comprehensive, all-embracing condition of security is surely something both Foucault and Agamben would be sceptical about. The implications of an Agambenite and a Foucauldian critique of human security are, nevertheless, quite different. Foucault's thought appears to be more local and historical, and interested in the detail compared to Agamben's more metaphysical account of biopolitics. In terms of human security, this means that a Foucauldian critique is able to offer a more nuanced account of the object of its critique. An Agambenite critique, in contrast, sees human security simply as part of the transhistorical workings of biopower that pervade our whole understanding of life and politics. Because of this transhistorical essence of power, one may end up missing the specific workings of power, with the latter appearing as being always the same; and always as something to be opposed. A Foucauldian account would thus appear to offer a more differentiated way of thinking about human security.

Foucault's thought is better able to ground political agency in the conditions of the contemporary world but Agamben's thought is nevertheless incredibly intriguing in its advocation of 'that which has never been.' Hence, the differences between Agamben and Foucault can be seen as culminating in their understandings of the possibility of politics. Agamben's conception of politics does not locate the possibility for social transformation within the contemporary conditions of the world (Schaap 2008: 20) but rather envisions something that still largely remains to be thought. In contrast, Foucault's work helps us to recognize both the mundane character of power as well as the equally mundane character of resistance to it. A Foucauldian critique of human security entails a micro-politics of resistance as opposed to an Agambenite critique that proposes an outright rejection and refusal of all normative discourse. At the same time, however, Agamben's work is of course normative in itself as it expresses a specific conception and judgement of the state of the contemporary world.

In conclusion, the discourse of human security refuses to recognize solutions that come from outside the form of political-economic organization, characteristic of liberal democratic market economies. It also refuses to recognize knowledge and values that are not by its standards considered 'rational', 'well-informed' and 'ethical'. And it also fails to accept lifestyles that deviate from the 'healthy' norm. Also, the Foucauldian critique of human security presented here has its limitations as it is predicated on the centrality of the individual 'self', thus ignoring more collective ways of understanding human beings in general and political agency in particular. These are questions that those individuals, peoples and policy groups who wish to use the discourse of human security should take into account. Human security also fails to recognize that through its promotion of a certain form of 'secure' human being, it may be making others all the more 'insecure'. Indeed, in its promotion of security as the core of *human* being, it may also be producing the insecure as the *inhuman*.

Notes

1 The author wishes to thank Julian Reid, for support and guidance in the preparation of this chapter. She is also particularly grateful to Eine Alt, Saija Ekorre and Jan Gaspers for their valuable comments and critique. All omissions and mistakes remain the author's alone.
2 Traditional critiques of human security, such as those by Buzan (2004), Newman (2004), MacFarlane (2004), Paris (2004) and Khong (2001) most often point towards problems resulting from the lack of definitional clarity and analytical precision within human security debates.
3 For Foucault-inspired critiques of human security, see Grayson (2008), de Larrinaga and Doucet (2008), Youssef (2008), Duffield (2007), Duffield and Waddell (2006) and Grayson (2004).
4 For other discussions of different accounts of biopolitics and biopower, see Coleman and Grove (2009), Dillon and Lobo-Guerrero (2009), Patton (2007), Prozorov (2007), Dillon (2005) and Ojakangas (2005).
5 Edkins (2007), for example, has identified various positive possibilities for political agency in Agamben's work. In this respect, also see Edkins and Pin-Fat (2005) and Zevnik (2009).

References

Agamben, G. (1993) *The Coming Community*, trans. M. Hardt, Minnesota: University of Minnesota Press.
—— (1998) *Homo Sacer: Sovereign Power and Bare Life*, trans. D. Heller-Roazen, Stanford: Stanford University Press.
—— (1999) *Potentialities: Collected Essays in Philosophy*, ed. D. Heller-Roazen, Stanford: Stanford University Press.
—— (2000) *Means without End: Notes on Politics*, trans. V. Binetti and C. Casarino, Minnesota: University of Minnesota Press.
—— (2002) *Remnants of Auschwitz: The Witness and the Archive*, trans. D. Heller-Roazen, New York: Zone Books.
—— (2007) 'The Work of Man', in M. Calarco and S. DeCaroli (eds) *Giorgio Agamben: Sovereignty and Life*, Stanford: Stanford University Press.
Buzan, B. (2004) 'A Reductionist, Idealistic Notion that Adds Little Analytical Value', *Security Dialogue*, 35(3): 369–70.
Chandler, D. (2008) 'Human Security II: Waiting for the Tail to Wag the Dog: A Rejoinder to Ambrosetti, Owen and Wibben', *Security Dialogue*, 39(4): 463–69.
Coleman, M. and Grove, K. (2009) 'Biopolitics, Biopower and the Return of Sovereignty', *Society and Space*, 27(3): 489–507.
Commission on Human Security, Survival, Livelihood and Dignity (CHS) (2003) *Human Security Now*, New York: United Nations Publications.
Connolly, W. E. (2004) 'The Complexity of Sovereignty', in J. Edkins, V. Pin-Fat and M. Shapiro (eds) *Sovereign Lives: Power in Global Politics*, New York: Routledge.
de Larrinaga, M. and Doucet, M. G. (2008) 'Sovereign Power and the Biopolitics of Human Security', *Security Dialogue*, 39(5): 517–37.
Diken, B. and Laustsen, C. B. (2002) 'Zones of Indistinction: Security, Terror, and Bare Life', *Space and Culture*, 5(3): 290–307.
Dillon, M. (2004) 'Correlating Sovereign and Biopower', in J. Edkins, V. Pin-Fat and M. Shapiro (eds) *Sovereign Lives: Power in Global Politics*, New York: Routledge.
—— (2005) 'Cared to Death: The Biopoliticized Time of Your Life', *Foucault Studies*, 2: 37–46.
Dillon, M. and Lobo-Guerrero, L. (2009) 'The Biopolitical Imaginary of Species Being', *Theory, Culture & Society*, 26(1): 1–23.
Duffield, M. (2007) *Development, Security and Unending War*, New York: Polity Press.
Duffield, M. and Waddell, N. (2006) 'Securing Humans in a Dangerous World', *International Politics*, 43(1): 1–23.
Edkins, J. (2007) 'Whatever Politics', in M. Calarco and S. DeCaroli (eds) *Giorgio Agamben: Sovereignty and Life*, Stanford: Stanford University Press.
Edkins, J. and Pin-Fat, V. (2005) 'Through the Wire: Relations of Power and Relations of Violence', *Millenium: Journal of International Studies*, 31(1): 1–22.
Foucault, M. (1977) 'Nietzsche, Genealogy, History', in D. F. Bouchard (ed.) *Language, Counter-Memory, Practice: Selected Essays and Interviews*, Ithaca: Cornell University Press.
—— (1990) *The History of Sexuality: Volume 1*, trans. R. Hurley, London: Penguin Books.
—— (1991) *Discipline and Punish*, London: Penguin Books.
—— (1997) 'Sexuality and Solitude', in M. Foucault, *Ethics: Subjectivity and Truth*, ed. P. Rabinow, trans. R. Hurley and others, New York: The New Press.
—— (2002) 'Confronting Governments: Human Rights', in M. Foucault, *Power: Essential*

Works of Foucault 1954–1984 Volume 3, ed. J. Faubion, trans. R. Hurley and others, London: Penguin Books.
—— (2004) *Society Must Be Defended: Lectures at the College de France 1975–76*, trans. D. Macey, London: Penguin Books.
—— (2008) *The Birth of Biopolitics: Lectures at the College de France 1978–79*, trans. G. Burchell, Basingstoke: Palgrave Macmillan.
Gasper, D. (2005) 'Securing Humanity: Situating "Human Security" as Concept and Discourse', *Journal of Human Development*, 6(2): 221–45.
Grayson, K. (2004) 'A Challenge to the Power over Knowledge of Traditional Security Studies', *Security Dialogue*, 35(3): 357.
—— (2008) 'Human Security as Power/Knowledge: The Biopolitics of a Definitional Debate', *Cambridge Review of International Affairs*, 21(3): 383–401.
Hardt, M. and Negri, A. (2004) *Multitude: War and Democracy in the Age of Empire*, London: Penguin Books.
Khong, Y. F. (2001) 'Human Security: A Shotgun Approach to Alleviating Human Misery?', *Global Governance*, 7(3): 231–36.
Lemke, T. (2002) 'Foucault, Governmentality, and Critique', *Rethinking Marxism*, 14(3): 49–64.
Macfarlane, S. N. (2004) 'A Useful Concept that Risks Losing Its Political Salience', *Security Dialogue*, 35(3): 368–69.
Mills, C. (2004) 'Agamben's Messianic Politics: Biopolitics, Abandonment and Happy Life', *Contretemps 5*, December 2004: 42–62.
—— (2008) *The Philosophy of Agamben*, Stocksfield: Acumen.
Neal, A. W. (2006) 'Foucault in Guantánamo: Towards an Archaeology of the Exception', *Security Dialogue*, 37(1): 31–46.
Newman, E. (2004) 'A Normatively Attractive but Analytically Weak Concept', *Security Dialogue*, 35(3): 358–59.
Ojakangas, M. (2005) 'Impossible Dialogue on Bio-Power', *Foucault Studies*, 2(2): 5–28.
Paris, R. (2004) 'Still an Inscrutable Concept', *Security Dialogue*, 35(3): 370–72.
Patton, P. (2007) 'Agamben and Foucault on Biopower and Biopolitics', in M. Calarco and S. DeCaroli (eds) *Giorgio Agamben: Sovereignty and Life*, Stanford: Stanford University Press.
Prozorov, S. (2007) 'The Unrequited Love of Power: Biopolitical Investment and the Refusal of Care', *Foucault Studies*, 4(4): 53–77.
Reid, J. (2006) *The Biopolitics of the War on Terror: Life Struggles, Liberal Modernity, and the Defence of Logistical Societies*, Manchester: Manchester University Press.
Rose, N. (2001) 'The Politics of Life Itself', *Theory, Culture & Society*, 18(6): 1–30.
Schaap, A. (2008) 'Political Abandonment and the Abandonment of Politics in Agamben's Critique of Human Rights', Available URL: http://eric.exeter.ac.uk/exeter/bitstream/10036/42438/2/Agamben%e2%80%99s%20critique%20of%20Human%20 Rights.pdf (accessed 2 February 2009).
Tadjbakhsh, S. and Chenoy, A. (2009) *Human Security: Concepts and Implications*, London: Routledge.
United Nations Development Programme (UNDP) (1994) *Human Development Report 1994: New Dimensions of Human Security*, Oxford: Oxford University Press.
Youssef, M. (2008) 'Suffering Men of Empire: Human Security and the War on Iraq', *Cultural Dynamics*, 20(2): 149–66.
Zevnik, A. (2009) 'Sovereign-less Subject and the Possibility of Resistance', *Millenium: Journal of International Studies*, 38(1): 83–106.

12 Rethinking human security

History, economy, governmentality

Nik Hynek[1]

Introduction

Conventional understanding reveals that human security has been examined as a policy-making enterprise *par excellence*. The 'official history' of human security is full of references to political documents, with the UNDP Report of 1994 being highlighted as the most important one as it, allegedly, established this alternative paradigm. Some analysts go even further and trace its origins in a series of reports (the Brandt Report, the Palme Report and the Brundtland Report) that broadened the concept of security during the 1980s. It is not surprising that some scholars go even further back into the past, as is always the case with any search for roots of anything. What *is* surprising, however, is that the obsession with the roots at the policy-making level has structured almost all academic debates which have concerned human security as the centrepiece till date.

In this light, it makes sense that one can often hardly differentiate between policy-making documents concerned with human security and academic studies of it, the situation given by the fact that the latter have merely been a derivative of the former (not to speak about another, complementary fact that a number of authors have been writing at both levels). The aforementioned situation is not a problem in itself; rather, the problem quickly emerges when the debate is centred on the question of what is the structural plane upon which human security has been unfolded, both historically and in the contemporary era. Heuristically speaking, the conventional understanding of human security has considerably reduced the ability to assess the notion critically, especially to appreciate its potential and limits in both practical and theoretical terms. Thinking through policy-making categories that are often cast in a binary language of opposites (e.g. narrow/broad; hard/soft; human/national) is not a particularly productive starting point, though these categories deserve to be analysed too.

The proposed chapter attempts to investigate human security as a liberal project that has indeed drawn on certain theoretical information and had practical effects. The observation on which the chapter rests is that one needs to direct his/her attention to deeper levels from which a certain version of human security emerged, to which it later retreated, and from which it, again, re-emerged in its most recent manifestation of an explicit and successfully sedimented doctrine. It will be argued that human security needs to be analysed through an examination of individuals in their dual, hybrid quality of subjects of security and objects of security against the backdrop of liberal order. In order to do so, historical trajectories of economic and political liberalism and their links to political and security rationalities need to be the central part of such an analysis.

In concrete terms, this is achieved in the chapter as follows. In the first step, relevant conceptualization of civil society and the state in the work of the French philosopher of the systems of thought, Michel Foucault, is outlined and discussed. In the second step, and contrary to the commonly viewed newness of human security, a nascent, nineteenth-century human security is examined and its echoes visible in the post-Cold War world are highlighted. The emphasis will be laid on the intersection between the liberal order and humanitarian disarmament, including an analysis of the hybrid role of individuals as subjects of security (agents of change) and objects of security (a discourse on individuals suffering at war). Finally, a post-Cold War version of human security (the freedom-from-fear doctrine) is investigated and discussed against the background of neo-liberal rationality of government. It will be shown that it represents an interesting mixture of old elements (the nineteenth century) and distinctively new characteristics (e.g. the use of a service-delivery model; disciplinary management of NGOs).

Civil society and the state in Foucault's work

Rationalities of early liberal government

In this section, I will show how Foucault's sketches of liberalism serve an important role of the background for apprehending past and recent processes in human security and humanitarian action. Foucault's only detailed discussion of neo-liberalism can be found in his Collège de France lectures of 1979, published for the first time in English in June 2008. They are further complemented by Foucault and Gordon's insightful chapters in *The Foucault Effect* (1991). Although Foucault remained as neutral in his analysis of liberalism and its neo-versions as he could, one can sense his fascination with related political rationalities.[2] His growing disillusionment with a welfare state was certainly a stimulus: unlike a liberal order, welfarism never possessed its own distinctive art of governing (Foucault 2008: 93–94). Foucault starts his analysis in the sixteenth century, recognizing an early modern governmentality defined as an autonomous rationality based on raison d'état and science of police (Foucault 1991: 87–104).

Foucault (2008: 51–74) continues his study by an investigation of governmental naturalism which cannot be considered a mere doctrine as it critiques state reason and argues for limited government, restraint and the improvement of state reason by 'displaying to it the intrinsic bounds of its power to know' (Gordon 1991: 14). It was Adam Smith, the representative of the new liberal art of government, who pointed out the impossibility of an economic sovereignty, with a result of the previous firm bond between raison d'état and science of police to dissolve and be replaced by governmental rationality derived from economics, the approach that became epitomized by the label *laissez-faire* (Foucault 2008: 20, 61, 284–86). Subsequently, Foucault draws one's attention to emerging inter-penetration between the structure of private and public order, resulting in the beginning of a more statist liberal perspective: 'the private domain [is regarded] as a "virtual" public space. . . . It is . . . the historical point from which it becomes decreasingly possible to think of civil society as an autonomous order which confronts and experiences the state as an alien, incursive force' (Gordon 1991: 33–34).

Neo-liberal rationalities of government

The aforementioned sketches show how laissez-faire liberalism with a sharp division between autonomous and spontaneous civil society and the minimal state faded out as an idea and practice. Instead, liberalism transmutated into a pluralized interconnected system of government with a blurring division between state and society. In Gordon's words,

> [a]mong these processes might be numbered the initiating roles of private individuals and organizations in the exploring and defining new governmental tasks; . . . the cross-fertilizing interplay between different agencies and expertises, public and private alike; . . . the different forms of delegation represented by the 'quangos', and the renewed mobilization of voluntary sector . . . [T]he interface between state and society [can be portrayed] in the form of something like a second-order market of governmental goods and services. It becomes the ambition of neo-liberalism to implicate the individual citizen, as player and partner, into this market game.
>
> (Gordon 1991: 36)

Foucault did not understand modern neo-liberal governmentality as a neo-laissez-faire order as is sometimes wrongly believed, but as a rationality that is simultaneously *individualizing* and *totalizing*.

In his 1979 lectures, Foucault discussed different versions of neo-liberalism, focusing particularly on German post-war neo-liberalism (the Freiburg School of Ordo-liberals) and US neo-liberalism (the Chicago School) which evolved as a much more radical version from the former. The Ordo-liberals were concerned with the social market economy and held an anti-naturalistic notion of the market and of competition as well as a constructivist concept of law and of juridical institutions. This School essentially believed in an active role of state in constituting the market and spurring competition, although it firmly refused any direct state interventionism into the realm of economy. It is then no surprise that proponents held that the economic order should be an object of indirect political regulation and social intervention (Foucault 2008: 101–28). Put differently, the Ordo-liberals generally aimed at creating a social framework within which the enterprise and entrepreneurial activity would take place, complemented by the so-called Vitalpolitik concerned with the reproduction and re-activation of cultural and moral values that would be able to challenge free economic play (Foucault 2008: 148).

According to Foucault, neo-liberals of the Chicago School tried to redress the problem of indirect state activism by eliminating it altogether. The key strategy in this was their systematic expansion of the economic form into all other areas, including the social sphere, with a result of reducing any remaining difference between the economic and the social. Therefore, unlike the Ordo-liberals justifying the social being conducted in the name of the economic, the Chicago School neo-liberals advocated a global re-inscription of the social sphere as a form of the economic domain (Foucault 2008: 215–38). Gordon summarizes the arrival of the Chicago School neo-liberalism as follows:

> [T]his operation works by a progressive enlargement of the territory of economic theory by a series of redefinitions of its object ... Now it is proposed that economics concerns the study of ... *all rational conduct*. ... But the great departure here from eighteen-century precedent is that, whereas *homo economicus* originally meant that subject the springs of whose activity must remain forever untouchable by government, the American neo-liberal *homo economicus* is *manipulable man*, man who is perpetually responsive to modifications in his environment.
>
> (Gordon 1991: 43, emphasis in original)

Individualizing and totalizing dimensions

In light of the earlier analysis, it is somewhat perplexing that a number of recent studies working in the governmentality approach portray neo-liberalism in a too simplified fashion when compared with Foucault's original conceptualization. Not only does such a portrayal blackbox neo-liberal nuances, but it also presents a significant obstacle in terms of further positive heuristics in this area. In order to expose this problem, I will focus on the issue that is central to my own analysis of peace machinery of new humanitarianism, i.e. the relationship between responsibility and autonomy of NGOs from the government in this field. The key problem with deeper implications poses the assertion that as the government (in the sense of the executive) in advanced liberal countries transfers to an ever greater extent the actual government (mainly the provision of public goods) to various external/quasi-external actors and agencies, NGOs become more and more *responsible and autonomous*.

Sending and Neumann (2006: 651) thus, for instance, argue that 'civil society is redefined from a passive object of government to be acted upon into an entity that is both an object and a subject of government' (Sending and Neumann 2006: 651).They make a distinction between NGOs being 'passive objects' during the Cold War as opposed to becoming 'free and autonomous subjects' in the post-Cold War era (Sending and Neumann 2006: 667, 669). These authors (Sending and Neumann 2006: 663) as well as O'Connor and Ilcan (2005: 6) specifically for Canada suggest that responsibility and autonomy go hand in hand. This assertion is, however, flawed on two fronts: conceptually, such an argument does not take notice of Foucault's important observation about the *totalizing* dimension of neo-liberalism as discussed earlier; empirically, my own findings presented in the following lines indicate that such an assertion is problematic at best since *more* responsibility for NGOs has in fact been accompanied by *less* autonomy for them.

Nascent human security in nineteenth-century liberal governmentality

Nineteenth century and post-Cold War echoes

The following part will show that an increase in humanitarianism after the end of the Cold War and the role of NGOs in this process cannot be considered an unprecedented phenomenon. If one speaks about *new* humanitarianism, then the attention really needs to be directed to the nineteenth century. New humanitarianism of the nineteenth century emerges in connection with the establishment of new types of actors: non-state actors (Boli and Thomas 1999). What both the nineteenth-century humanitarianism and the post-Cold War humanitarianism have in common is precisely their strong attachment to liberal and neo-liberal political rationality of government respectively. It was for this reason that related conceptual issues were discussed in the previous part of the chapter. In both of these instances, humanitarian action and campaign was discursively built around the notion of a suffering individual.

The legitimization of humanitarian-disarmament campaigns suggest that both actions were framed as human-security issues: in the case of the nineteenth century without an accompanying political doctrine; in the case of a campaign to ban landmines this was a part of an explicit human-security doctrine (the freedom-from-fear doctrine). However important this difference can be, common characteristics of both versions of humanitarianisms are visible too, including the discursive transfer from the former to the latter. Indeed, in line with the earlier conceptual debate concerning the development of liberal rationality of government, one cannot really expect the post-Cold War humanitarianism to merely replicate the experiences from the nineteenth century. As the following analysis will demonstrate, on the contrary, a number of characteristics are different due to historical and political contingencies that have shaped economy, security and politics in between. To this study, the crucial issue is that of normative resonance between the humanitarianisms and the central role of non-state actors in their articulation, the fact enabled in both cases by a certain version of liberal order.

In both cases, one can speak about a shift in a security dispositif, or apparatus. Foucault defines the dispositif as 'the system of relations that can be established between . . . elements [such as] discourses, institutions, architectural forms, regulatory decisions, laws, administrative measures, scientific statements, philosophical, moral and philanthropic propositions' (Foucault 1980:194). As Deleuze aptly adds, each dispositif 'has its way of structuring light, the way in which it falls, blurs and disperses, distributing the visible and the invisible, giving birth to objects which are dependent on it for their existence, and causing them to disappear' (Deleuze 1992:160). An examination of the security dispositif can be conducted in terms of relations of knowledge (discourse), power and subjectivity (cf. Foucault 1980:196–97). The shift in the security dispositif will therefore be investigated through changes in the referent object of security problématique; and through wider changes in the field of security. As I showed elsewhere (Hynek 2008a), there is an intimate link between the constitution of active subjects in the security field (here non-state actors) and the emergence of the suffering individual as an object, or a referent point, of security.

Although the Antipersonnel Landmines (APL) campaign has been celebrated in a majority of existing studies (Matthew 2004; Cameron *et al.* 1998; Goose and Williams 2004; Price 1998) as an important part of an unprecedented phenomenon that was itself brought about by the new macro-structural organization of world politics after the end of the Cold War, such an image cannot withstand the confrontation with empirical evidence. Contrary to this popular belief, the APL campaign in fact includes similar dynamics to nineteenth-century humanitarian campaigns concerned with humanitarian disarmament. Specifically, types of actors involved, organization of campaigns, styles of argumentation and issue-framing, as well as legal outputs of these campaigns are not all that different. Such a perspective is in line with Foucault's observations regarding similarities between the classical liberal rationality of government in the nineteenth century and the neo-liberal rationality. This does not support, on the other hand, fashionable though flawed assertions made by Wapner (2000; 2004) and others about the unprecedented transformation of the current world politics, allegedly caused by an increase of NGOs and information technologies. Among campaigns that were founded on liberal rationalities of government, one can mention the campaign for women's suffrage, though it is humanitarian-disarmament campaigns which are central to this chapter.

Humanitarian disarmament as Liberal practice

In this respect, key events of the nineteenth Century were the St Petersburg Conference of 1868 and, most importantly, the First Hague Conference of 1899. The legal output of the former was the St Petersburg Declaration and its rationale was explained on grounds of the need to establish a link between the progress of civilization and alleviating as much as possible the horrors of war. It banned all projectiles of a weight below 400 grammes, which were either explosive or charged with fulminating or inflammable substances. As for the latter, its legal output in the area of humanitarian disarmament comprised three declarations. These banned any use of expanding bullets (so-called dum dum bullets), asphyxiating or deleterious gases and the discharge of projectiles and explosives from balloons (Goldblat 2002). One of the common traits of the St Petersburg Conference of 1868, the Hague Conference of 1899 and the Ottawa Conference of 1997 is the fact that these were convened as a result of successful efforts of political norm entrepreneurs (Rutherford 1999). In concrete terms, the nineteenth-century conferences were connected to the Russian Tzar Nicholas II; the Ottawa Conference was organized by the Canadian Minister of Foreign Affairs, Lloyd Axworthy. Despite the fact that

Nicholas II – unlike Lloyd Axworthy, cannot be considered a representative of liberal order as such (though he introduced measures in this direction), he played an important role in promoting ideas of non-state actors campaigning for disarmament and it was also due to his efforts that they were allowed a close scrutiny during the conferences' negotiations.

Non-state actors took advantage of this climate and shaped the views of politicians, both directly and also indirectly through the printed media (Tuchman 1996: Chapter 5). Their argumentation aiming at the creation of new human-security-based legal norms reveals the essence of what Foucault (1991) calls the transformation of the individual in effective and efficient political subject. Disarmament was promoted as a part of the human-security frame instead of the national-security frame. As Foucault (1991: 26–27) notes, liberal rationality of government does not concern purely economic matters; rather, it engulfs the entire functional mechanism of the exercise of political sovereignty. In this light, it is not surprising that the President of the First Plenary Session during the Hague Conference of 1899 mentioned the liberal purpose of maintaining harmony and reduction of horrors of war as the basic reason why diplomatic delegations gathered in the Hague. Similarly, the Dutch government which hosted and co-financed the conference appeals in its conference invitation to states to do their utmost to secure the peace and disarmament (Rutherford 1999: 36, 42).

The reason for banning certain types of weapons that were deemed odious was to reduce suffering of individuals: in the nineteenth-century campaigns mainly of soldiers and in the APL campaign chiefly of civilians. One hundred years later, the imagery of the suffering individual served as the basis for the Canadian Minister of Foreign Affairs, Lloyd Axworthy. He successfully linked his own human-security project to the Hague Conference:

> I cannot think of a subject more important at the dawn of the next millennium than that of civilians in war . . . In 1899, the Hague Conference on Peace set an agenda. In 1999, the world needs a new agenda – one that puts people at the heart of foreign policy. The impetus for the generation involved in the first Hague Conference was a desire to make the act of war itself more humane, establishing rules to protect combatants at a time when civilians were largely bystanders . . . In World War I, 5 percent of casualties were civilians: today that figure is closer to 80 percent. In 1999, civilians are direct targets of war, and live on its battlefields . . . The point is that the onus is on our generation – 100 years after the Hague Conference – to respond to these new realities. We need to change the discourse of diplomacy. And we need to change its practice. Fundamentally, we need to make human security at least as important as state privilege.
>
> (Axworthy 1999: not numbered)

Liberal rationality of government can be discerned in the nineteenth-century campaigns concerned with humanitarian disarmament in several directions. First of all, it is visible in related knowledge production. Knowledge was generated by non-state actors and subsequently used to target governments that were present at the conferences. Apart from that, liberal rationality was, too, visible through medialization of this knowledge, with the aim to pressurize the governments and to hold them accountable. More and more, governments had to pay attention to public opinion in liberalizing polities and were under pressure from non-state opinion-makers, organizations promoting humanitarian ideals and peace, associations of lawyers and teachers, and so on.

Anatomo- and bio-politics as two poles of liberal security

It can be maintained that the nature of the shift from the discourse on national security to that of human security – or to paraphrase Deleuze, the politics of restructuring light (the shining individual/population vs the unilluminated state), was largely informed by the reconstitution of the role of the individual in the society. Specifically, an intimate relationship between the constitution of an active subject/citizen in the society and the emergence of the individual in need of protection as the referent point in the security discourse can be discerned. By virtue of this relationship, one can argue that the human body began to be perceived as a *vulnerable organism* as far as the people-centred security was concerned. In other words, while anatomo-politics disciplined the individual-as-a-subject, in both body and mind, bio-politics approached it through life sciences, regulating it at the level of population (Foucault 1978:139–44). In line with Foucault, bio-politics can be conceived of as the point of the strategic coordination between economy, population and government with the aim of extracting from the population what I term 'bio-energy'. This is to be accomplished through the use of biopower which includes 'numerous and diverse techniques for achieving the subjugation of bodies and the control of populations . . . [i.e.] techniques that govern and administer . . . human life' (Foucault 1978:140,143). The essential characteristic of biopower is its capillarity: once it is exercised, it works through the minds of subjects with the aim of introducing certain attitudes and behavioural patterns.

Certainly, the International Committee of the Red Cross can be considered one of the most important actors of that time (and, also, later in the APL campaign) and its importance for the generation of new type of humanitarian knowledge in the field of security (Finnemore 1999). The organization was founded by a Swiss citizen, Henry Dunant, in a reaction to his immediate experience of the Battle of Solferino (1859). Subsequently, Dunant wrote a book containing his memories of the battle and sent it out to all important non-governmental actors, governments and military personnel alike. In 1863, the ICRC invited governments, international lawyers, and representatives of international pacifist and peace federation movements for a conference to discuss principles of international humanitarian law. These principles were later inserted to the Geneva Conventions (Lavoyer and Maresca 1999). Discussed proposals and humanitarian-oriented knowledge about security were successfully linked to disarmament efforts. The uniting element was precisely the suffering individual as a cornerstone of humanitarian disarmament and human security.

As far as non-state actors in the discussed field are concerned, other important players, apart from the International Committee of the Red Cross, were mainly associations promoting peace and humanitarian disarmament from a pacifistic perspective. The decision to organize the two nineteenth-century conferences is usually explained in the available literature as a result of intensive lobbying activities of Dr Darby, the Secretary of the Peace Society of London, Bertha von Suttner, co-founder of the Austrian Peace Society and a Nobel Peace Prize laureate (Goldblat 2002; Abrams 1962) and Ivan Bloch, a Polish writer who systematically examined political and economic consequences of modern industrial warfare and had great personal influence on Tzar Nicholas II. Nicholas II used his diplomatic position to allow a number of these opinion-makers to attend the Hague Conference of 1899 and disseminate their work. Immediate access of non-state actors to the conference, including their presence in corridors of buildings in which negotiations were held, as well as significant room they were given in the media to share their opinions and demands (Eyffinger 1999), is what British historian Alfred Zimmem (cited in Caron 2000: 14) summarized under the rubrics of the so-called *open diplomacy*. That was the space within which diplomats, lawyers, and human-rights defenders and peace activists mingled and exchanged their views.

What is more, people-centred liberal rationality of government in the field of humanitarian disarmament was also embodied in the so-called Martens Clause during the First Hague Conference of 1899. This clause establishes the protection of civilians and soldiers in those cases that are not explicitly covered by the Laws and Customs of War in the Land. The key argument of the Martens Clause is the importance of public conscience. The clause was also inserted in the Ottawa Treaty of 1997 that banned APLs. Although with a 100 years hiatus, both humanitarian processes rested on analogous, liberal conception of normative change with human-security legitimization.

The doctrine of human security and neo-liberal humanitarian practice[3]

Domestic structural conditions

From a Foucauldian perspective, locating the origins of the human security agenda in direct governmental attempts to engage the public misses the point. The same is true for interpreting the subsequent unfolding of events into a more narrow Freedom-from-Fear (FFF) doctrine as a linear and somewhat natural and logical development. It is crucial to 'dig deeper' and search for structural conditions that allowed the human security agenda to emerge. As far as the FFF doctrine is concerned, it means to go back to Canada of the 1960s. The most important enabling structural condition for FFF were repeated, government-initiated, transformations of Canada's non-profit and voluntary sector in the late 1960s/early 1970s (first crisis of welfare liberalism) and the late 1980s/early 1990s (second crisis of welfare liberalism). These resulted in both a quantitative increase in NGOs as well as in a qualitative trend of delegating more social responsibility to them.

During these eras, the notion of the state as a universal caretaker of the population and its needs was increasingly under fire from two sides. First, there was growing disillusionment with the government in economic matters, especially its ability to distribute wealth and deliver public goods. The main governmental aim during the 1990s could thus be summarized as 'engage more NGOs for less money' as the federal budget was in deficit and severe funding cutbacks were imposed. Second, economic difficulties were coupled with an increase in citizens' activism, mainly rights-based movements. The two sides were closely interconnected as one of the effects of the aforementioned development was government's successful pressure on then heterogeneous Canada's 'peace movement' to professionalize. Consequently, a number of specialized international-development/humanitarian NGOs, such as Project Ploughshares, were founded (Hynek 2008a: 99–100).

By the 1993 general elections, earlier efforts of the Progressive Conservative government to tame the peace movement were further intensified in the Liberals' electoral campaign, which promised a radical change in Canadian foreign and security policy. The clear mandate obtained by the Liberals' landslide victory in the elections marked the key and perhaps permanent change in the procedure and substance of Canadian foreign and security policy. The Liberal Party's *Foreign Policy Handbook* noted that '[t]here must be more involvement by *our* NGOs . . . in defining *our* role in the globe' (Liberal Party of Canada 1993, emphasis added). Liberal leader Jean Chrétien promoted his vision, arguing that 'NGOs are often very good at what they do – often better than governments – whether it is delivering aid or assistance, or . . . working to promote a greater public awareness of international issues . . . No one government can do it all' (Chrétien 1995: not numbered). There was, however, a key difference in the motivation of governmental attempts to bring NGOs closer. While the earlier neo-conservative government had consulted NGOs in its dual efforts to tame them and to boost its popularity among voters, the Liberals saw NGO engagement as an opportunity to transfer the burden of responsibility from the government to NGOs in a fiscally difficult period. Thus, it is appropriate to see this change as an important indicator of the shift from welfare liberalism to advanced liberalism that 'outsourced' many state responsibilities to NGOs.

Desecuritization and the service-delivery model

As far as the substance, human security was introduced and sought to replace an earlier emphasis on national security, as a part of a renewed attempt to make defence policy subordinate to foreign policy. It was no surprise, then, that *Canada and the World* argued that '[m]ore and more, the concept of security is focussing on the economic, social and political needs of the *individual* . . . [, i.e.] *human security*' (DFAIT 1995: not numbered). Human security can be seen, especially from the international level, as a result of a combination of successful securitization of the traditional development agenda and deepening of previously dominant national security. Nevertheless, a Foucauldian perspective that focuses on domestic factors and conditions brings less expected insights. Specifically, the FFF doctrine can be understood as *desecuritization and domestication-at-a-distance of the international development agenda*. One should emphasize that the aforementioned trend, particularly visible when actual *practices* get examined, is not mutually exclusive with a trend of securitization of the foreign policy *discourse*. The two have in fact successfully co-existed alongside each other for some time. One could even think about their mutual reinforcement, however paradoxical that seems.

The landmine case has usually been seen as the most important issue within FFF doctrine and the one that has been hailed as a big victory for civil society, both locally and globally. It is for these reasons that the case serves as an important example to understand the counter-intuitive argument about desecuritization of practices and domestication of the international development. Specifically, the successful conclusion of the Ottawa Convention in 1997 can be considered, from a Foucauldian perspective, the beginning of an era that would connect hitherto separated realms: the realm of (domestic) public-service delivery and the realm of (international) security/development. The oft-neglected post-1997 development in the landmine case therefore suggests that landmines were reframed from a security/development issues to an issue modelled on public-goods provision that was previously used mainly for domestic issues. While the pre-1997 phase of the issue was largely about the securitization of discourse, the post-1997 phase was dominated by the desecuritization of practices.

Human security and disciplinary management

The result of the aforementioned was the shift from the technology of involvement/citizenship to the technology of new contractualism. The aim of the former was to involve actors in consultations and negotiations, to give them a voice. With the conclusion of the Ottawa Convention, the latter technology emerged as a dominant one. It is precisely this lesson that challenges the victorious discourse on human security as a policy that empowers people and that is related to the rise of a politically-aware global civil society. This is because the introduction of the technology of new contractualism generally brings about the de-politicization of NGOs. They are essentially transformed from participating political stakeholders into responsible service-delivery agents, or arms of the state. This has been made possible by the government's detachment of human security policy-making from service delivery, wherein the main aim is to ensure an equal opportunity for NGOs to compete for funding. The most important feature of the latter's technology has been the departure from core funding to project funding. This phenomenon has been clearly demonstrated by the ongoing abandonment of transfer payments in the form of grants, which are not subject to audit, and their replacement by conditioned and audited contributions. One of the consequences has been the homogenization of Canada's NGOs involved in the implementation of human security. This trend has been visible through an emergence of two cleavages: small vs large organizations, and advocacy vs service delivery organizations. The technology of new contractualism has heavily favoured the latter in each cleavage (Hynek 2008a: 107).

The analysed link between the logic of domestic service delivery and its subsequent extension to the field of international security/development is cardinal for one more reason: it allows one to explain why Canada's human security has been defined in negative terms as FFF doctrine (freedom from fear, i.e. from physical violence) and not otherwise. This has been given by the reconstitution of individual's role in the society as manifested by the responsibilization of Canada's NGOs active in international security/development. Specifically, an intimate relationship between the constitution of an active subject/citizen in the society and the emergence of the individual in need of protection as the referent point in the security discourse can be discerned. By virtue of this relationship, one can argue that the human body, which was previously seen purely as an efficient-and-effective performance machine as institutionalized in the technology of the new contractualism, also began to be perceived as a *vulnerable organism* as far as the FFF doctrine is concerned. This is clear from the governmental document in which the latter is described and which reads as follows: 'Human security means freedom from pervasive threats to people's . . . safety or lives' (DFAIT 2000: 2). This understanding of human security has stood in direct opposition to a conceptually much wider and emancipatory Japanese human-security approach that has emphasized the importance of human empowerment and socio-economic development (Hynek 2008b, Bosold and Werthes 2005). Unlike Canada, Japan has not gone through the similar transformation of political rationalities with large responsibilization of subjects/NGOs and therefore also has not focused on the protection of bare lives in their human security.

Finally, the process of responsibilization of individuals in Canadian human security dealt with in this part of the article cannot be seen as *mutually exclusive* of the process of militarization of human security discussed in the first part of the article. While one could argue that there are instances where Canadian human security agenda – more specifically its militarization and the subsequent introduction of the Responsibility-to-Protect (R2P) norm – can be seen as the responsibilization of states, not individuals, it would be a mistake to think that this process cannot co-exist with that of human security desecuritization and the introduction of the service-delivery model. In reality, the opposite has been true. The narrowing of the FFF doctrine has been a result of both the militarization of human security (including the introduction of R2P), where international factors were dominant, and of the transfer of responsibility and competency to NGOs in the areas of earlier human security focus, such as landmines (domestic factors were decisive here). Such understanding is fully in line with a more general argument done by Mark Duffield, maintaining that the responsibilization of NGOs and the reinstatement of the state in human security are complementary technologies of governance in the period of permanent complex emergency (Duffield 2007: 32–38, 111–31). In other words, humanitarian activism (NGOs) and humanitarian interventionism (states) are *mutually dependent*, as can be seen in a number of examples, be it Bosnia, Kosovo or East Timor.

Conclusion

The presented analysis shed light on two concrete manifestations of human security: the nineteenth-century liberal disarmament and the post-Cold War

Freedom-from-Fear doctrine. As the analysis of nineteenth-century disarmament conferences and the campaign to ban anti-personnel landmines showed, both shared a number of liberal features. Thus, the examination of liberal rationalities of government was a crucial part of deeper understanding of human security, the one that goes beyond the policy-making derived analyses. The present chapter also demonstrated that one needs to focus on political micro-sites and microprocesses and on the ways in which they grow in importance. In the case of the nineteenth-century humanitarian disarmament, the venue of the Hague conference was one such micro-site. As for the FFF doctrine, the Canada-based dynamics related to APLs ban was another such a micro-site.

Although the role of NGOs in post-Cold War human security and humanitarian disarmament processes was shown to have certain echoes in the nineteenth-Century, it, too, possessed distinct traits. The most visible departure has been the use of domestic service-delivery model as the basis for twenty first-century human security practices. Competition for funding and the introduction of disciplinary management techniques have shaped actions of humanitarian NGOs in unprecedented ways. The result has been what Duffield (2001: 50–51) calls the emergence of 'liberal strategic complexes' of human security. The difference could also be seen at the general level. Unlike a common-sense understanding of liberalism (welfare, neo-, etc.) as a political ideology, Foucauldian analytics allowed us to look at liberalism in a much broader sense, i.e. as a political rationality, or governmentality, which elevated what was thought to be an economic policy or political ideology to the status of rationality, or as Foucault described it as 'the art of exercising power in the form of the economy' (Foucault 1991: 92).

Notes

1 Nik Hynek is Research Fellow, Institute of International Relations, Prague, Czech Republic; Lecturer, Charles University and Metropolitan University, Prague; and Visiting Research Scholar, Saltzman Institute of War and Peace Studies, Columbia University, New York, USA. The financial support of the Czech Academy of Science (grant identification number KJB708140803) is gratefully acknowledged.
2 In this chapter, I treat the terms 'governmentality', 'political rationality' and 'rationality of government' interchangeably.
3 The following part also appears in Hynek and Bosold (2009). The author thanks for the reprint permission.

Bibliography

Abrams, I. (1962) 'Bertha von Suttner and the Nobel Peace Prize', *Journal of Central European Affairs* 22 (3): 286–307.
Axworthy, L. (1999) *Notes for an Address by the Honourable Lloyd Axworthy to the Symposium "Civilians in War: 100 Years after the Hague Conference, 99/49"*, Ottawa: Library and Archives Canada.
Boli, J. and Thomas, G. (eds) (1999) *Constructing World Culture: International Nongovernmental Organizations since 1875*, Palo Alto: Stanford University Press.
Bosold, D. and Werthes, S. (2005) 'Human Security in Practice: Canadian and Japanese Experiences', *Internationale Politik und Gesellschaft* 1 (1): 84–102.

Burchell, G., Gordon, C. and Miller, P. (eds) (1991) *The Foucault Effect: Studies in Governmentality*, Hemel Hempstead: Harvester Wheatsheaf.

Cameron, M. A., Lawson, R. J. and Tomlin, B. W. (eds) (1998) *To Walk without Fear: The Global Movement to Ban Landmines*, Oxford: Oxford University Press.

Caron, D. (2000) 'War and International Adjudication: Reflections on the 1899 Peace Conference', *American Journal of International Law* 94 (4): 4–30.

Chrétien, J. (1995) *Speech by Prime Minister Jean Chrétien to the National Forum on Canada's International Relations*, Toronto, 11 September.

Deleuze, G. (1992) 'What is a Dispositif?', in T. J. Armstrong (ed.) *Michel Foucault Philosopher*, New York: Routledge, 159–68.

Department of Foreign Affairs and International Trade (DFAIT) (1995) *Canada in the World*, Ottawa: DFAIT.

—— (2000) *Freedom from Fear: Canada's Foreign Policy for Human Security*, Ottawa: DFAIT.

Duffield, M. (2001) *Global Governance and the New Wars: The Merging of Development and Security*, London: Zed Books.

—— (2007) *Development, Security and Unending War: Governing the World of Peoples*, London: Polity.

Eyffinger, A. (1999) *The 1899 Hague Peace Conference: The Parliament of Man, the Federation of the World*, Leiden and Boston: Martinus Nijhoff Publishers.

Finnemore, M. (1999) 'Rules of War and Wars of Rules: The International Red Cross and the Restraint of State Violence', in J. Boli and G. Thomas (eds) *Constructing World Culture: International Nongovernmental Organizations since 1875*, Palo Alto: Stanford University Press, 149–68.

Foucault, M. (1978) *The History of Sexuality, Volume I: An Introduction*, New York: Pantheon Books.

—— (1980) *Power/Knowledge: Selected Interviews and Other Writings 1972–1977* (collected by C. Gordon), Brighton: Harvester.

—— (1991) 'Governmentality', in G. Burchell, C. Gordon and P. Miller (eds) *The Foucault Effect: Studies in Governmentality*, Hemel Hempstead: Harvester Wheatsheaf, 87–104.

—— (2008) *The Birth of Biopolitics: Lectures at the Collège de France, 1978–1979*, Houndmills: Palgrave Macmillan.

Goldblat, J. (2002) *Arms Control: The New Guide to Negotiations and Agreements*, Thousand Oaks: Sage.

Goose, S. and Williams, J. (2004) 'The Campaign to Ban Antipersonnel Landmines: Potential Lessons', in Richard A. Matthew, Bryan McDonald, and Kenneth Rutherford (eds) *Landmines and Human Security: International Politics and War's Hidden Legacy*, New York: SUNY Press, 239–50.

Gordon, C. (1991) 'Governmental Rationality: An Introduction', in G. Burchell, C. Gordon and P. Miller (eds) *The Foucault Effect: Studies in Governmentality*, Hemel Hempstead: Harvester Wheatsheaf, 1–52.

Hynek, N. (2008a) 'Conditions of Emergence and Their Effects: Political Rationalities, Governmental Programs and Technologies of Power in the Landmine Case', *Journal of International Relations and Development* 11 (2): 93–120.

—— (2008b) 'Japanese Human Security: A Conceptual and Institutional Analysis', *Ritsumeikan Annual Review of International Studies* 7: 1–20.

Hynek, N. and Bosold, D. (2009) 'A History and Genealogy of the Freedom-from-Fear Doctrine', *International Journal* 64 (3) (Summer): 143–58.

Lavoyer, J. P. and Maresca, L. (1999) 'The Role of the ICRC in the Development of International Humanitarian Law', *International Negotiation* 4 (3): 503–27.

Liberal Party of Canada (1993) *Creating Opportunity: The Liberal Plan for Canada*, Ottawa: Liberal Party of Canada.

Matthew, R. A. (2004) 'Human Security and the Mine Ban Movement II: Conclusions', in R. A. Matthew, B. McDonald and K. Rutherford (ed.) *Landmines and Human Security*, New York: SUNY Press.

O'Connor, D. and Ilcan, S. (2005) 'The Folding of Liberal Government: Contract Governance and the Transformation of the Canadian Public Service in Canada', *Alternatives* 30 (1): 1–23.

Price, R. (1998) 'Reversing the Gun Sights: Transnational Civil Society Targets Land Mines', *International Organization* 52 (3): 613–44.

Rutherford, K. (1999) 'The Hague and Ottawa Conventions: A Model for Future Weapons-Prohibition Regimes?', *Non-Proliferation Review* 6 (3): 36–50.

Sending, O. and Neumann, I. (2006) 'Governance to Governmentality: Analyzing NGOs, States, and Power', *International Studies Quarterly* 50 (3): 651–72.

Tuchman, B. W. (1996) *The Proud Tower: A Portrait of the World Before the War, 1890–1914*, New York: Ballantine Books.

Wapner, P. (2000) 'The Resurgence and Metamorphosis of Normative International Relations: Principled Commitment and Scholarship in a New Millennium', in P. Wapner and L. E. Ruiz (eds) *Principled World Politics: The Challenge of Normative International Relations*, Lanham, MD: Rowman & Littlefield, 1–22.

—— (2004) 'The Campaign to Ban Antipersonnel Landmines: Potential Lessons', in R. A. Matthew, B. McDonald and K. Rutherford (eds) *Landmines and Human Security*, New York: SUNY Press, 251–68.

13 Human security

Sovereignty and disorder

Kyle Grayson

Introduction

In July 2009, a story about mass killings of Taliban prisoners of war in Afghanistan – thought to number in the thousands – returned to the front pages of the western press. The killings were alleged to have been committed during the 2001 invasion under the orders of Gen. Abdul Rashid Dostum, a former warlord within the Coalition-backed Northern Alliance.[1]

According to the *New York Times*, eyewitnesses reported that:

> [o]ver a three-day period, Taliban prisoners were stuffed into closed metal shipping containers and given no food or water; many suffocated while being trucked to the prison. Other prisoners were killed when guards shot into the containers. The bodies were said to have been buried in a mass grave in Dasht-i-Leili, a stretch of desert just outside Shibarghan.
>
> (Risen 2009)

Despite the 2002 US State Department Report that corroborated previous allegations of mass killing, a United Nations' forensics team investigation that uncovered evidence of human remains, and calls from international humanitarian groups including Physicians for Human Rights and the International Committee of the Red Cross, no further investigation of the incident has taken place.

Why bring this event up, a horror amongst the horrors that have been supplied by eight years of war? That people die in terrible ways for terrible reasons during armed conflict is not new. Nor, is the downloading by liberal regimes of the responsibility for war-fighting onto local forces a novel development. As Mark Duffield (2005) has shown, the colonial practice of getting 'savages to fight barbarians' remains central to managing contemporary geopolitical entanglements and the biopolitical rationalities underpinning them. Thus, while the acts of violence themselves can be clearly located within the strategies and tactics of a global governmentality that has fixated on taming a diverse spectrum of ungovernable populations – terrorists, the poor, Arabs, Muslims, drug-users and producers, pirates, insurgents and migrants – as well as those who operate at odds with or outside of capitalist market relations – hackers, indigenous farmers, file-sharers, worker collectives amongst others – less attention has focussed on how these kinds of violence get reabsorbed into a political imaginary that has made a series of 'humanitarian' interventions possible.

Given the reflex to seek out forms of measurement in order to establish optimums that can be transposed into new rules for prudential ruling, one would imagine that abject failures to transform societies and their constitutive populations through the imposition of particular forms of democracy, human rights, market relations and culture – the elements that are said to trickle security down into the everyday lives of individuals and the collectives to which they belong – would be a political crisis of existential proportions for current configurations of governance (Grayson 2008; Dillon and Reid 2009; Reid 2004). And yet, with a solution for how to tackle complex emergencies remaining as vexing as ever and with bodies continuing to pile up, the senses and sources of crisis are contained within the populations and territories of the intervened as opposed to the interveners. How then can we account for the lack of crisis? How might we understand the assemblage of institutions, rules, norms and rationales that capriciously kills humans and/or lets them die in the name of human security?

The following analysis will explore how the theory/practice of human security is linked to more general disciplinary and biopolitical relations of power. Taking human security's own narrative of origins as the starting point, this chapter asks – paraphrasing Foucault – has human security as an aspect of global governance acted in opposition to power mechanisms that have been operating unimpeded prior to its political emergence, or is it a part of the same historico-political network as those things it denounces? (Foucault 1990:10). It will be shown that by digging beneath the narrative of genesis that is shared by many in the field – including its inclusions and exclusions – a different perception of what is at stake in discussions of human security and the function or role of human security in contemporary global politics is revealed.

Many have argued both within the academic and policy communities that human security and state security are complementary (Axworthy 1997; Axworthy and Taylor 1998; Commission on Human Security 2003; DFAIT 2003; UN 2004; FAC 2005). In a sense they are, but not in the way that is commonly understood. This chapter will conduct a critical investigation of the type of state that ideally is supposed to be conceived and produced through the theory/practice of human security in order to illustrate the difference. In conclusion, this chapter will ask if human security has shed the geopolitical baggage of state security's primary concern with the containment of perceived disorder? The potential answers to this question shape how one ultimately understands what is being rendered secure through the practices of human security provision.

A point of origin? Biopolitics and human security[2]

In orthodox narratives of the genesis of human security, it is analysed as a concept whose emergence was made possible by the political vacuum and loss of *raison d'etre* for western state security architectures with the close of the Cold War (Alkire 2002). But rather than understand human security as a concept that emerged detached from everything but its immediate geopolitical context, what if we look at the emergence of human security as a longer process situated in a diverse complex of knowledges and practices? In other words, rather than understanding the development of the concept of human security as a response to outside stimuli, what if we conceive of it as a framework that made these stimuli perceivable? As Miller and Rose (2008) argue doing so would suggest that:

> problems [to be addressed through human security] are not pregiven, lying there waiting to be revealed. They have to be constructed and made visible, and this construction of a field of problems is a complex and often slow process. Issues and concerns have to be made to appear problematic, often in different ways, in different sites, and by different agents . . . [And] the activity of problematizing is intrinsically linked to devising ways to seek to remedy it.
> (Miller and Rose 2008: 14–15)

The process that makes human security possible is reflective of longer standing changes to the way in which mechanisms for governing have been viewed by those who govern. As Foucault outlined in a series of lectures at the end of the 1970s, what it means to govern begins to transform in the eighteenth century in western Europe as the means and ends of government shifted from being primarily concerned with the (geopolitical) aggrandizement of the state towards the mastering of population as an instrument through the use of newly developing statistical sciences (Foucault 2003b: 244; Foucault 2007). Identifying advantages in populations that had to that point remained hidden and mitigating those underlying risks and/or uncertainties that could generate disruptive manifestations became both the definition of, and goal for, effective governing. What Foucault referred to as 'governmentality therefore required that a whole novel series of security apparatuses and complexes of knowledge – particularly the statistical sciences – be utilized to improve the welfare, living conditions, health, wealth, and longevity of population' (Grayson 2008: 385).

Public sanitation, universal education, the growth of psychiatry and criminology, the professionalization of key occupations such as medicine and policing, the development of public insurance schemes and the problems that these measures were said to be solving became central concerns for government. Thus biopolitics – a means to rationalize the problems presented to governmental practice by the phenomena characteristics of living human beings constituted as a population – was also 'an ends that practices of governmentality sought to achieve, that is to provide a compelling rationalization of the phenomena characteristics of populations' (Rabinow and Rose 2003: xxix; Grayson 2008: 385). As Grayson outlines:

> [b]iopolitics identified specific phenomena that not just should, but more importantly could, be managed by the state (e.g., communicable disease) while fuelling the creation of specific 'scientific' classifications such as the homosex-

ual, the criminal-addict, or the immigrant as sub-sets of the general population that needed to be directly managed. The aim was to reduce the prevalence and potential impacts of what were represented as their associated phenomena.

(Grayson 2008: 385)

Deviations from the norm of acceptable ways of life, their prevention – or correction if efforts failed to prevent their manifestation – became the central problematique for governing. The art of government therefore required prudential balancing to promote the 'right ways' of living in 'a system anxious to have the respect of legal subjects and to ensure the free enterprise of individuals' (Foucault 2003a: 202 quoted in Grayson 2008: 385). The concerns of experts and authorities in the ensuing centuries have thus revolved around the extent to which government could be done without and conversely those instances when it is necessary (and therefore legitimate) to intervene in order to promote health, production and economic circulation (Rabinow and Rose 2003: xxix; Foucault 2003a: 203). The primary purpose is to reap the benefits said to derive from governing through freedom rather than coercive control, while recognizing that there are instances in which coercion may become necessary, though the exact amount of coercion and what constitutes necessity remained contested.

It has been these contending accounts of what constitutes proper biopolitical management that help to define differences between liberalism and other forms of governance as well as differences within forms of liberalism itself. However, while 'what must be known in order to govern' and what might constitute 'the good use of forces' remains contentious, shared foundations for making these determinations developed over the ensuing decades (Foucault 2007: 273; 314). Despite shifts between various forms of rule – liberalisms, fascisms, socialisms, welfarisms – all shared a presupposition that 'the real is programmable by authorities' (Miller and Rose 2008: 211). All thought of the objects of government in a manner so that problems and shortcomings would be 'amenable to diagnosis, prescription, and cure' (Miller and Rose 2008: 211). Thus, all maintained a 'will to govern', a desire to invent new strategies of governing that could succeed where others had failed (Miller and Rose 2008: 211).

Those who have conducted genealogies of security and military warfare, such as David Campbell (1998), James Der Derian (1995), Michael Dillon and Julian Reid (2009) and Antoine Bousquet (2009), have suggested, security and defence as elements of governing both constituted and reflected dominant corpuses – scientific, national, diplomatic, legal and cultural – at a given time. Security was increasingly understood 'as a series of political rationalities and technologies with the aim of regulating circulation in order to manage contingency' (de Larringa and Doucet 2008: 524). The advent of new technologies and forms of community identity within the restrictions offered by internationally recognized juridical sovereignty combined with thinking from the life sciences that emphasized adaptation and mutation. This resulted in a dramatic increase in the perceived magnitude of potential risks at a time when the ability to mitigate them through the traditional practices of national defence was diminishing (Dillon and Reid 2009). The myth of national invulnerability through security provision faded in the aftermath of the two world wars that featured massive aerial bombardments which evaded all forms of defence and was supplemented by nuclear weapons development and the establishment of a cold war security architecture rooted in a balance of terror through mutually assured destruction. Without hyperbole, the consequences of war could now threaten the life of the entire species.

In contrast, Nikolas Rose (2007) has shown that concurrently in the human sciences, discovery and advancements in knowledge of the human genome had ramifications that began to shift into everyday socio-political life. Increasingly – albeit sometimes in haphazard forms as witnessed by the recent financial crisis – the art of government and the very definition of personal responsibility became framed in terms of susceptibility and enhancement. In other words, the key to good conduct of governments, populations and individuals was to determine their susceptibilities and then partake in activities, treatments or policies that had been shown to enhance characteristics, skills, technologies and/or social structures that were thought by the experts to prevent susceptibilities from transforming into full blown threats with negative social and/or individual consequences. Thus, the proliferation of CCTV cameras, anti-bacterial cleaning agents, self-checking credit services, medications for the treatment of latent conditions, and the requirements to be satisfied for citizenship, are developments that can be associated with this gradual shift that has constituted the contemporary ethics of liberal humanism: the ethos of enhanced capability through the suppression of susceptibility.

These developments are left out of orthodox discussions of the emergence of human security in global politics. Instead, these accounts privilege specific geopolitical developments – i.e. the collapse of the Eastern Bloc and the ensuing 'chaos' that arose in the political vacuum – as root causes for human security as a concept and as a policy posture (Hubert and McRae 2001; ICISS 2001). In other words, human security encapsulated a set of problems and solutions that were apparent to anyone willing to accept the 'new' realities of the post-Cold War global system. As some commentators observed, human security was an idea whose time had come (Krause 2005). Focussing on the longer processes outlined earlier puts such a narrow perspective into question.

Calls for the expansion of security beyond a military focus with the state as a referent object had a provenance before the end of the Cold War. Moreover, issues like economic development and global health as means of risk alleviation – e.g. the Marshall Plan or the eradication of smallpox – had also been a part of global governance structures for the previous five decades.[3] But it was not until the 1990s that the range of factors outlined previously created the discursive space for human security to be formally articulated as a discrete policy platform. The primary – though not the only, nor necessarily the first – venue to present human security as a governing agenda was the United Nations Development Programme that featured human security in the 1994 Human Development Report.

As an assemblage of knowledges, procedures, mechanisms and ideologies that constituted a human subject in biological, economic, social and political forms, the UNDP report argued that orthodox visions of security and the relationship between state and society were no longer relevant to the geopolitical realities of the post-Cold War world. To tackle the new and emerging threats of the time, it was argued that the focus for security policy ought to be on the promotion of human life and dignity. In the hubris provided by the 'end of history', a commitment to the values of liberal humanism was understood as the key to stemming the tide of the 'coming anarchy' unleashed by the proliferation of complex emergencies – Somalia, Sierra Leone, Haiti, Bosnia and Herzegovina – that arose from the vacuums of disintegrating Cold War relations of power and clientelism.

The authors of the UNDP report argued that human security – like human rights – was to be understood as universal, applicable to all individuals and communities across geographic space and community organization (UNDP 1995). The focus of human security was to be people-centred. Public policy at the national, regional and global levels should be concerned with their effects on people and priority should be given to those phenomena that unduly threatened the ability of individuals to go about their everyday lives safely and freely (UNDP 1995). To achieve this level of security, the focus had to be on preventing threats before they became manifest – and entrenched – rather than relying on after-the-fact intervention. Human security was therefore positioned by proponents as a proactive governing agenda that required extensive engagement anywhere in the world where human life and dignity were understood to be under threat (UNDP 1995).

More specifically, human security was said to be constituted by seven interdependent and indivisible elements: personal security, environmental security, food security, health security, economic security, political security and community security (UNDP 1995). This equation marked an extension of phenomena to be securitized under governmental practice. No longer was global security policy said to entail a narrow realm of conducting the defence of the nation-state from external military attack. Security was now extended to a concern with the interactive dimensions of human vitality and existence. Development and democratization were no longer optional tactics in a strategy of geopolitical aggrandizement. They were deemed as essential to the life of the human species insofar as they created the requisite levels of docility and governability of people and places that allowed for the 'right' types of flows – of goods, services, finance capital and people – and rights kinds of adaption (e.g. increasingly self-regulating markets) central to the maintenance of neoliberal dynamics. This required an extension of biopolitical rationalities to regional and global spheres, levels not previously contemplated. Thus, in the (geo)political space made available after the fall of socialism, an imperative emerged to manage, even as the specific means, processes, mechanisms, forms of knowledge and rationalities underpinning these practices remained works-in-progress.

Concurrently, the proposed solutions to the threats outlined in the human security matrix themselves became securitized. Not only did this provide a needed resource base to pursue a series of interventions, rebuilding projects and attempted socio-political transformations, it also discursively elevated key policy concepts like democracy, development and human rights to a realm of technical policy deliberation where challenges to their meanings and/or their links to specific forms of militarization could be safely ignored as political non-starters (Beall *et al.* 2006). In this way, principles for conflict intervention, resolution and rebuilding – like those outlined in the *Responsibility to Protect* – became shared across a wide body of actors – state, inter-governmental, non-governmental and the private sector – creating a network of mutual understanding and a sense of shared mission (Duffield 2001; Berger and Weber 2009). Free markets, democracy, community development, political rights, civil rights, western cultural norms and an entitlement to 'feel responsible' became entrenched as the common-sense starting points through which specific instances of intervention – or non-intervention – were to be filtered (McCormack 2008). Thus, one could argue that a 'humanitarian-industrial complex' was formed, a shifting alliance of groups who despite differing on means – depending on the context – shared material stakes in the industry of humanitarianism, as well as common points of reference and purpose.

This complex has initiated changes to the organizational form of states as symbiotic relations between the military and agencies of development, first forged in the hearts and minds campaigns of the Cold War, became further entangled. From Canada's 3-d approach (defence, development, diplomacy) to contemporary complex emergencies to the attempts of international agencies to re-engineer state–civil society relations in places like Cambodia, all aspects of external policy have been securitized in the name of addressing crises that are said to threaten the vitality and existence of the species (Beall *et al.* 2006; Christie 2006; Christie 2008). Similarly, at the global level, the cultural emphasis on susceptibility and the responsibility to enhance has reconfigured relations between the state and civil society into a tighter interlinking than was already taking place within the neoliberal environments found within specific national jurisdictions like the United Kingdom, the United States, Japan, Canada and Australia.

At the same time, human security has played an important role within states identified as human security providers. While Chandler (2003) has noted that the affected moves undertaken to present foreign policy as ethical to domestic polities results in both popular support for particular interventions with limited risks to the credibility and accountability of the intervening party, the human security agenda has also given a sense of purpose and legitimacy that makes possible the performative enactment of positive identities that would not be compelling through appeals to domestic policy alone (Grayson 2004; Grayson 2006). Moreover, the hybrid policy space that is engendered by the various levels and actors of human security provision has created a consensus on the legitimacy of the new politics of global responsibility – as enacted through (non)intervention – while neglecting notions of collective accountability for any crises that arise or remain in the process.[4] As a problematization of global risks centred around the vitality and the existence of the species, human security has been able to function politically as a means of identifying and geographing problematic people and spaces (Dalby 2000). Chandler (2008) has noted that these danger zones are generally understood to be located in the global south. That the epicentres of human insecurity are argued to be primarily – if not exclusively – found in the global south are not a result of an objective assessment of the real as argued by Owen (2008), but rather result from the conceptual framework that is predisposed to identify and focus on human insecurities that may be located there. It is in the geographic space of the global south that adaptations to global neoliberal dynamics are perceived as dangerous mutations in need of rectification.

Pasha (2007) goes even further than Chandler by demonstrating that Islamic Cultural Zones (ICZs) – like Afghanistan, Iraq and Somalia – are now positioned as the epicentres of global human insecurity within contemporary security discourses tempered by the war on terror and the perceived threat of Islamic violence. He argues that 'the materialization of human insecurity in the ICZs, is not a religious/cultural issue, but a problem of the political, with perennial and new ambivalences surrounding the question of the Other, how to manage it under altered states' (Pasha 2007: 178). Human security then as a form of biopolitical regulation and geopolitical imagination has contributed to an erosion of the space for political possibility in global governance comparable to anything experienced within the Cold War. Moreover, it has done so while limiting the possibilities for communities of interest to exercise even the limited forms of agency and self-determination that are available (McCormack 2008).

Rather than proxy wars, mutually assured destruction and spheres of influence – although the recent conflict in Georgia would point to the returning significance of the latter concept – we have constrictions brought about by the entrenchment of capitalist modes of production, free markets, liberal constitutional forms, particular ideas of what constitutes an 'advanced' society and the imposition of a bandwidth of tolerable deviation being applied as universal norms by institutions and states that are not directly accountable to their objects of intervention (McCormack 2008). As a case like Somalia illustrates – the *bête noir* of failed states and human insecurity for the international community – these have then been applied regardless of their appropriateness to the local context (Hagmann and Hoehne 2009; Menkhaus 2004; Menkhaus 2006/07; Menkhaus 2007; World Bank 2005). Not only have these projects of biopolitical enhancement overlooked existing socio-political dynamics that demonstrate strong linkages to global circulatory flows, but they have also imposed models of state development that – at their historical best – have a close association with decades of violence and disorder (Hagmann and Hoehne 2009). It is the problem of the state, as much as the problem of the human, that has defined the theory/practice of contemporary human (in)security.

The state of human (in)security

Typically within the human security literature, the relationship between the security of the state and the security of the human is seen as linked and interdependent. However, whether one adheres to a 'freedom from fear' or 'freedom from want' conceptualization of human security, the security of the state is seen as a necessary – though not necessarily sufficient – condition for human security (Shani 2007: 6–7). Under 'freedom from fear' equations that seek to mitigate the deleterious effects of armed conflict, warlordism, crime, small arms proliferation, genocide and other forms of large-scale human rights violations, a strong state is necessary.[5] This is required so that the state – often with the help of the international community – can regain and/or retain a monopoly on the use of force – or the legitimate farming out of this monopoly – to end armed violence. Perversely, a strong state structure – even in the commissioning of prohibited forms of violence – has the advantage of providing a focal point for interventions that seek to end specific violations of human security, a focal point that might be absent in a more fluid environment. The argument is that other threats to human life and dignity cannot possibly be confronted until requisite levels of peace and stability – defined in terms of the absence of systemic levels of violence at a local level – have been achieved.

Under 'freedom from want', a strong state capable of maintaining order is necessary in order to coordinate development initiatives and to liaize with the range of other actors linked within the governance structures of contemporary development.[6] The argument for the privileging of development is that poverty and underdevelopment are typically the root causes of contemporary armed conflicts. Thus, if one wants to reduce levels of human insecurity, the prudential first step is to address issues of resource allocation, economic opportunity and financial viability upwards from local to national levels (Sato 2007: 88–90).

While often presented as polar ends on the spectrum of potential human security orientations, many analysts argue that in practice, these views have congealed into the security–development nexus (Duffield 2001). Practices to be pursued are therefore not done in isolation or prior to one another. Rather, the art of governing relates to which particular element needs to be emphasized at any given time. Thus, their symbiosis is conceived temporally as concurrent rather than evolutionary with respect to addressing the root causes of marginalization, exclusion and violence said to constitute human insecurity.

There has therefore been a double movement with respect to human security and the state. As Berger and Weber argue,

> there is an increasing elaboration of humanitarian networks and activities by the UN and a wide range of aid organisations. There are also important military interventions by outside governments in the 'marginalized' regions, sometimes under UN auspices and at other times operating under the authority of a particular national government or group of national governments, or a regional organisation.
>
> (Berger and Weber 2009: 9)

At the same time, these biopolitical interventions, strategies and attempts to alter state–society dynamics into more governable forms wish to reconstruct a state structure that is – eventually – able to conduct the orchestration of these interventions itself. Thus, while Miguel de Larrinaga and Marc Doucet (2008) perceptively allude to how biopolitical technologies and rationalities concurrently augment sovereign power's ability to launch international interventions to provide human security by invoking the terms of exceptionality, the ultimate signal of a success would be to have these specific locales exercise the sovereign exception over themselves and their constitutive populations (de Larrinaga and Doucet 2008: 517).

As much as proponents might believe that the human security agenda is about the extension of rights and responsibilities through the structures of global governance, the underlying rationality blends biopolitical concerns with those of geopolitics (Hubert 2004; Thomas 2002). That is, the imperatives of productivity, circulation and positive adaptation become imbricated in understandings of stability and order, while the recognition that populations by their very nature exhibit dynamic evolutionary properties remains an inescapable concern. As de Larrinaga and Doucet (2008) remark, ultimately the function of human security 'is to help define the exceptional circumstances that require the international community's intervention, whether on behalf of humanitarian imperatives as initially conceived or in the service of maintaining global order . . .' (532).

Such a perspective also provides a reading on the numerous instances of non-intervention. While some critical analyses wish to explain non-interventions in contexts like Darfur or Burma as an extension of narrow self-interests and/or geopolitical constraints, a view sensitive to the global governmentality of human security is able to draw out a richer bounty of contributing elements. First, the emphasis on military intervention obscures the multiple forms that intervention may take in contemporary global politics, from the economic to the religious, in attempting to transform problematic entities into safe hands. Thus, intervention is better viewed as a continuum than as a binary partner to non-intervention. Second, interventions are mostly undertaken in relation to disorder, even if the logics are biopolitical. But rather than revert to an orthodox anxiety that perceives disorder in terms of state failure – whether it be juridical or de facto – there needs to be a sensitivity shown to the ways in which such locales experience other forms of intervention, particularly financial and economic, that ensnare them into the global economy. At the same time, this does not preclude recognition that forms of integration that result – for example, piracy – may not necessarily be in ways determined to be acceptable, potentially requiring increased levels of management (Duffield 2001). Third, instances of gross humanitarian violations, despite the rhetoric of the responsibility to protect, only become defined as a problem for global governance requiring direct intervention when such instances are perceived to have destabilizing spillover effects. A gross violator of human rights norms yet reasonably effective regime with regards to the exertion of local authority – North Korea, Sudan, Burma, the United States, China – is not calculated to be the same kind of liability in terms of foreseeable spillover effects to productive circulation as other jurisdictions with less control. The metaphor of containment remains the trope through which circulation is to be secured from disarray within the constraints of the contemporary global order.

In securing circulation, de Larrinaga and Doucet argue that since the UN Secretary General's *High Level Report on Threats, Challenges, and Change* (2004), there has been a shift in the governing strategies of human security from an 'emphasis . . . [on] an understanding of threats that stem from a broad set of quotidian political, social, economic and environmental contingencies, to what are deemed to be "avoidable catastrophe[s]"' (526). Catastrophe becomes the key enabler of overt intervention, but the term itself – through a reading of recent (non)interventions –

appears to be operationally defined in relation to the species as a whole – with some populations of the species receiving an elevated weighting – as opposed to the value of localized populations in and of themselves. The killing or letting die of parts of the sum need not be perceived as an imperative to intervene and this has – in part – been reflected in the grafting of the laws of war onto the criteria for the norms of legitimate armed intervention including balance of consequence considerations in policy statements like the *High Level Report* (62–67). When one's referent object for security policy is the existence and vitality of the species as a whole and the dynamics of the system that allows these proper types of life to flourish, the levels of concern would seem to diminish as the standards for legitimate management rise. Thus, we return to the importance of the state vis-à-vis its capacity to keep catastrophe localized. As de Larrinaga and Doucet (2008) argue, 'within this context . . . it is through the nexus of the state that the provision of both security and insecurity, by state and non-state actors, is predominantly understood' (526).

Conclusion

This chapter can be but an introduction to the governmentality of human security. In merging what Michael Dillon has referred to as the 'toxic combination' of biopolitical and geopolitical rationalities, legitimations and interpretive frameworks, human security has constituted relations of power and exclusions that necessarily become a part of any emancipatory project pursued under its name (Dillon 2007). These relations and exclusions should not be seen as abnormalities or deviations that can be eliminated through further tinkering. Nor does it mean that is it necessary to argue that the global focus on human security has made no positive contributions in particular contexts.

But the issue of concern should be power. Every project, whether emancipatory or otherwise, is both constitutive and productive of relations of power. The projects of liberalism have mastered the sleights of hand necessary to present themselves as either power neutral or as emancipatory by standing in direct opposition to existing relations of power. Human security showcases the skill with which liberal regimes are able to hide in plain view mechanisms for the commission of arbitrary killing by the state in the name of 'security', whether for the state or for the species. These claims, and the violences that they can enable, are what should not escape our gaze.

Similar to the way in which we must be sensitive to the complex web of power-relations contributing to contemporary global politics – juridical, disciplinary, biopolitical, control – we must also not discount the ongoing importance of the state as an instigator, facilitator, conduit or even barrier to their operation. Although the primary focus of security may now rest upon the species, its life and propagation, the state and its proper roles (i.e. 'the correct use of forces') in achieving these goals remains central to the theory/practice of human security. The presence of the state, even if this presence serves no other role than to derogate authority to others, must not escape our accounts.

But beyond remaining cognizant of the importance of the state as a referent object for security interventions, there is much work to be done on fleshing out the further contradictions inherent to the emancipatory project of human security and how these play out in localized forms.[7] Thus, attention needs to be paid to the ways in which human security is rationalized, the forms of measurement that are developed, the ways in which these are deployed, the authorities who are consulted, and the forms of knowledge that are drawn upon in specific contexts of intervention. In doing so, the underlying war that constitutes the politics of human security can be revealed.

Notes

1. Gen. Dostum is currently serving as a defence official in the government of President Harmid Karzai.
2. This section contains revised elements from Grayson (2008).
3. Colonial projects of the nineteenth century had also contained elements of 'improving' local populations, whether through intervention schemes to implement personal hygiene to the 'letting die' strategies of famine management.
4. Dillon and Reid (2009) argue that the legitimacy of biopolitical rule has been computed through measures of effectiveness. Thus, the liberal idealism of political philosophy has always been tempered by a de facto pragmatism of the human sciences.
5. This approach to human security is most commonly associated with Canadian and Norwegian initiatives since the 1990s.
6. This view of human security is most commonly associated with Japanese global policy efforts that have earmarked a significant sum of resources to UN human security initiatives.
7. For a comprehensive account, see Dillon and Reid (2009).

Bibliography

Alkire, S. (2002) *Conceptual Framework for Human Security*, Commission on Human Security 2002. Available URL: http://www.humansecurity-chs.org/activities/outreach/frame.pdf (accessed July 2009).
Axworthy, L. (1997) 'Canada and Human Security: The Need for Leadership', *International Journal* 52 (2): 183–96.
—— (2001) 'Human Security and Global Governance: Putting People First', *Global Governance* 7 (2): 19–23.
Axworthy, L. and Taylor, S. (1998) 'A Ban for All Seasons: The Landmines Convention and its Implications for Canadian Diplomacy', *International Journal* 53 (1): 183–96.
Beall, J., Goodfellow, T. and Putzel, J. (2006) 'On the Discourse of Terrorism, Security, and Development', *Journal of International Development* 18 (1): 51–57.
Berger, M. T. and Weber, H. (2009) 'War, Peace and Progress: Conflict, Development, (In)security and Violence in the 21st Century', *Third World Quarterly* 30 (1): 1–16.
Bousquet, A. (2009) *The Scientific Way of Warfare: Order and Chaos on the Battlefields of Modernity*, London: Hurst and Co.
Campbell, D. (1998) *Writing Security: United States Foreign Policy and the Politics of Identity*, 2nd edition, Minneapolis: University of Minnesota Press.
Chandler, D. (2003) 'Rhetoric Without Responsibility: The Attraction of Ethical Foreign Policy', *British Journal of Politics and International Relations* 5 (3): 295–316.
—— (2008) 'Human Security: The Dog That Didn't Bark', *Security Dialogue* 39 (4): 427–38.

Christie, R. (2006) 'Partners or Competitors: A Critical Examination of State/NGO Interaction in Cambodia', Paper presented at the *International Studies Association Annual Convention*, San Diego.

—— (2008) 'The Human Security Dilemma: Lost Opportunities, Appropriated Concepts, or Actual Change?' in *Environmental Change and Human Security: Recognizing and Acting on Hazard Impacts*, edited by P. H. Liotta, William G. Kepner and Judith M. Lancaster, AA Dordrecht: Springer.

Commission on Human Security (2003) *Human Security Now*, New York: United Nations.

Dalby, S. (2000) *Geopolitical Change and Contemporary Security Studies: Contextualizing the Human Security Agenda. IIR Working Paper Series*, Vancouver: Institute for International Relations, University of British Columbia.

de Larrinaga, M. and Doucet, M. G. (2008) 'Sovereign Power and the Biopolitics of Human Security', *Security Dialogue* 39 (5): 517–37.

Department of Foreign Affairs and International Trade (1998) *The Lysoen Declaration*, Lysoen: Government of Canada.

—— (2003) *Freedom From Fear: Canada's Foreign Policy for Human Security*, Ottawa: Government of Canada.

Der Derian, J. (1995) 'The Value of Security: Hobbes, Marx, Nietzsche, and Baudrillard', in *On Security*, edited by R. Lipschutz, New York: Columbia.

Dillon, M. (2007) 'Governing through Contingency: The Security of Biopolitical Governance', *Political Geography* 26 (1): 41–47.

Dillon, M. and Reid, J. (2009) *The Liberal Way of War: Killing to Make Life Live*, London: Routledge.

Duffield, M. (2001) *Global Governance and the New Wars: The Merging of Development and Security*, London: Zed Books.

—— (2005) 'Getting Savages to Fight Barbarians: Development, Security, and the Colonial Present', *Conflict, Security & Development* 5 (2): 141–59.

Foreign Affairs Canada (2005) *Canada's International Policy Statement: A Role of Pride and Influence in the World*, Ottawa: Government of Canada.

Foucault, M. (1990) *The History of Sexuality: An Introduction*, 3 Vols, Vol. 1, New York: Random House.

—— (2003a) 'The Birth of Biopolitics', in *The Essential Foucault: Selections from Essential Works of Foucault 1954–1984*, edited by Paul Rabinow and Nikolas Rose, New York: The New Press.

—— (2003b) *Society Must Be Defended: Lectures at the College de France 1975–1976*, Translated by D. Macey, New York: Picador.

—— (2007) *Security, Territory, Population: Lectures at the College de France 1977–1978*, Translated by G. Burchell, Basingstoke: Palgrave.

Grayson, K. (2004) 'Branding Transformation in Canadian Foreign Policy: Human Security', *Canadian Foreign Policy* 11 (2): 41–68.

—— (2006) 'Promoting Responsibility and Accountability: Human Security and Canadian Corporate Conduct', *International Journal* 56 (1): 479–95.

—— (2008) 'Human Security as Power/Knowledge: The Biopolitics of a Definitional Debate', *Cambridge Review of International Affairs* 21 (3): 383–401.

Hagmann, T. and Hoehne, M. V. (2009) 'Failures of the State Failure Debate: Evidence from the Somali Territories', *Journal of International Development* 21 (1): 42–57.

Hubert, D. (2004) 'An Idea that Works in Practice', *Security Dialogue* 35 (3): 351.

Hubert, D. and McRae, R. (eds) (2001) *Human Security and the New Diplomacy: Protecting People, Promoting Peace*, Montreal and Kingston: McGill-Queen's University Press.

McCormack, T. (2008) 'Power and Agency in the Human Security Framework', *Cambridge Review of International Affairs* 21 (1): 113–28.

Menkhaus, K. (2004) 'Vicious Circles and the Security Development Nexus in Somalia', *Conflict, Security, & Development* 4 (2): 149–65.

—— (2006/07) 'Governance Without Government in Somalia: Spoilers, State Building, and the Politics of Coping', *International Security* 31 (3): 74–106.

—— (2007) 'The Crisis in Somalia: Tragedy in Five Acts', *African Affairs* 106 (424): 357–90.

Miller, P. and Rose, N. (2008) *Governing the Present*, Cambridge: Polity Press.

Owen, T. (2008) 'The Critique That Doesn't Bite: A Response to David Chandler's "Human Security: The Dog That Didn't Bark"', *Security Dialogue* 39 (4): 445–53.

Pasha, M. K. (2007) 'Human Security and Exceptionalism(s): Securitization, Neoliberalism, and Islam', in *Protecting Human Security in a Post 9/11 World: Critical and Global Insights*, edited by Giorgio Shani, Makoto Sato and Mustapha Kamal Pasha, Basingstoke: Palgrave.

Rabinow, P. and Rose, N. (2003) 'Introduction: Foucault Today', in *The Essential Foucault: Selections from Essential Works of Foucault 1954–1984*, edited by Paul Rabinow and Nikolas Rose, New York: The New Press.

Reid, J. (2004) 'War, Liberalism, and Modernity: The Biopolitical Provocations of "Empire"', *Cambridge Review of International Affairs* 17 (1): 63–79.

Risen, J. (2009) 'U.S. Inaction Seen After Taliban P.O.W.'s Died', *New York Times*, July 10.

Rose, N. (2007) *The Politics of Life Itself: Biomedicine, Power, and Subjectivity in the Twenty-First Century*, Princeton: Princeton University Press.

Sato, M. (2007) 'Human Security and Japanese Diplomacy: Debates on the Role of Human Security in Japanese Policy', in *Protecting Human Security in a Post 9/11 World: Critical and Global Insights*, edited by Giorgio Shani, Makoto Sato and Mustapha Kamal Pasha, Basingstoke: Palgrave.

Secretary-General's High-Level Panel on Threats, Challenges and Change (2004) *A More Secure World: Our Shared Responsibility*, New York: United Nations.

Shani, G. (2007) 'Protecting Human Security in a Post 9/11 World', in *Protecting Human Security in a Post 9/11 World: Critical and Global Insights*, edited by Giorgio Shani, Makoto Sato and Mustapha Kamal Pasha, Basingstoke: Palgrave.

Thomas, C. (2001) 'Global Governance, Development, and Human Security: Exploring the Links', *Third World Quarterly* 22(2): 159–175.

United Nations Development Programme (1995) 'Redefining Security: The Human Dimension', *Current History* 94 (592): 229–36.

World Bank (2005) *Conflict in Somalia: Drivers and Dynamics*, World Bank.

14 Inhuman security

Mark Neocleous

'Human security'. It's a lovely phrase. It encourages the view that security can be rescued from its long association with states and the armed defence of their territories and connected in a more progressive, even emancipatory way, with the human. Security, it suggests, is so important to being human that it can and should form the foundation of freedom, democracy and the good society. Regardless of the misery conducted in its name, the bombing and the maiming, the slaughter and the torture, security is *still* a 'good thing'. All it needs is to be *humanized*.

Either explicitly or implicitly this relies on the assumption that security has to be oriented around the notion of emancipation. 'Security and emancipation are two sides of the same coin', we are told. Emancipation *is* security, both theoretically and empirically, because 'emancipation, not power or order, produces true security' (Booth 1991: 319, 323). Simply put, the logic of the work generated around the label 'human security', and to a large degree also the work in 'critical security studies', is that 'security' can be reconfigured in such a way as to render the fundamental dimension of both global and local politics as human. The project is to humanize one of the most important aspects of state power in the service of emancipation. In this chapter I want to challenge this set of assumptions. I want to do so by linking security not to emancipation, but to fascism.

A number of writers have noted that there is a real Schmittian logic underpinning security politics (for example, Williams 2003). Casting an issue as one of 'security' tends to situate that issue within the logic of friend and enemy. In so doing it ratchets up strategic 'security' fears and dangers and so encourages a political decisionism concerning the 'state of exception' (Neocleous 2006a: 2008: 39–75). Such political reason is the core of Schmitt's concept of the political. 'The political is the most intense and extreme antagonism', says Schmitt, 'and every concrete antagonism becomes that much more political the closer it approaches the most extreme point, that of the friend-enemy grouping'. The nature of friendship lies in a set of common values distinguishing the friend from the 'other, the stranger' (Schmitt 1932: 29).

> The political enemy need not be morally evil or aesthetically ugly; he need not appear as an economic competitor, and it may even be advantageous to engage with him in business; and it is sufficient for his nature that he is, in a specially

intense way, existentially something different and alien, so that in the extreme case conflicts with him are possible.

(Schmitt 1932: 27)

For Schmitt, this friend-enemy antagonism is the essence of the political, reaching its highpoint in a state of exception which allows sovereignty to be asserted and reinstated: 'sovereign is he who decides on the exception' (Schmitt 1922: 5). It is fair to say that this kind of argument has been a powerful undercurrent in a fair amount of recent thinking around security. For example, in their influential work aiming to develop security concepts away from classical and realist arguments centred on the security of the state and towards a wider range of 'societal sectors', Barry Buzan, Ole Waever and Jaap de Wilde nonetheless still resort to Schmittian concepts and language. Something becomes a security issue 'when [that] issue is presented as posing an existential threat to a designated referent object'. In such a context, 'by saying "security", a state representative declares an emergency condition' (Buzan *et al.* 1998: 21). For these writers, the broadening of the sphere of security does little to change the assumptions underpinning the existential threat. Now, I have no desire to rehearse the fascist dimensions of Schmitt's work (see Neocleous 1996). But if there is a real Schmittian logic to much of the language of security, and if Schmitt can legitimately be described as a 'theorist' or even 'Crown jurist' for the Reich (Bendersky 1983; Stirk 2005), then this must at least demand a proper exploration of the relationship between the logic of security and fascism.

'Speaking and writing about security is never innocent', says Jef Huysmans, 'it always risks contributing to the opening of a window of opportunity for a "fascist mobilization"' (2002: 43). Recent events bear witness to this, and it is by no means far-fetched to say that any revival of fascism will come through a political mobilization in the name of security (Harootunian 2007). I therefore want to push this idea by exploring the connections between security and fascism. As far as I am aware, this has not been done within security studies, a fact that is especially odd when one considers that fascism is often understood in terms of the idea of a 'police state' and that security is the core category of police (Neocleous 2000). The initial question I want to ask is: what happens to our understanding of fascism if we view it through the lens of security? But then a far more interesting question emerges: what happens to our understanding of security if we view it through the lens of fascism?

Perhaps these questions could be framed in a different way: what would a revolutionary emancipation in the name of security actually look like, politically speaking? This never seems to be addressed by those who speak of security and emancipation, an omission that seems especially odd given that this is often done in the name of 'critical theory'. But it is hard to imagine such a 'revolution' other than one which reinforces the fundamental instrumentality at the heart of security, and which therefore reinforces domination over freedom. That is, it is hard to imagine such a revolution other than as a counter-revolution or revolutionary reaction; as getting rather uncomfortably close to fascism; as a politics of *inhuman security*.

'Anti-Semitism fused with security issues'

It is well-known that the Nazis constantly used euphemism to mask the deeds of the Nazi state and played around with language in order to reframe political questions, as Victor Klemperer (1946) has shown at length: 'productive work' rather than slave labour or being taken into 'protective custody' rather than being arrested, to give just two examples. In similar fashion, people who had been robbed of their valuables found that in fact the state had simply 'secured' (*sichergestellt*) their property. And rather a lot of such 'securing' went on. From the moment communists started being detained 'for security reasons', in Dachau in March 1933, security became integral to the glossary of Nazi ideas. As such, we need to examine what can only be described as the 'securitization' of German society from 1933 onwards.[1]

In April 1933, a new 'Secret State Police' (*Geheime Staatspolizei*, or *Gestapo*) was formed as part of the new Nazi state. The law creating this new body claimed that it was necessary 'in order to assure the effective struggle against all of the efforts directed against the existence and security of the state' (cited in Gellately 1991: 29). Concerns had been widespread since the seizure of power at the end of January 1933 that not enough was being done in terms of security. For example, Adolf Wagner, *Staatskommissar* at the Bavarian Ministry of the Interior, wrote on 13 March, 1933, to Hans Frank, *Staatskommissar* at the Bavarian Ministry of Justice, that 'the order for the arrest of all communist officials and *Reichsbannerführer* [Social Democrat squad leaders] has not so far been carried out as thoroughly as necessary for the preservation of peace and security' (cited in Broszat 1965: 144). From the initial seizure of power, then, the securitization of German society was afoot. Yet the feeling that the 'security of the state' was not being properly defended was still in place three years later, and led to a huge reorganization of the security apparatus, in June 1936, as major changes were made to the organization of certain aspects of the Nazi state. Hitler appointed Himmler as head of the German police, allowing him to combine this with his role as head of the SS. Himmler divided the police into two sections: the Order Police (*Ordnungspolizei*, or Orpo) and the Security Police (*Sicherheitspolizei*, or Sipo). The latter was a new organization combining the Gestapo and Kripo (*Kriminalpolizei*, the Criminal Police). The Security Police was to be headed by Reinhard Heydrich, who was also head of the *Sicherheitsdienst* (SD), the Nazi Party's Security Service. Later, at the beginning of the war in September 1939 the Security Police and the SD were combined into a new Reich Security Head Office (*Reichssicherheitshauptamt*, the RSHA). As we shall see, it is no coincidence that the birth of a new major institution with overall control of 'security' occurred at the same time as the extermination in the East was intensified.

Drawing together these complementary party and state agencies created a powerful new organizational tool which was to become crucial in the war against the communist–Jewish enemy, for a number of reasons. First, many Nazis believed that the project of extermination could be conducted only by those willing and able to undertake it. 'Only the Security Police has the necessary experience in this area', commented Franz Rademacher, head of the Jewish desk in the German Foreign Office (cited in Browning 2005: 85). Despite his role as supreme commander of the

Wehrmacht, Hitler had concerns about the regular army's ability to carry out the necessary actions, and had therefore appointed Himmler, as security chief, to the task (Förster 1986; Mazower 2009: 143, 190–91; Wildt 2005: 345). Time and again the experience of the Security Police in 'security matters' was used by the Nazis as an explanation for the institution's role in dealing with the 'Jewish problem'. To give just one further example, Eichmann's close associate Theodore Dannecker commented in January 1941 on the importance of the 'extensive experience' of the security services in carrying out the final solution (cited in Browing 2005: 103–4). Second, just as the military is the least likely institution to resist a military coup, and the police the least likely institution to resist a police state, so the 'security services' are the least likely to question, resist or refuse actions carried out in the name of security. And third, having such actions carried out by the Security Police gave the whole project an air of legitimacy. For example, Rudolf Lehmann, Chief of the legal division of the Armed Forces High Command (OKW) commented in a document on the jurisdiction of military courts that to make the use of military courts 'somewhat more palatable' he would omit references to 'the carriers of the Jewish-Bolshevik worldview' and 'Jewish-Bolshevik system' and would instead emphasize the rationale of security (Browning 2005: 220).

Thus to point to the institutional mish-mash of police and security organizations – Sipo, Kripo, Orpo, Gestapo, SS, SD and so on – as a way of highlighting 'confusion about the nature and mission of the organizations charged with "security" in the Third Reich' (Gellately 1991: 143), is in some sense to miss the point, which is that 'security' was the *raison d'être* of the institutional framework as a whole. The institutional mish-mash is therefore somewhat irrelevant; indeed, is there any state which does not have an institutional overlap and confusion between institutions concerned with 'security'? What is crucial is that security was the logic which underpinned the whole system. As Browder's (1996) work has suggested, the institutional identity conferred by security work had a kind of elective affinity with Nazism. That this should be so should not surprise, since in *Mein Kampf* Hitler had referred many times to the importance of security: of economic security for the nation and the insecurity generated by trade unions; the security of the living space for the race and the security of the state within this living space; the security of Germany in the international system; the importance of a food supply and national honour to the nation's security; the security of the means of executing a movement's ideas; the list of 'security issues' goes on and on (Hitler 1925: 50, 130, 131, 133, 136, 150, 177, 325, 601). By the time the Nazis came to power, and consolidated this power within the wider international system in the 1930s, a system in which the new ideology of security was becoming increasingly important, this thematic could very easily be used to underpin the whole system. Symptomatically, the SA often denied that they were a 'storm section' (*Sturm Abteilung*), and preferred to present themselves in a guise more consistent with this *raison d'être*: as a 'security section' (*Sicherheits Abteilung*); the initials 'SA' conveniently stood for both (Heiden 1944: 234).

Security thereby permeated the system of legal terror exercised by the Nazis. The *Sicherungslager* (security camp) was one of the main categories of the concentration camp system. Nikolaus Wachsmann (2004) has also shown that the regular legal system – that is, the system of trial and punishment that imprisoned people to such an extent that until August 1944 the numbers in the regular prisons outnumbered those in concentration camps – was also founded on the notion of security. The whole system was based on the notion of 'security confinement' (*Sicherungsverwahrung*), derived from the Law against Dangerous Habitual Criminals of 24 November, 1933, and aimed at imprisoning people said to be a danger to the security of the community – the *sicherungsverwahrter Krimineller*, who wore a triangle with the letter 'S'. Judges made extensive use of security confinement sentences, which were eagerly carried out by prison officials committed to the notion, to the extent that both retrospective security confinements (even for people who had not actually been sentenced by the courts for anything) and the indefinite imprisonment of offenders even after the end of their original sentence became common. Security confinement was not just a weapon of criminal policy, but was explicitly political: it was central to Nazism's attempt to reorder the German polity and society by excluding 'security threats' – 'inferiors', 'outsiders', 'deviants', critics and resisters – from the national community. Eventually *Sicherungsverwahrung* became a euphemism for concentration camp incarceration and 'security confinement prisoners' (*Sicherungsverwahrungshaftlinger*), including Jews (often arrested for their political opposition to the regime rather than as 'racial aliens'), trade unionists, communists and other problematic outsiders, were taken into 'protective custody' (*Schutzhaft*). This term, *Schutzhaft*, was applied initially following the proclamation of the emergency decree of 28 February, 1933, but became widespread from April 1933. (In the intervening weeks such arrests were often referred to as a transfer into *Polizeihaft* [police custody], and relevant orders throughout 1933 refer varyingly to 'political protective custody', 'police custody for political reasons' and 'political custody' [Broszat 1965: 144], reminding us of the extent to which security and police overlap as political concepts.) The key to such custody was that those taken into it were regarded as enemies of security – a term which in effect 'provided the Gestapo with virtually unlimited powers of arrest and confinement' (Gellately 1991: 13).

The logic of security helped legitimize not only the acts of exclusion on which Nazism was initially founded, but also led to the final act of extermination. The Wannsee conference of 20 January, 1942, taken by many to be the formal meeting to launch the Final Solution, was essentially a meeting of security police. Overall control of the Final Solution lay with the Reichsfuhrer SS and chief of the German police (Himmler, with Heydrich as his representative). Indeed, it has been suggested that the purpose of the Wannsee conference was not merely to finalize the plans for the Final Solution, but 'to reinforce the RSHA's pre-eminence in all aspects of the Jewish question' (Roseman 2002: 83). It might also be pointed out that the key administrative agency for supervising the concentration camps alongside the RSHA was the Office of Economic Policy (WVHA), giving us not only another nice euphemism – extermination as economic policy – but also another suitable example of the conjunction between security and conceptions of economic order.

'What explains the decision to extend killing to the whole of European Jewry?' asks Michael Burleigh.

> Warning bells began to sound in the autumn of 1941, when notice was dramatically served on the Jews of Western Europe too. It is important to grasp . . . that what follows had nothing whatsoever to do with rationalising economies or settlement plans, but involved anti-Semitism fused with security issues.
>
> (2001: 645)

Whenever the extermination was to be stepped up, such as following the Warsaw uprising in April 1943, it was always as a 'security threat' that Jews were depicted, a depiction which of course countervailed against any arguments concerning, say, their economic utility. As Christopher Browning puts it, 'with the exception of artisans, Jews were not an important labor factor. Instead, they presented a security threat that had to be neutralized in the interest of the "absolutely necessary, quick pacification of the east"'. Thus, 'in the eyes of German officials, especially outside the civil administration, the economic usefulness of Jews as forced laborers was far outweighed by their being perceived as a threat to security' (Browning 2005: 285–86, 297).

Security was thus the major theme in managing the occupied states and the extermination policies carried out there, and for the measures carried out against other social groups for which 'exclusion' wasn't quite enough. Let me briefly discuss the case of the Lithuanian Jews as an illustration of the point about occupied states, and gypsies and homosexuals as illustrative of the point about social groups.

The initial pogroms and shootings of Lithuanian Jews in the summer of 1941 were conducted under the guise of security. Heydrich authorized the Lithuanian police to carry out 'cleansing operations' to secure the movement of the *Einsatzgruppen* and *Einsatzkommandos*. The local understanding was that the project was a security measure: since the Jewish people were the active agents of Bolshevism, their initial exclusion and eventual destruction was necessary on security grounds. Asked under interrogation in 1958 about his role in the shooting of Jewish men in Kretinga in 1941, *SS-Unterführer* Krumbach from the police station in Tilsit commented:

> It was explained to me then that according to an order from the Fuhrer, the whole of eastern Jewry had to be exterminated so that there would no longer be Jewish blood available there to maintain a world Jewry, thus bringing about the decisive destruction of world Jewry. This affirmation was by itself not new at that time and was rooted in the ideology of the Party. The *Einsatzkommandos* of the Sipo and of the SD were instituted for this task by the Fuhrer.
>
> (cited in Dieckmann 2000: 246)

Once the pogroms against the Jews were set in place, the second dimension of the Nazi obsession with security could then be set into play. The leaders of the *Einsatzgruppen* had to give the pogroms the appearance of being carried out spontaneously by Lithuanians as revenge against the Jews for their supposed Bolshevik activities. In this way, the responsibility of the Security Police for the killings would not become widely known – one of the many instances in which the exercise of violence is erased from the concept of security. The Sipo, as the agent of this particular security project, could thereby be protected from accusations of uncontrolled brutality. Dieckmann (2000: 269) cites the report of *Einsatzgruppe A*, from 15 October, 1941:

> It was however not undesirable that they [the German Security Police] ... did not give the appearance of using the clearly unusually harsh measures, which would certainly elicit a stir in German circles. It must be shown to the outside world that the native population itself took the first measures, of its own accord, in a natural reaction against centuries of oppression by the Jews and the terror of the Communists in former times.

This then served to facilitate a further dimension to the importance of security: that the Security Police could then be seen to step in as the guarantor of order – as some kind of institutional check on the 'wild wrath of the people'. Thus the Security Police would be needed to restore order, reaffirming once more security's 'positive' role. For reasons such as these, Dieckmann suggests that in the Lithuanian context 'National Socialist security policy was the most important element'.

> The intent to exterminate the Jews was clear from the plans for deportations. The analysis of the policy as it actually developed makes it seem possible that further factors were also necessary. The modification of the racist starvation policy ... meant first and foremost the pauperization of the Jewish population, which was to be denied the right to live. The mass killings were in this connection legitimized on the grounds of National Socialist security policy.
> (Dieckmann 2000: 266)

His point applies to the whole of the Third Reich.

In terms of social groups, Guenter Lewy (2000: 70–77) has shown that the persecution against the gypsies was conducted under a range of security measures. The notion easily spread that gypsies were not merely 'plague' or 'nuisance', the traditional ways of distancing them, but were also in fact working for foreign intelligence services. This was the reason given to explain why gypsies liked to live in border areas. Thus on 31 January, 1940, the High Command of the Armed forces requested from Himmler an order prohibiting on the grounds of 'defence' gypsies from living in the border zone. On 27 April, 1940, Heydrich issued a decree on 'Resettlement of Gypsies' which gave orders to begin transporting 2,500 gypsies away from the western and north-western border zones and to the General Government. These requests and orders were gradually realized through 1940, during which period the security theme became prevalent. Lewy comments that the idea that the expulsion was based in the main on concern about military security is less than credible, for if it was then why did it take so long? And why limit the number to 2,500? Why send them to the General Government, which was also a border zone and where they could do as much damage? And why were foreign gypsies excluded? These are fair questions, but they only make sense if one takes the security project at face value. But no security project should ever be taken at face value. Security always functions as an underlying rationale for some political project: an exclusion here, an extermination there; a partial solution here, a final solution there. Moreover, security could play this foundational role precisely because of the way it obliterates any distinction between inside and outside, domestic and foreign. The internal enemy needed to be exterminated because it was in fact integral to the external enemy – international communism. The external security project which identified the Soviet state as the key enemy could thus slide into an internal security project aimed at the supposed agents of the Soviet state, namely the Jewish–Bolshevik conspiracy.

At the same time, and in common with many security forces in the west, the Nazis perceived homosexuals as a security threat, part of a broader range of 'non-conformist' activities which were the basis for one security measure after another (Browder 1996: 65–66, 72). Gellately suggests that everyday life became so politicized in Nazi Germany that *even* the sphere of sexuality and friendship became an issue and the Nazis criminalized any behaviour that appeared oppositional (1991: 147, 157). Indeed, but that's where the logic of security takes us. It presupposes that every aspect of our human being is part of a general security problem (Neocleous 2006c; 2008: 123–41).

Another six million

'I have talked a good deal about Hitler', says Aimé Césaire in his *Discourse on Colonialism* in 1955. Why? 'Because he deserves it: he makes it possible to see things on a large scale'. 'At the end of capitalism', Césaire writes, 'there is Hitler. At the end of formal humanism and philosophical renunciation, there is Hitler' (1955: 37). He might well have said: at the end of security, there is Hitler.

This is precisely why the Schmittian logic underpinning so much of the security discourse is so telling. For in Schmittian terms the question of security unveils the nature of the political, inherent in which is the idea of combat and annihilation (Schmitt 1932: 32). 'War is neither the aim nor the purpose nor even the very content of politics. But as an ever present possibility it is the leading presupposition which ... thereby creates a specifically political behaviour' (ibid: 34). As much as the state presupposes the concept of the political, so the political presupposes the concept of war. To this end, Hobbes's war of all against all becomes the 'fundamental presupposition of a specific political philosophy' (ibid: 65). However, whilst Hobbes's state of nature is a war of individuals, Schmitt's account posits collectivities at war, albeit undefined: 'An enemy exists only when, at least potentially, one fighting collectivity of people confronts a similar collectivity' (ibid: 28). And it is clear that this enemy may be domestic as well as foreign: the fight in question may be a civil war as much as war between nations, a war of extermination against internal as well as external enemies. This is the main reason Schmitt so despises liberalism: because it *demilitarizes* politics and reduces intensely political concepts such as combat to either economic competition or intellectual discussion (ibid: 71). In so doing 'the decisive bloody battle' is transformed into a parliamentary debate

(Schmitt 1922: 63). Regardless of Schmitt's misreading of liberalism on this point – liberal social orders have been more than happy to carry out, and liberals more than happy to justify, 'decisive' acts of violence against either external or internal enemies on the grounds of emergency and in the name of security – the point is that for Schmitt the decisive bloody battle becomes the *defining characteristic* of the political, the key to the nature of the decision and to the identification of friends and enemies. 'A world in which the possibility of war is eliminated, a completely pacified globe, would be a world without the distinction of friend and enemy and hence a world without politics' (Schmitt 1932: 35, 78).

For Schmitt, war is the pinnacle of great politics and the highest form of human behaviour: 'What always matters is the possibility of the extreme case taking place, the real war' (Schmitt 1932: 35). War therefore needs no real justification as such; or, rather, its existence *is* its justification: 'the justification of war does not reside in its being fought for ideals or norms of justice, but in its being fought against a real enemy' (ibid: 49). Being at war with one's enemy follows logically from the decision to identify the 'other', the 'stranger', as different and alien – an enemy and therefore geared for combat. But because Schmitt's decisionism is an essentially existentialist politics, war is not just a perpetual phenomenon of the political, but is its *highest form*. 'The high points of politics are simultaneously the moments in which the enemy is, in concrete clarity, recognized as the enemy' (Schmitt 1932: 67). The concrete clarity of the enemy raises the possibility of 'life' and the struggles surrounding it being accorded an existential meaning. In this context, the importance of the state of exception is that it breaks through the torpid, repetitive everdayness of bourgeois norms. Just as in existential philosophy moments of peril call forth individual 'authenticity', so the state of exception, as moment of *political* peril, calls forth a *political* authenticity. The state of exception – the clampdown in the name of security – is thus granted an existential significance. But because the enemy, as other, is existentially alien, *exclusion* is not enough. Rather, its *physical annihilation* takes on an existential meaning: 'the friend, enemy, and combat concepts receive their real meaning precisely because they refer to the real possibility of physical killing' (Schmitt 1932: 33). Extermination is thus beyond the requirement of any normative meaning; it is justified for its own sake, for the meaning it brings to the political.

Reflecting in 1953 on some of these themes, Franz Neumann commented that the integrating element of liberal democracy always purports to be a moral one, such as 'freedom' or 'justice', but that 'there is opposed to this a second integrating principle of a political system: fear of an enemy'. Such fear, he notes, is a key feature of fascism, which 'asserts that the creation of a national community is conditioned by the existence of an enemy whom one must be willing to exterminate physically'. Yet Neumann adds that when the concepts of 'enemy' and 'fear' come to constitute the most energetic principle of politics, democracy becomes impossible and the system is ripe for dictatorship (1953: 223–24). His reference is to Schmitt, and reflects also on his own experience of having lived through the rise of fascism in Germany. But he also had in mind the kind of practices then being carried out in the name of security by liberal democracies, such as the Loyalty Program in the US. This Program replicated and in some ways surpassed the practices for consolidating loyalty, national identity and political unity used by the fascist regimes: lack of toleration of different political opinions in public life; police incursions into personal lives; the proscription of lawful associations; Star Chamber proceedings on the basis of anonymous testimony; persecution for political beliefs entailing no criminal conduct; and the enforcement of rigid political orthodoxy through the use of vague and sweeping standards of loyalty. The fear of the enemy, and the equally substantive fear of being denounced as part of the enemy, meant the continual reiteration of 'Patriot Acts' – no other term is more appropriate – on the part of the good citizen-subjects. The Program was also being conducted at a time when the national security state in question was happily employing known fascists in its own struggle for security against the communist enemy.

Neumann clearly sensed that much of what he said about fascism could be used to point to dangers that actually lie within liberalism, dangers rooted in allowing a mythical security to become the only measure of political judgement and fear the basis of order. But Neumann was also trying to contribute to one of critical theory's insights, namely that the fascist potential *within* liberal democracy is more dangerous than the fascist tendency *against* democracy (Adorno 1959: 90). Bearing in mind that fascism thrives in the crises of liberalism, that the crises of liberalism are more often than not expressed as crises threatening the security of the state and the social order of capital, and bearing in mind too the extent to which fascism comes draped in its own security blanket and can speak the language of security as well as anyone else, it really is no exaggeration to say that were such tendencies to be realized now then they would do so in the name of security.

It strikes me that this poses a very real political problem for those who think that if only we could 'humanize' security then everything will be all right. In constantly harping on about the need for a new security agenda, the various 'solutions' recently proposed to redefine, re-vision, re-map, re-civilize or just generally rethink security around the human might actually be part of the problem. The solution lies not in yet another, more human, vision of security, but in the way Marx originally understood the purpose of critical theory: not as a search for security, but as the ruthless criticism of all that exists. If we are to turn such ruthless criticism on to security – that is, if we are to focus critical theory on the question of security – then we must do so not in search of security's 'humanization', but in search of its critique.

As I suggest elsewhere, the critique of security suggests that at the heart of the logic of security lies not a vision of freedom or emancipation, but a means of modelling the whole of human society around capital and the state (Neocleous 2008). Through security, authority inscribes itself deeply into human experience, neutralizing political action and encouraging us to surrender ourselves to the state and the institutional violence which underpins it. In so doing the critique of security reminds us of the fascist potential within some of the core categories within liberalism and its order of capital. Rather than rethink such categories through an attempt at 'humanizing' them, we need instead to consider the kind of project Walter Benjamin had in mind in his essay 'The Work of Art in the Age of its Reproducibility', where he comments that as well as contributing to the creation of conditions which would make it possible to abolish capitalism itself, the essay also tries to develop concepts which 'are completely useless for the purposes of fascism'. The critique of security is part of this project. But given the extent to which the ideology of security has become the dominant ideological trope of contemporary politics, such critique is not without its difficulties. Faced with such difficulties in the context of the rise of European fascism, Benjamin enquired in 1929 about 'the conditions for revolution'. In bleak tone, he suggested that surrealism had come close to the communist answer: 'pessimism all along the line. Absolutely'. 'Mistrust in the fate of literature', he continues, 'mistrust in the fate of freedom, mistrust in the fate of European humanity, but three times mistrust in all reconciliation: between classes, between nations, between individuals (Benjamin 1929: 216–17). To this list we should add 'security'. Mistrust in security, all along the line.

Note

1 The bulk of the following section is reproduced from Neocleous 2009.

Bibliography

Adorno, T. (1959) 'The Meaning of Working Through the Past', in *Critical Models: Interventions and Catchwords* (1998), trans. Henry W. Pickford, New York: Columbia University Press.
Bendersky, J. (1983) *Carl Schmitt: Theorist for the Reich*, Princeton, NJ: Princeton University Press.
Benjamin, W. (1929) 'Surrealism: The Last Snapshot of the European Intelligentsia', trans. Edmund Jephcott; reprinted in M. W. Jennings, H. Eiland and G. Smith (eds) (1999), *Walter Benjamin: Selected Writings, Volume 2: 1927–1934*, Cambridge, MA: Belknap/Harvard University Press.
—— (1936) 'The Work of Art in the Age of Its Reproducibility', trans. Edmund Jephcott and Harry Zohn; reprinted in H. Eiland and M. Jennings (eds) (2002), *Walter Benjamin: Selected Writings, Vol. 3: 1935–1938*, Cambridge, MA: Belknap/Harvard University Press.
Booth, K. (1991) 'Security and Emancipation', *Review of International Studies*, 1(17): 313–26.
Broszat, M. (1965) 'The Concentration Camps 1933–45', trans. Marian Jackson, in Helmut Krausnick and Martin Broszat, *Anatomy of the SS State*, St Albans, Hertfordshire: Paladin.
Browder, G. C. (1996) *Hitler's Enforcers: The Gestapo and the SS Security Service in the Nazi Revolution*, Oxford: Oxford University Press.
Browning, C. R. (2005) *The Origins of the Final Solution: The Evolution of Nazi Jewish Policy, September 1939-March 1942*, London: Arrow Books.
Burleigh, M. (2001) *The Third Reich: A New History*, London: Pan Macmillan.
Buzan, B., Waever, O. and de Wilde, J. (1998) *Security: A New Framework for Analysis*, Boulder, CO: Lynne Rienner.
Césaire, A. (1955 [2000]) *Discourse on Colonialism*, trans. Joan Pinkham, New York: Monthly Review Press.
Dieckmann, C. (2000) 'The War and the Killing of the Lithuanian Jews', in U. Herbert (ed.), *National Socialist Extermination Policies: Contemporary German Perspectives and Controversies*, New York: Berghahn Books.
Förster, J. (1986) 'The German Army and the Ideological War Against the Soviet Union', in G. Hirschfeld (ed.), *The Policies of Genocide: Jews and Soviet Prisoners of War in Nazi Germany*, London: Allen & Unwin.

Gellately, R. (1991) *The Gestapo and German Society: Enforcing Racial Policy 1933–1945*, Oxford: Clarendon Press.
Harootunian, H. (2007) 'The Imperial Present and the Second Coming of Fascism', *boundary 2*, 34(1): 1–15.
Heiden, K. (1944) *Der Fuehrer, Book 1*, trans. Ralph Manheim, London: Victor Gollanz.
Hitler, A. (1925) *Mein Kampf*, trans. Ralph Manheim, Boston, MA: Houghton Mifflin Company.
Huysmans, J. (2002) 'Defining Social Constructivism in Security Studies: The Normative Dilemma in Writing Security', *Alternatives*, 27 (Special Issue): 41–62.
Klemperer, V. (1946) *The Language of the Third Reich: LTI – Lingua Tertii Imperii: A Philologist's Notebook* (2000), trans. Martin Brady, London: The Athlone Press.
Lewy, G. (2000) *The Nazi Persecution of the Gypsies*, Oxford: Oxford University Press.
Mazower, M. (2009) *Hitler's Empire: Nazi Rule in Occupied Europe*, London: Penguin.
Neocleous, M. (1996) 'Friend or Enemy? Reading Schmitt Politically', *Radical Philosophy*, 79: 13–23.
—— (2000) *The Fabrication of Social Order: A Critical Theory of Police Power*, London: Pluto Press.
—— (2006a) 'The Problem with Normality, or, Taking Exception to "Permanent Emergency"', *Alternatives*, 31(2): 191–213.
—— (2006b) 'From Social to National Security: On the Fabrication of Economic Order', *Security Dialogue*, 37(3): 363–84.
—— (2006c) '"What Do You Think of Female Chastity?" Identity and Loyalty in the National Security State', *Journal of Historical Sociology*, 19(4): 374–79.
—— (2008) *Critique of Security*, Edinburgh: University of Edinburgh Press.
—— (2009) 'The Fascist Moment: Security, Exclusion, Extermination', *Studies in Social Justice*, 3(1): 23–37.
Neumann, F. L. (1953) 'The Concept of Political Freedom', reprinted in W. E. Scheuerman (ed.) (1996) *The Rule of Law Under Siege: Selected Essays of Franz L. Neumann and Otto Kirchheimer*, Berkeley, CA: University of California Press.
Roseman, M. (2002) *The Villa, The Lake, The Meeting: Wannsee and the Final Solution*, London: Penguin.
Schmitt, C. (1922) *Political Theology* (1985), trans. George Schwab, Cambridge, MA: MIT Press.
—— (1932) *The Concept of the Political* (1996), trans. George Schwab, Chicago, IL: University of Chicago Press.
Stirk, P. (2005) *Carl Schmitt, Crown Jurist of the Third Reich: On Preemptive War, Military Occupation, and World Empire*, Ceredigion: Edwin Mellen Press.
Wachsmann, N. (2004) *Hitler's Prisons: Legal Terror in Nazi Germany*, New Haven, CT: Yale University Press.
Wildt, M. (2005) 'The Spirit of the Reich Security Main Office (RSHA)', *Totalitarian Movements and Political Religions*, 6(3): 333–49.
Williams, M. (2003) 'Words, Images, Enemies: Securitization and International Politics', *International Studies Quarterly*, 47(4): 511–31.

Further reading

Agamben, G. (1993) *The Coming Community*, trans. M. Hardt, Minnesota: University of Minnesota Press.
—— (1998) *Homo Sacer: Sovereign Power and Bare Life*, trans. D. Heller-Roazen, Stanford, CA: Stanford University Press.
—— (2002) *Remnants of Auschwitz: The Witness and the Archive*, trans. D. Heller-Roazen, New York: Zone Books.
Axworthy, L. (1997) 'Canada and Human Security: The Need for Leadership', *International Journal* 52 (Spring): 183–96.
Barnett, M. and Duvall, R. (eds) *Power in Global Governance*, Cambridge: Cambridge University Press.
Bellamy, A. J. and McDonald, M. (2002) 'The Utility of Human Security: Which Humans? What Security? A Reply to Thomas & Tow', *Security Dialogue* 33 (3): 373–77.
Berenskoetter, F. (2007) 'Thinking about Power', in F. Berenskoetter (ed.) *Power in World Politics*, London: Routledge, 1–23.
Berger, M. T. and Weber, H. (2009) 'War, Peace and Progress: Conflict, Development', in 'Security and Violence in the 21st Century', *Third World Quarterly* 30 (1): 1–16.
Berman, J. (2007) 'The "Vital Core": from Bare Life to the Biopolitics of Human Security', in G. Shani, M. Sato and M. K. Pasha (eds) *Protecting Human Security in a Post 9/11 World: Critical and Global Insights*, Houndmills, Basingstoke, Hants: Palgrave Macmillan, 30–50.
Booth, K. (1999) 'Three Tyrannies', in T. Dunne and N. J. Wheeler (eds) *Human Rights in Global Politics*, Cambridge: Cambridge University Press.
—— (2005) 'Beyond Critical Security Studies', in K. Booth (ed.) *Critical Security Studies and World Politics*, Boulder, CO: Lynne Rienner, 259–79.
Bosold, D. and Werthes, S. (2005) 'Human Security in Practice: Canadian and Japanese Experiences', *International Politics and Society* 1 (2005): 84–101.
Browning, C. R. (2005) *The Origins of the Final Solution: The Evolution of Nazi Jewish Policy, September 1939 – March 1942*, London: Arrow Books.
Buzan, B. (2004) 'A Reductionist, Idealistic Notion that Adds Little Analytical Value', *Security Dialogue* 35 (3): 369–70.
Buzan, B., Waever, O. and de Wilde, J. (1998) *Security: A New Framework for Analysis*, Boulder, CO: Lynne Rienner.
Caldwell, A. (2004) 'Bio-Sovereignty and the Emergence of Humanity', *Theory & Event* 7 (2): pages n.a.
Chandler, D. (2008) 'Human Security: The Dog That Didn't Bark', *Security Dialogue* 39 (4): 427–38.

Commission on Global Governance (CGG) (1995) *Our Global Neighbourhood*, Oxford: Oxford University Press.

Commission on Human Security (2003) *Human Security Now*, New York: United Nations.

Connolly, W. E. (2004) 'The Complexity of Sovereignty', in J. Edkins, V. Pin-Fat and M. Shapiro (eds) *Sovereign Lives: Power in Global Politics*, New York: Routledge.

de Larrinaga, M. and Doucet, M. G. (2008) 'Sovereign Power and the Biopolitics of Human Security', *Security Dialogue* 39 (5): 497–517.

Dillon, M. and Reid, J. (2001) 'Global Liberal Governance: Biopolitics, Security and War', *Millennium: Journal of International Studies* 30 (1): 41–66.

Douzinas, C. (2007) *Human Rights and Empire: The Political Philosophy of Cosmopolitanism*, London: Routledge Cavendish.

Duffield, M. (2001) *Global Governance and the New Wars, the Merging of Development and Security*, London: Zed Books.

—— (2007) *Development, Security and Unending War*, New York: Polity Press.

Duffield, M. and Waddell, N. (2004) *'Human Security and Global Danger: Exploring a Governmental Assemblage'*, Department of Politics and International Relations, University of Lancaster. Online. Available URL: http://www.bond.org.uk/pubs/gsd/duffield.pdf (accessed 21 December 2006).

—— (2006) 'Securing Humans in a Dangerous World', *International Politics* 43 (1): 1–23.

Edkins, J. and Pin-Fat, V. (2005) 'Through the Wire: Relations of Power and Relations of Violence', *Millennium: Journal of International Studies* 34 (1): 1–24.

Edström, B. (2003) 'Japan's Foreign Policy and Human Security', *Japan Forum* 15 (2): 209–25.

—— (2008) *Japan and the Challenge of Human Security. The Founding of a New Policy 1995–2003*, Stockholm: Institute for Security and Development Policy.

Fierke, K. M. (2007) *Critical Approaches to International Security*, Cambridge: Polity Press.

Foucault, M. (1976; 1979; 1990) *The History of Sexuality*, Vol.1, London: Penguin.

—— (1991) 'Governmentality', in G. Burchell, C. Gordon and P. Miller (eds) *The Foucault Effect: Studies in Governmentality*, Hemel Hempstead: Harvester Wheatsheaf, 87–104.

—— (2003) *Society Must Be Defended: Lectures at the College de France 1975–1976*, New York: Picador.

—— (2007) *Security, Territory, Population: Lectures at the College de France, 1977–1978*, trans. G. Burchell, Houndmills, Basingstoke, Hants: Palgrave Macmillan.

—— (2008) *The Birth of Biopolitics: Lectures at the College de France 1978–79*, trans. G. Burchell, Basingstoke: Palgrave Macmillan.

Gasper, D. (2005) 'Securing Humanity: Situating "Human Security" as Concept and Discourse', *Journal of Human Development* 6 (2): 221–45.

Gordon, C. (1991) 'Governmental Rationality: An Introduction', in G. Burchell, C. Gordon and P. Miller (eds) *The Foucault Effect: Studies in Governmentality*, Hemel Hempstead: Harvester Wheatsheaf, 1–52.

Grayson, K. (2004) 'A Challenge to the Power over Knowledge of Traditional Security Studies', *Security Dialogue* 35 (3): 357.

—— (2008) 'Human Security as Power/Knowledge: The Biopolitics of a Definitional Debate', *Cambridge Review of International Affairs* 21 (3): 383–401.

Human Security Centre (HSC) (2005) *Human Security Report 2005, War and Peace in the 21st Century*, Oxford: Oxford University Press.

Hynek, N. (2008a) 'Conditions of Emergence and Their Effects: Political Rationalities, Governmental Programs and Technologies of Power in the Landmine Case', *Journal of International Relations and Development* 11(2): 93–120.

Further reading

—— (2008b) 'Japan's Human Security: A Conceptual and Institutional Analysis', *Ritsumeikan Annual Review of International Studies* 7(1): 1–20.

International Commission on Intervention and State Sovereignty (ICISS) (2001) *The Responsibility to Protect*, Ottawa: International Development Research Centre.

Jabri, V. (2007) *War and the Transformation of Global Politics*, Basingstoke: Palgrave.

Jolly, R. and Basu Ray, D. (2006) *National Human Development Reports and the Human Security Framework: A Review of Analysis and Experience*, Institute of Development Studies, Sussex. Produced for: The Human Development Report.

Kaldor, M. (1999) 'Transnational Civil Society', in T. Dunne and N. J. Wheeler (eds) *Human Rights in Global Politics*, Cambridge: Cambridge University Press.

—— (2007) *Human Security: Reflections on Globalization and Intervention*, Cambridge: Polity.

Kaldor, M., Martin, M. and Selchow, S. (2007) 'Human Security: A New Strategic Narrative for Europe', *International Affairs* 83 (2): 273–88.

Krause, K. (2004) 'The Key to a Powerful Agenda if Properly Delimited', *Security Dialogue* 35 (3): 367–68.

MacFarlane, S. N. (2004) 'A Useful Concept that Risks Losing Its Political Salience', *Security Dialogue* 35 (3): 368–69.

MacFarlane, S. N. and Khong, Y. F. (eds) (2006) *Human Security and the UN*, Bloomington, IN: Indiana University Press.

Mack, A. (2005) *The Human Security Report 2005: War and Peace in the 21st Century*, Oxford: Oxford University Press.

MacLean, S. J., Black, D. R. and Shaw, T. M. (eds) (2006) *A Decade of Human Security: Global Governance and New Multilateralisms*, Hampshire: Ashgate.

McRae, R. (2001) 'Human Security in a Globalized World', in R. McRae and D. Hubert (eds) *Human Security and the New Diplomacy*, Canada: McGill-Queen's University Press, 45–58.

Modood, T. (2005) *Multicultural Politics: Racism, Ethnicity and Muslims in Britain*, Minneapolis, MN: University of Minnesota Press.

Muggah, R. and Krause, K. (2006) 'A True Measure of Success? The Discourse and Practice of Human Security in Haiti', in S. J. MacLean , David R. Black and Timothy M. Shaw (eds) *A Decade of Human Security. Global Governance and New Multilateralisms*, Aldershot: Ashgate, 113–26.

Newman, E. (2001) 'Human Security and Constructivism', *International Studies Perspectives* 2: 239–51.

—— (2004) 'A Normatively Attractive but Analytically Weak Concept', *Security Dialogue* 35 (3): 358–59.

Owen, T. (2008) 'The Critique That Doesn't Bite: A Response to David Chandler's "Human Security: The Dog That Didn't Bark"' *Security Dialogue* 39 (4): 445–53.

Owens, P. (forthcoming) 'Beyond Bare Life: Refugees and the Right to Have Rights', in A. Betts and G. Loescher (eds) *Refugees in International Relations*, Oxford: Oxford University Press.

Paris, R. (2001) 'Human Security, Paradigm Shift or Hot Air', *International Security* 26 (2): 87–102.

—— (2004) 'Still an Inscrutable Concept', in J. P. Burgess and T. Owen (eds) 'Special Section: What is "Human Security?"' *Security Dialogue* 35 (3): 370–72.

Price, R. (1998) 'Reversing the Gun Sights: Transnational Civil Society Targets Land Mines', *International Organization* 52 (3): 613–44.

Richmond, O. P. (2007) 'Emancipatory Forms of Human Security and Liberal Peacebuilding', *International Journal* 62 (3): 459-478.

Rosenau, J. (1995) 'Governance in the Twenty-First Century', *Global Governance* 1 (1): 13–43.

Schaap, A. (2008) 'Political Abandonment and the Abandonment of Politics in Agamben's Critique of Human Rights', Available URL: http://eric.exeter.ac.uk/exeter/bitstream/10036/42438/2/Agamben%e2%80%99s%20critique%20of%20Human%20Rights.pdf (accessed 2 February 2009).

Schmitt, C. (1922, 1996) *The Concept of the Political*, Chicago, IL: University of Chicago Press.

—— (1932, 1985) *Political Theology: Four Chapters on the Concept of Sovereignty*, Massachusetts: MIT Press.

Shani, G., Sato, M. and Pasha, M. K. (eds) (2007) *Protecting Human Security in a Post 9/11 World. Critical and Global Insights*, Houndmills, Basingstoke: Routledge.

Tadjbakhsh, S. (2005) 'Human Security: Concepts and Implications', *Les Etudes du CERI CERI*/Sciences Po, Paris, France, 117–18 (September).

Tadjbakhsh, S. and Chenoy, A. M. (2007) *Human Security: Concepts and Implications*, London and New York: Routledge.

Thomas, C. (2000) *Global Governance, Development and Human Security. The Challenge of Poverty and Inequality*, London: Pluto Press.

Thomas, N. and Tow, W. T. (2002) 'The Utility of Human Security: Sovereignty and Humanitarian Intervention', *Security Dialogue* 33 (2): 177–92.

United Nations (UN) (1992; 1995) *An Agenda for Peace*, Second Edition, New York: UN.

—— (2004) *A More Secure World: Our Shared Responsibility*. Report of the Secretary-General's High Level Panel on Threats, Challenges and Change, New York: UN, December.

—— (2005) *In Larger Freedom: Towards Development, Security and Human Rights for All*. Report of the Secretary-General, UN doc. A/59/2005, 21 March.

United Nations Development Programme (UNDP) (1994) *Human Development Report: New Dimensions of Human Security*, New York: Oxford University Press.

Index

Afghanistan 1, 25, 44, 86, 104, 108, 172, 179
Africa 20, 23, 86, 91, 92
Agamben, Giorgio 65, 75, 129, 148–51; comparison with Foucault 8, 144–6, 152–4; poststructuralism 121; potentiality 149, 150; sovereign power 132–4, 139, 140; *zoē* 60–1, 132, 148
agency 8, 51, 108, 123, 125, 149, 179
Agenda for Peace (UN) 33, 34, 35, 36, 84
aid 47–8, 85–6, 91
Alkire, Sabine 57–8, 65n3, 66n5
al-Qaeda 15, 25, 111n7
Alt, Suvi 8, 144–56
Amnesty International 16, 21, 22–3, 25, 73
Angola 47
Annan, Kofi 59, 106
Antipersonnel Landmines (APL) campaign 162, 163, 165
anti-Semitism 188–9, 190–2, 193
Arendt, Hannah 134
arms control 21, 87–90, 93, 162–4
assimilation 62, 65
Australia 178
Axworthy, Lloyd 100, 162–3

'bare life' 5, 8, 57, 129, 132, 148–9, 151; human rights 134; modern biopolitics 152; sovereign power 133, 134; *zoē* 60–1, 64–5
Barnett, M. 71
'basic rights' 22
Baxi, Upendra 74
Beetham, David 23
Benjamin, Walter 195–6
Berenskoetter, Felix 72
Berger, M. T. 180
Berman, J. 59

biopolitics 7, 121–3, 129, 137, 174–9; Agambenite perspective 61, 132, 145–6, 149, 151, 152–3; empowerment 58; Foucauldian perspective 72, 80, 145–6, 152–3, 164; global governance 74–5; human rights 134–5; North-South relations 59–60; sovereign power 138–40, 180–1
biopoverty 6, 75–6
biopower 8, 121–3, 129–43, 144–56; Agambenite perspective 132, 145–6, 148–51, 152–3; Foucauldian perspective 59, 145, 146–8, 152–3, 164; liberal peacebuilding 48
Black, M. 78
Blair, Tony 25n4
Bloch, Ivan 165
Booth, Ken 59, 60, 66n6, 117–18, 186
Bosnia 47, 49, 168, 177
Bosold, David 4–5, 28–42
bottom-up approaches 77–9
Boutros-Ghali, Boutros 34, 36
Brahimi Report (2000) 47, 85, 107
Browning, Christopher 191
Bull, Hedley 17, 21
Burleigh, Michael 190–1
Burma (Myanmar) 22, 137, 181
Burundi 16
Bush, George H. 19
Bush, George W. 15
Buzan, Barry 60, 187

Caldwell, A. 140
Cambodia 47
Canada 5, 83, 84, 115, 183n5; 3-d approach 178; 'narrow' conception of human security 33, 37, 101, 102; NGOs and FFF doctrine 165–6, 167–8
capacity building 86–7, 91

Index

capitalism 74, 93–4, 195; 'casino crisis' 90, 92; co-option of human security 83; development agenda 92; global regulatory norms 7, 114
Carr, E. H. 13
CBOs *see* Community-Based Organisations
Césaire, Aimé 193
CGG *see* Commission on Global Governance
Chandler, David 1–10, 83, 84, 114–28, 148, 178
Chenoy, Anuradha M. 83, 101, 118, 119
Chicago School 159, 160
child mortality 76–80
child soldiers 21
China 181
Chomsky, Noam 19, 89
Chrétien, Jean 166
CHS *see* Commission on Human Security
citizenship 9, 134
civil society 45, 159; global 22–3, 24, 117, 167; liberal peacebuilding 46, 48, 50–1; state relationship 178
Clinton, Bill 19
cluster munitions 87–8, 89, 90, 93
Cold War 34, 115, 121, 144, 174; end of 5; NGOs 160; realist discourse 15
Commission on Global Governance (CGG) 36, 105–6
Commission on Human Security (CHS) 35, 37, 57, 83, 84–5, 136, 144–5; definition of human security 101; development agenda 91–2; governance 148; health 146–7
Community-Based Organisations (CBOs) 77–8, 79
Congo, Democratic Republic of 16
Connolly, W. E. 149
conservatism 51, 99, 100
constructivism 7, 114–17, 119–20
Cooper, Neil 6, 83–96
co-option 6, 59, 83–96; development agenda 90–2; pariah weapons 87–90; peacebuilding 84–7
corruption 79
cosmopolitanism 13, 46, 65, 117
Cox, Robert 23
critical theory 13, 14, 60, 117, 123, 187, 195
cultural diversity 5–6, 57, 65

DAC *see* Development Assistance Committee
Darby, Dr 165

Darfur 181
de Soto, A. 36
de Wilde, Jaap 60, 187
del Castillo, G. 36
Deleuze, Gilles 161, 164
democracy 46, 60–1, 123, 149, 173, 177–8
democratisation 47, 61, 102, 144, 177
Department for International Development (DFID) 86, 92, 120
de-securitisation 60, 65, 94, 166–7
development 90–2, 93, 102–5, 138, 177–8; de-securitisation 166–7; 'Security-Development Nexus' 69, 180; UN concept of human security 33
Development Assistance Committee (DAC) 86
DFID *see* Department for International Development
diasporas 86
Dieckmann, C. 192
dignity 57, 61, 65, 151, 177
Diken, B. 152
Dillon, Michael 73, 153, 182, 183n4
disarmament *see* arms control
disciplinary management 167–8
disease 20, 146–7
Donnelly, Jack 18, 116
donors 85–6
Doucet, Marc 8, 60, 129–43, 144, 145, 180–2
Douzinas, Costas 121
Duffield, Mark 59, 121–3, 137, 168, 169, 172
Dunant, Henry 164
Dunne, Tim 4, 13–27
Duvall, R. 71

East Timor (Timor Leste) 44, 47, 49, 50, 168
Eastern Europe 18–19, 92
economics 71, 160
'economy of power' 4
El Salvador 36, 47, 137
Elden, Stuart 130
emancipation 3, 4, 9–10, 66n6, 186, 187
emancipatory approach 2–3, 4–5, 43–4, 83–4, 186; critiques of 7, 9, 49, 50–1, 52, 99, 110, 119; liberal peacebuilding 46; pluralism 100
empowerment 3, 7, 50, 57, 58, 110, 168; definition of human security 101; individual sovereignty 106, 108; initiatives 101–2; neo-liberal logic 147; UNTFHS 93

204 Index

'equity-security' 33
ethics 119
European Convention on Human Rights 64
Evans, Gareth 35–6
exclusion 62, 63

Falk, Richard 14
fascism 10, 17, 187, 188–93, 194–6
FFF *see* freedom from fear
Foucault, Michel 3–4, 9, 70, 75, 137, 158–60; biopolitics 6, 164; biopower 59, 122, 130–2; comparison with Agamben 8, 144–6, 152–4; global governance 72–3, 173; governmentality 73, 74, 76, 129, 136, 174; liberal rationality 163, 169; poststructuralism 121; resistance 151–2; security dispositif 161–2
France 6, 62, 63–5
freedom from fear (FFF) 29, 45, 166–7, 169; Canada 165, 168; 'Just War' interventions 120; 'narrow' conception of human security 58, 101, 135; strong state 179–80; UN system 31
freedom from want 29, 45, 120, 180; 'broad' conception of human security 58, 101, 135; UN system 31
freedom of thought, conscience and religion 64
friend-enemy distinction 131, 186–7
funding issues 35, 167

GECHS *see* Global Environmental Change and Human Security
genocide 18
Georgia 179
Germany 62, 188–93
Gill, Stephen 61
global civil society 22–3, 24, 117, 167
Global Environmental Change and Human Security (GECHS) 38
global governance 80, 114, 117, 181; Foucauldian perspective 72–3, 173; neo-imperialism 59; neo-liberalism 74–5; non-state actors 47; power 69, 70–2
Global Water Bank 77–8
globalisation 56, 123, 144; cultural diversity 5–6, 57; neo-liberal 62, 65; vulnerabilities of 90
'good governance' 85–6, 90, 91, 93
Gordon, C. 158, 159, 160
governmentality 48, 130, 135–6, 172; Agambenite perspective 133; biopower 129; capitalist 61; development 138; economy of power 4; Foucauldian perspective 72–3, 76, 80, 122, 169, 174; neo-liberal 58, 74–5, 159
Grayson, Kyle 9, 74, 101, 172–85
Great Britain: Department for International Development 86, 92, 120; neo-liberal ideology 20; state/civil society relationship 178; support for South Africa 19
Grin, Rabbi Hugo 23
gypsies 192–3

Hague Conference on Peace (1899) 163, 165, 169
Haiti 39, 83, 102, 120, 177
Hamas 86, 87
Hardt, M. 122, 152–3
health 146–7, 176
Helsinki Final Act (1975) 18
Hitler, Adolf 188–9, 193
HIV/AIDS 20, 23, 147
Hobbes, Thomas 193
homosexuals 193
HSN *see* Human Security Network
HSR *see* Human Security Report
Human Development Report 7, 26n12, 28–36, 38–9, 56, 100, 102, 176–7
human rights 4, 14, 19, 25, 173; biopolitics 134–5; gross abuses 20, 181; indivisibility of security and 21–3, 24; liberal peacebuilding 46; military interventions 138–40; pluralist discourse 17; post-colonial/post-liberal 52–3; realist discourse 16–17; securitisation 177–8; sovereignty relationship 140; universal 118
Human Rights Watch 22, 73
human security 1–2, 21–3; Agambenite perspective 145–6, 148–51, 152–4; analysing 28–9; biopolitics 74–5, 121–3, 174–9; biopoverty 6, 75–6; biopower 8, 48, 129–43, 144–5; as challenge to power 117–20; collapse of 43; competing paradigms 7, 114, 117, 126; 'conceptual overstretch' 137; constructivist perspective 7, 114–17, 119–20; co-option 6, 83–96; critical perspectives 58–62; critiques of 7–8, 69, 99–113, 117, 120, 123–6, 144; depoliticisation of western intervention 109; development 102–5, 138; disciplinary management 167–8;

Foucauldian perspective 3–4, 8, 80, 145, 146–8, 152–4, 165; histories of 4–5, 29, 30–1; individual focus 56–7, 100, 105–6, 118, 135–6, 166; liberal peacebuilding 44–9; measurement of 38; as mechanism of power 121–3; militarisation 168; 'narrow' and 'broad' definitions 37, 38–9, 57–8, 101–2, 106, 135; pluralist framework 99–100; as policy-making enterprise 157; post-colonial approaches 44; reproduction of power 3–4; semantic dimension 29–30; sovereignty 8, 105–9; state security 9, 179–82; United Nations 31–7; water resources 75, 76–80; *see also* emancipatory approach
Human Security Network (HSN) 56, 57, 58, 66n4, 83
Human Security Report (HSR) 56, 57, 76, 136
humanitarian intervention 43, 115–16, 139–40, 168, 173
humanitarianism 8, 14, 23, 48, 161, 178; Agambenite perspective 148, 149; arms trade regulation 88, 90; co-option of human security 93; disarmament 162–4; NGOs 168
Huysmans, Jef 187
Hynek, Nik 1–10, 157–71

ICC *see* International Criminal Court
ICISS *see* International Commission on Intervention and State Sovereignty
ICRC *see* International Committee of the Red Cross
idealist approach 7–8, 123–4
Ignatieff, Michael 14, 25
IMF *see* International Monetary Fund
immigrants 62–3
inequalities 7, 20, 71, 99, 105, 108–9, 110, 114
institutionalist approach 46–7, 49, 52, 70–1
International Commission on Intervention and State Sovereignty (ICISS) 102–3, 106–7, 109, 138, 139
International Committee of the Red Cross (ICRC) 22, 164, 172
International Criminal Court (ICC) 24, 58, 102, 134
international law 139
International Monetary Fund (IMF) 20, 61, 75, 105
International Relations 13, 16, 70, 74, 116, 152–3

intervention 109, 122, 138; biopower 129; catastrophes 182; continuum of 181; gross human rights abuses 138–40, 181; humanitarian 43, 115–16, 139–40, 168, 173; liberal peace 2, 45, 47
Iran 15
Iraq 1, 15, 25, 86, 179
Islamic Cultural Zones (ICZs) 179
Israel 87

Jabri, Vivienne 121
Japan 83, 84, 138, 183n6; 'broad' approach to human security 37, 101, 168; guns as pariah weapons 88, 89; migrants 62; state/civil society relationship 178; Trust Fund for Human Security 35
Jews 188–9, 190–2, 193
Johnstone, Ian 71

Kaldor, Mary 90, 115–16, 118
Kapstein, P. 71
Keohane, Robert 70–1
Khong, Y. F. 31, 59
Klemperer, Victor 188
Kosovo 39, 47, 49, 50, 102, 137, 168
Krause, Keith 83, 88, 120

landmines 58, 87–8, 89–90, 102, 162, 163, 165, 167
Larrinaga, Miguel de 8, 60, 129–43, 144, 145, 180–2
Laustsen, C. B. 152
Lemke, Thomas 131
Lewis, Norman 16–17
Lewy, Guenter 192
liberal institutionalism 47, 49, 52
liberal peace 3, 4, 5, 43, 44–9; critique of 49–51, 52; global governance 70; international intervention 2; pariah weapons 90; *see also* peacebuilding
liberalism 2, 69, 80, 158; biopolitics 175; Canada 166; conservative wing 43; dangers of 195; disarmament 162–4; Foucauldian perspective 169; global governance 70; humanitarianism 161; laissez-faire 159; power 182; Schmitt's critique of 193–4; securitisation of 5, 44
Liberia 85, 137
'life welfare' paradigm 6–7, 94
LIP *see* Local Initiatives Project
Lippmann, Walter 15
Lipschutz, Ronnie 73
Lithuanian Jews 191–2

206　*Index*

Local Initiatives Project (LIP) 79

MacDonald, Mary K. 88
MacFarlane, S. N. 31, 59
Marriage, Zoë 120
Martens Clause 165
Marx, Karl 195
McCormack, Tara 7, 99–113
MDGs *see* Millennium Development Goals
Médecins Sans Frontières 22
Merlingen, Michael 73
migration 62, 84
militarism 88, 89
Millennium Development Goals (MDGs) 35, 85, 90–1, 93
Miller, P. 174
Mills, C. 149
Modood, T. 62
Moldova 137
Morgenthau, Hans J. 16
Mozambique 47
Muggah, Robert 83, 120
multiculturalism 62–3
multilateralism 126
Myanmar (Burma) 22, 137, 181

national security 2, 5, 14–17, 19, 56, 59, 173
National Security Strategy (NSS) 104
Nazism 61, 132, 188–93
Neal, A. W. 149
Negri, A. 122, 152–3
Neocleous, Mark 9–10, 186–97
neo-liberalism 1, 20, 50, 80, 147; arms trade 88–9; biopolitics 123; control technologies 6; co-option of human security 83, 90, 93; development agenda 91, 92; disciplinary 61; economies of power 4; Foucault on 158, 159–60; global governance 69, 72–3, 117; global regulatory norms 7, 114; governmentality 58, 74–5, 159; humanitarianism 161; water projects 77
Neumann, Franz 194–5
Neumann, I. 160
Newman, Edward 105
NGOs *see* non-governmental organisations
Nicholas II, Tzar of Russia 162–3, 165
non-governmental organisations (NGOs) 4, 23, 45, 83–4, 85, 169; autonomy and responsibility 160–1; Canada 165–6, 167, 168; constructivist perspective 116; humanitarianism 161; liberal peacebuilding 47, 48, 52; unaccountability 108
non-intervention 17, 36, 103, 106, 107, 109, 181
norms 71, 115–16
North Korea 15, 181
NSS *see* National Security Strategy
nuclear weapons 15, 176
Nye, Joseph 70–1

OECD *see* Organisation for Economic Cooperation and Development
Ogata, Sadako 57
Ohiorhenuan, J. 79
Ojakangas, M. 153
Ordo-liberals 159
Organisation for Economic Cooperation and Development (OECD) 35, 86
Ottawa Convention on Anti-personnel Landmines (1997) 58, 102, 165, 167
Owen, Taylor 101, 178
Oxfam 22, 25, 73

Palestine 86–7
pariah weapons 87–90, 93, 162–3
Paris, Roland 28, 58
partnerships 85–6
Pasha, M. K. 179
peacebuilding 3, 5, 39, 44–9, 50, 89; co-option of human security 6, 84–7, 93; critique of 49–51; hybrid agencies 44; post-colonial/post-liberal 52–3; *see also* liberal peace
Peru 137
pluralism 4, 17–19, 102; critique of 19, 20–1, 99–100; ideological framework 110; state sovereignty 106, 107, 109
Pogge, Thomas 76
policy making 125–6, 157
post-colonial approaches 5, 44, 49, 52–3
post-liberalism 44, 49, 52–3
poststructuralism 117, 121, 123, 125
potentiality 149, 150
poverty 20, 60, 91, 92, 105; biopoverty 6, 75–6; merging of development and security 102, 103; terrorism link 104; weak states 103–4
power 8, 9, 104, 124, 182; Agambenite perspective 145; asymmetric 3, 6; disciplinary 61, 130; emancipatory approach 100; Foucauldian perspective 72–3, 145, 151–2, 154, 169; global governance 69, 70–2; human security as challenge to 117–20; human security as

mechanism of 121–3; ideational 71, 72, 73, 80; inequalities 7, 99, 105, 108–9, 110, 114; reproduction of 3–4; sovereign 8, 59–60, 129, 130–5, 138–40, 180–1; *see also* biopower
preventive war 15, 25n5
prisons 189–90
'problem-solving' 100, 101, 117
protection 59, 93, 101
Pugh, Michael 6, 74, 83–96

racism 131–2
rationalist approach 7–8, 115, 119
realism 4, 14, 39, 43, 56, 80, 84, 119; biopolitics 122; critical 117; end of Cold War 115; global governance 70; institutionalist approach 49; moral indifference 24; power relations 123; realist discourse 14–17; securitisation of 5, 44; state interests 116; 'war on terror' 125
regulation 4; global regulatory norms 7; pariah weapons 88, 89, 93
Reid, Julian 73, 183n4
religion 63–5
resistance 53, 145, 151–2
Richmond, Oliver 5, 43–55
rights 22, 58, 134, 145, 151; *see also* human rights
Roberts, David 6, 69–82
Robertson, Geoffrey 24–5
Rogers, Paul 120
Roosevelt, Franklin D. 31
Rose, Nikolas 174, 176
Rosenau, James 70–1
Rumsfeld, Donald 15
Russia 92
Rwanda 16, 18

Sachs, Jeffrey D. 92
SAPs *see* Structural Adjustment Programmes
Save the Children 22
Schaap, A. 149
Schittecatte, Catherine 120
Schmitt, Carl 61, 121, 131, 133, 186–7, 193–4
Schümer, Tanja 120
Sector Wide Approach (SWAp) 76
securitisation 5, 44, 84, 124–5, 177–8; biopower 59; development agenda 166; foreign policy discourse 167; migration 62; Nazi Germany 188; weapons technology 89; welfare 3; *zoē* 61

security 13, 175–6; critique of 195–6; fascism link 10, 187; friend-enemy antagonism 186–7; 'hard' vs 'soft' 73; individualised 9; limits of traditional discourses 19–21; Nazi Germany 188–93; 'new' forms of 28; pluralist discourse 17–19; politics of emancipation 9–10; realist discourse 14–17; reconfiguration of 4–5, 186, 195; *see also* human security; national security
security dispositif 161–2
security sector reform (SSR) 85, 86–7
'Security-Development Nexus' 69, 180
self, technologies of the 147–8, 152
self-determination 5, 51, 179
self-interest 116, 119
Sen, Amartya 57, 118
Sending, O. 160
September 11th 2001 terrorist attacks 14, 25, 103
Shani, Giorgio 5–6, 56–68
Shue, Henry 22
Sierra Leone 49, 85, 86, 102, 120, 177
Sikhs 6, 63–5
Sikkink, Kathryn 116
Smith, Adam 158
social contract 50–1, 53
Solomon Islands 44
Somalia 19, 177, 179
South Africa 19
sovereign power 8, 59–60, 129, 130–5, 138–40, 180–1
sovereignty 8, 45, 105–9, 110, 118; Agambenite perspective 133, 150; constructivist perspective 116; contingent 85, 93; Foucault on 130–1; friend-enemy antagonism 187; human rights abuses 17; individual 57; suspension of rights of 129–30; UN Charter 17–18
Soviet Union, former (USSR) 15, 18, 115
SSR *see* security sector reform
state 8, 9, 135, 138–9, 179–83; biopolitics 175; citizen relationship 30–1; civil society relationship 178; constructivist perspective 116, 119; crimes against people 100; disciplinary neo-liberalism 61; global civil society 24; national security 15; non-intervention 103; realism 56; sovereignty 105–9, 118, 131
state of exception 132–3, 139, 140, 149, 186–7, 194
statebuilding 43, 50, 85, 86
statism 16, 59, 118, 159

Stewart, F. 79
Structural Adjustment Programmes (SAPs) 61, 75, 92
submarines 88
Sudan 181
Suttner, Bertha von 165
Suu Kyi, Daw Aung San 22
SWAp *see* Sector Wide Approach

Tadjbakhsh, Shahrbanou 83, 101, 118, 119
Taliban 25, 44, 172
territorial integrity 35–6, 129–30
terrorism 14, 25, 84, 92, 102, 103–4, 111n7; *see also* 'war on terror'
Third Reich 10, 188–93
Timor Leste (East Timor) 44, 47, 49, 50, 168
Tocqueville, Alexis de 28
torture 23
Turner, Mandy 6, 83–96

U Thant, Sithu 30
UDHR *see* Universal Declaration of Human Rights
ul Haq, Mahbub 30, 32, 34, 83, 93
underdevelopment 102, 103, 105
UNDP *see* United Nations Development Programme
United Nations (UN) 31–7, 45, 83, 138, 180; Charter of the 13, 17–18, 19, 21, 24; development agenda 91; empowerment initiatives 101–2; Haiti missions 120; *High Level Report on Threats, Challenges and Change* 36, 45, 47, 52, 85, 91, 103, 106, 138, 181–2; institutionalist approach 49; post-liberal peacebuilding 53; state sovereignty 106; statism 16
United Nations Development Programme (UNDP) 7, 56, 176–7; development agenda 90; history of human security 4–5, 28, 29–30, 31–5, 36, 38–9; individual focus 135; migration 62; neo-liberal logic 147
United Nations Trust Fund for Human Security (UNTFHS) 83, 93, 136

United States (US): arms exports 21; democratic imperialism 66n8; human rights 19, 181; immigrants 62; Loyalty Program 194–5; National Security Strategy 104; neo-liberal ideology 20; realist discourse 15–16; state/civil society relationship 178; subjective conceptions 115; submarines 88; support for South Africa 19; 'war on terror' 14
Universal Declaration of Human Rights (UDHR) 14, 16, 18, 19
UNTFHS *see* United Nations Trust Fund for Human Security

Vankovska, Biljana 85
Vincent, R.J. 18, 22

Wachsmann, Nikolaus 189–90
Waever, Ole 60, 187
war 15, 36, 163, 172, 175–6, 193–4
'war on terror' 14, 25n4, 45, 104, 125, 179; *see also* terrorism
water resources 75, 76–80
weapons of mass destruction (WMD) 15, 104
Weber, H. 180
welfare: 'life welfare' paradigm 6–7, 94; securitisation of 3
Wendt, Alexander 115
Wheeler, Nicholas 4, 13–27
Wilkinson, Rorden 70
WMD *see* weapons of mass destruction
women 23, 100
World Bank 6, 20, 45, 105; development agenda 91, 92; post-liberal peacebuilding 53; Structural Adjustment Programmes 61, 75; water projects 76, 78
World Trade Organisation (WTO) 45, 61, 90

Youssef, M. 149

Zimmem, Alfred 165
zoē 60–1, 64–5, 132, 148